FRANK'S FANCY

FUNDING MADE POSSIBLE BY

THE FRANK PHILLIPS FOUNDATION, INC.

FRANK'S FANCY

FRANK PHILLIPS' WOOLAROC

by Gale Morgan Kane

OKLAHOMA HERITAGE ASSOCIATION
OKLAHOMA CITY

Library of Congress Card Catalog Number 2001089736

ISBN 1-885596-22-7

Printed in the United States of America

Jacket design by Todd Giles
Book design by Carol Haralson

Oklahoma Heritage Association
201 Northwest Fourteenth Street
Oklahoma City, Oklahoma 73103

LABELS, ABOVE: Woolaroc events featured Gingerock and Woolaroc bottled water. Though the springs at Woolaroc were all good potable water, it must have been particularly refreshing in those days to get a bottle of ice cold pure, good-tasting water. Frank even gave cases of them as Christmas gifts in 1930. He had the trade marks registered in New York in 1929. Courtesy Woolaroc.

CONTENTS PAGE, RIGHT: Chief Abbott and some Osage dancers pose with guests at the Traffic Club barbecue in October 1931. It was the waning years of Prohibition, but there are records of liquor supplies in those years. Some of the guests in this photograph are brandishing bottles of something. Courtesy Woolaroc.

Frank, Jane, and friends at Woolaroc. Courtesy Woolaroc.

ACKNOWLEDGMENTS

A GREAT DEAL of my information gathering began long, long before I ever dreamed of writing a history of Woolaroc. Since moving to Bartlesville 30 years ago, Woolaroc has been a constant part of my social life. It is that for most Bartians. Most of us, even those who have been personally involved in the ranch, hardly dreamed of all of the hilarity, audacity, calculation, joy, tragedy, frustration, and work that went into the place in the early days. I owe many thanks to those who assisted in my recovery of those old days and would like to express my gratitude.

This book was originally presented as a thesis for the degree of Master of Arts at the University of Tulsa with the title "8,000 Days: An Early History of Woolaroc." It is my duty to acknowledge the role of the university in my preparation of the thesis. I wish to thank the faculty of the History Department, especially my committee, Dr. James P. Ronda and Dr. Thomas H. Buckley. Anyone who has ever written such a paper understands the important role these men have played. It was Dr. Ronda who suggested that Woolaroc would be an apt subject. After preliminary investigation it was evident that there were sufficient resources, but only after some weeks of research did it become apparent that the complexity of the material went well beyond a usual thesis. I am grateful for the patience, liberality, and encouragement of Drs. Ronda and Buckley, and their continued interest in the development of this book.

Of course, I am immensely grateful to the trustees of the Frank Phillips Foundation for their enthusiastic support, and to Dick Miller, general manager, and the museum staff at Woolaroc. For most of a year I had openhanded access to the museum archives, and my very own working area in their office. Bob Lansdown, Ken Meek, and Linda Stone answered my questions, found what I was looking for, and brainstormed with me. I know it was not convenient to have me under foot and I am grateful to them.

I wish to remember with thanks to Margie Sydebotham for access to the lodge; to the men in the shop who shared their knowledge and skill, and their microwave; to Connie Collins, secretary in the business office, and Carol Fouts secretary in the museum for all their help and patience; and to the lodge staff for lots of those coveted Woolaroc lunches in the kitchen. The Woolaroc staff and docents are generous, interesting people and it is an honor to know them better.

Thank you to Phillips Petroleum Company in many ways. No one can visit the subject of Frank Phillips without recognizing the yeoman job of Phillips Archives in their stewardship of the early history of the company. I am grateful for access to their archival materials and for the company's help in copying photographs both for my thesis and for this book.

Many people around town have contributed snippets to this book. Mary Kane, John Hughes, Ann Preston, Art Gorman, Jean Campbell Brown, Jim Webb, and Dr. Miriam Steel-Petrovich were especially helpful. My father-in-law, Richard Kane, was the ornery little boy in the far right hand corner of the panoramic photograph taken at the 1928 Cow Thieves and Outlaws Picnic. He was at Woolaroc as a child, from its earliest days, right through his service as chairman of the board of trustees in recent years, and had many memories and corrections to contribute to this book.

Thanks to Bonnie Mills and Sigrid Williams who proofed my text when I was really tired of combing it for typographical errors.

I have never seen a writer who did not have profuse thanks to his or her family. My husband and children made many contributions of their own to this book, as well as sacrifices. Actually, it is hard to return appropriate thanks to family and friends who must have gotten very tired of hearing tales of how Frank Phillips handled some situation or other. I enjoyed the process and sharing it with them, and hope they, too, in their own ways, had some fun—even if it was only snickering at Gale's obsession.

Above all, I give God thanks and reaffirm the words of Isaiah, penned almost 2800 years ago,

> *. . . all that we have*
> *accomplished you have*
> *done for us.* (*Isaiah 26:12*)

—GMK

INTRODUCTION

DENSE CLOUDS of pallid cinnamon dust boil up from beneath the sleek black Chrysler limousine, speeding up the steep grade of the rugged dirt road into the Osage Hills. The year is 1934 or maybe 1936. In the back seat, Frank Phillips and his evening dinner guests, in business suits and light colored summer hats, are visiting jovially about their train ride to Bartlesville and excoriating the New Dealers. The automobile rocks and lurches over the rough dirt road at 25 miles per hour for most of the 40-minute drive. The men successively light up and puff casually on cigarettes, but they are careful not to toss out a smoldering butt for fear of grass fire. The tall Osage bluestem is cured golden after a parched August, and the leaves on the oaks are the tired green of late summer. The air has a dusty haze that gives the atmosphere an unreality; had the men paused in their conversation they might have noticed the surreal beauty. Even for the coastal sophisticates of their time, an invitation to Woolaroc was a prized social trophy, and these men eagerly anticipate their evening visit to the Old West.

The scene, in my mind's eye, fades as I approach the road sign. I am returned from my imagination to the present. An Indian arrow on a tasteful forest green sign with gold lettering and a buffalo medallion quietly directs visitors to the Frank Phillips ranch. It reads, "WOOLAROC 12 miles." From the stop light at the Phillips Petroleum Company Research Center, I turn my car left, going south on State Highway 123—still the Barnsdall Road to locals. Officially the Frank Phillips Memorial Highway, dedicated on 15 October 1985, it is a fine, "super" two-lane highway, arching through the bottoms of Sand Creek which drains into the Caney River about a mile east. Just across the bridge I set my speed control on 65 miles an hour. From the traffic light, it usually takes about 15 minutes to drive to the Woolaroc Museum where I am doing my research.

Left: An early photo of the living room in the lodge at Woolaroc. Courtesy Woolaroc.

Just beyond the Sand Creek Bridge, the road begins to ascend in gentle curves into the Osage Hills. For a while to the left in my rearview mirror I can overlook the river bottoms and glance towards the skyline of Bartlesville. Bartlesville has grown to a population of about 30,000 people. It boasts four moderate skyscrapers, belonging to Phillips Petroleum Company; a small Frank Lloyd Wright skyscraper, built by Price Pipeline Company in the 1950s; a John Duncan Forsythe high school that was finished in 1940; and a modern Community Center, designed by the Taliesin Group in 1982. Not so long ago this land was alive with pump jacks, and the night sky was lit by hundreds of natural gas flares atop derricks at each wellhead. From the days of a grubby little oil boomtown at the turn of the 20th century, progressive oil men in Bartlesville have always taken pride in the architecture of local homes and public buildings that today make this little city an Oklahoma showplace.

If I look to my right as I speed up the hill just ahead, the scene is the Hughes Ranch. John Hughes is a nationally-respected cattleman and a trustee of the Frank Phillips Foundation. His ranch borders on Woolaroc, on land that once belonged to Frank Phillips. The hills begin to become covered with blackjack oak, in various stages of de- or re-forestation. This land is a northern finger of the storied Cross Timbers, and John Hughes is at war with the blackjack. Only a little way on, the pastures to the left and right contain hundreds of horses. A small sign tells me it is the Prairie National Wild Horse Refuge. Hughes is under contract with the Department of the Interior to pasture these neutered mustangs for the rest of their lives. As I watch the scruffy creatures munch on this morning's haying, I am struck by this ironic turn for lands where mustangs once roamed free among vast herds of buffalo and where equus flourished until the late Pleistocene.

The horses are being hayed because there was a drought last summer, and this spring's rains promise to be sparse. The grass is very short and there will probably not be a spring burn this year. As I approach the entrance to Woolaroc, the blackjack forest is thicker and more of the trees are large and mature. No one has tried to control its growth since Frank Phillips tried brush goats. The drought in 1934 precipitously ended the effort. Drought is a regular feature of living in this land. Along the highway, the right of way becomes neatly mowed and soon the clean, manicured entry appears. Some Canadian geese are standing in the middle of the highway, just beyond the lily ponds at the Woolaroc gate.

The modern entry to Woolaroc has three lanes with an automatic barricade that lifts to allow visitors to be counted as they leave. I wave at Alice Barger, the gate attendant who has passed me in with a smile and wave most mornings for months now. Inside, I see the herd of elk just to the left, happily chewing cuds and napping in the same place as yesterday, which is their winter morning routine. I am carried back in time. I have spent so many hours reading the old letters of the 1920s and 1930s it is as if I have been transported back 70 years. The asphalt road is not the dusty dirt road Frank was constantly having oiled. Yet, the barns are the same, the fences are the same, the rock rip-rap along the road, the exotic animals, the haunted grove, the lodge, the tepees, the hokey Indian statue that waves good-bye as you cross the low-water bridge—they are all the same. There is a charm, a purposeful illusion at Woolaroc, as if you are standing at the threshold of a virtual reality. Woolaroc has a timeless sense of place. Fern Butler, Frank's early secretary, who grew to become assistant treasurer of Phillips Petroleum Company, and who was so intimately involved in the creation of the mystique of the ranch, understood this sense of place at a very early date. It was she who suggested its name: woods, lakes, rocks—Woolaroc.[1]

Inside the gates of this illusory place, driving through the herd of buffalo, picnicking by the picturesque lakes and springs, or perhaps discovering a broken flint along the hiking path can make a visitor feel he is partaking of nature. The red sandstone rocks along the draws tell an even longer tale. They tell us that Woolaroc was not always thus. Three hundred million years ago, during the Middle Pennsylvanian geological epoch, this place was under water. In fact, as far as the eye might see, water lapped along shallows and intermittent shorelines where the delta of a river emptied here into a shallow sea. The river carried reddish sand from the Wichita and Arbuckle Mountains to the southwest. That was the only land for hundreds of miles. The monsoon rains of the tropical climate washed red, sandy dirt from the youthful mountains into a long vanished river that deposited a delta that geologists now know as the Bigheart sandstone. There was abundant animal and plant life in that tropical world. It was an age in which fish, amphibians, and gigantic insects were prominent. On land there were forests of cane and lofty fern trees. The limestone around Bartlesville, only a few miles away, has abundant fossils to attest to the sea life of the time. The sandstone at Woolaroc reveals almost no shelly fauna. The porous, slightly acidic sands leeched away the calcium carbonate of the shells without a trace, but here and there a worm track or a mold is preserved as a witness to the sea life that once teemed here. The museum and barns of Woolaroc are built of sandstone quarried on the ranch, and today little children can run a finger along a wiggle worm track, never realizing they are touching a world 300,000,000 years old.[2]

As the hundreds of millennia passed, the tectonic plates gradually drifted back and forth, changing sea currents and land climates as the continents slowly emerged. The center of North America uplifted from below sea levels. The last ice age rapidly regressed only 11,000 years ago leaving a land that would, at last, be recognizable to us. Herds of big game, giant bison, mastodons, and horses roamed our continent then. The pine forests and giant mammals of the ice age disappeared as a warmer, drier climate developed, and hunters pressed the big game to extinction. By 4,000 years ago, eastern Oklahoma probably was a vast grassland.[3]

Indian foragers inhabited eastern Oklahoma very early as attested in radiocarbon dated sites as old as 9,416 years ago.[4] Archaeological survey of the Birch Creek area only seven miles south of Woolaroc shows that since the Archaic period the immediate area was traversed by hunters or small family bands, stopping to butcher a deer or do some fishing, but no major occupational sites were found. Those who are familiar with the frequent small collections at the Frank Phillips Ranch concur. The good springs were a reliable water source. Hunting and fishing must have been rewarding here, but resources would not support a long or large occupation. Museum director Bob Lansdown has walked the many paths and streams of Woolaroc for more than 30 years. He frequently makes small finds of flint points, chips, blades, and scrapers. There is a small display case in the first room of the museum that contains some nice specimens found in the area. Sources of the high quality local flint were not too distant, usually from Neosho or Hardy sources. Most points are the small triangular ones of more recent centuries. Only a few weeks ago Bob Lansdown found the top three-fourths of a Woodland Period blade of Neosho flint that was in a load of sand dredged that day from the creek.[5]

By the time of Francisco de Coronado's *entrada,* which passed as close as Cowley County, Kansas, the Wichita bands were moving into this area from northern Kansas. The Wichita were horticulturists who settled in large villages in the fertile flood plains, and they were formidable traders. Early in the 18th century the Wichita came under pressure from the powerful Osage who were on the move, pressing into eastern Oklahoma and Kansas. Lucrative trade with the French stimulated new competition for middlemen to deal with the fearful Comanche to the west. Osage ascendancy achieved dominance in precisely 1757, when the Wichita withdrew to the Red River. From that time, this area was essentially in Osage territory.[6]

In 1808, the Osage ceded a large portion of the territory under their control to the United States. Shortly, Cherokee families began to move into the ceded Arkansas Territory lands. By 1815, warfare broke out between the Osage and new interloper Cherokee. Several years of escalating outrages—Osage against Cherokee and then Cherokee against Osage—finally culminated in an alliance of the Eastern tribes that attacked and massacred many Osage in the winter of 1821. Thereafter, weakened by epidemics, continued war, and harangued by government agents and changed treaties, the harried Osage slowly found themselves reduced to the area that is now Osage County, a fateful and fortuitous allotment.[7] Chouteau Springs, along the road near the entrance of Woolaroc, is said to be the place where Louis Chouteau often traded with the Osage.[8] The chips and flints found at Woolaroc are remnants of the many peoples who lived on these lands: Osage and Wichita, unknown people groups now moved on or no longer existent, and ancient hunters of the most distant past.

The palpable presence of these Indian peoples weaves in and out among the blackjack trees and over the red sandstone rocks and crystalline springs. It is an essential part of the ambience of Oklahoma that the sense of place can not be divorced from the presence of Indians, animals, and oil. Woolaroc is a construction of the progressive and the modern in juxtaposition with the Romantic enthusiasm of a gentleman's estate. In Frank Phillips' time the ranch was a model of modern and scientific diversified farming, conservation, wildlife preservation, modern business practice, sophisticated sales, and public relations. The ranch was also a fictional world of exotic animals, eclectic collections, real Indians and outlaws, a genuine log cabin, old time charm, and a visionary collection of Western art. The business letters and appointment diaries of Frank Phillips in the Woolaroc and the Phillips Petroleum Company Archives, local history, interviews with locals and Phillips relatives, family movies, photos, public records, old newspapers, and publications all open a window to the past. Frank Phillips was not the first to collect Western art or begin a museum of ethnology or natural history or the first to promote a Romantic vision Old West. There is an intersection of the pragmatic and the Romantic at Woolaroc. Yet, his ranch has become a respected museum of these things and a living snapshot of a lifestyle in the heyday of Oklahoma oil. The history of Woolaroc is inextricably intertwined with the story of Frank Phillips and Phillips Petroleum Company—and with the land.

I

MOTHER NECESSITY: THE PRELUDE

SOMETIME DURING THE YEARS of World War I the world changed. The proof of the General Theory of Relativity in December of 1919 is regarded by some as the precise date of the paradigm shift that has defined our world since.[9] Certainly it was the time when the world witnessed the final dissolution of the ancien régime and, in the Soviet Union, the first emergence of totalitarianism. The world entered a war in horse-drawn vehicles and emerged in tanks, trucks, and aircraft. Before the turn of the century, Frederick Jackson Turner and Buffalo Bill Cody called America's attention to the end of the frontier and, as a way of life receded, America sensed that her frontier history embodied her unique identity. The United States took its place as a world industrial and political power after the Great War. American industry and technology took its place as a new sort of frontier. One American industrial giant that emerged in that time was Phillips Petroleum Company, a corporation that even from its early days was an innovator and pioneer within its industry.

The world changed in Osage County, Oklahoma, too. H.V. Foster's blanket oil lease of that county expired, and the Osage Tribe offered mineral leases in eastern Osage County at public auction in 1916.[10] At the time these things were eminent, in Bartlesville, Frank and L. E. Phillips had tired of the boom and bust cycles of the oil business and decided their fortunes were elsewhere. They were in the process of selling off the last of their oil leases and making plans to expand their banking interests into a proposed chain to be headquartered in Kansas City, Missouri.

Opposite: Frank and Jane Phillips' stylish Greek Revival town house was built in 1909. Its twenty-six rooms, including five bedrooms and nine bathrooms, were sumptuously decorated with oriental rugs, silks, and brocades of the era. For many years the mansion was the most imposing home in Bartlesville, rivaled only by Belle Meade which was just southwest of town. Before he built the ranch, the mansion was Frank's mainstay for entertaining visiting dignitaries. Courtesy Phillips Petroleum Company Archives.

The Phillipses owned a sublease in Osage County, designated Lot 185, which they acquired several years before from Foster. If they neglected to drill, by the terms of the agreement, the sublease would expire. The Foster lease provided that a subleasee could not sell his sublease, nor could he let it lie fallow without facing forfeiture. The Phillips brothers could not simply sell this lease to someone else, and they were loath to simply abandon their investment. Lucky for Frank and L. E., World War I increased the demand and price for crude oil so much that they decided to go ahead and develop their remaining Osage properties.[11] As a consequence, in 1916 their Lewcinda Oil & Gas Company received an extension of their lease from the Osage Tribe and test drilled six dry test wells on Lot 185. Finally, early in the next year, their seventh well came in at 100 barrels a day. Encouraged, they drilled one more well, just to the west. On March 22, 1917, Frank Phillips was standing on the drilling platform when a deep rumbling from the earth signaled a genuine gusher. That well, Number 8, came in at 1,000 barrels a day. It can be said that Number 8 was the beginning of Phillips Petroleum Company.[12]

Foster's lease gave the producer the right to acquire the acreage adjacent to a significant producing well. Because the earlier tests in Lot 185 were dry, the Phillipses released their lease on all but the quarter section containing Well Number 8 and exercised their option to lease the adjoining acreage in Lot 186, a total of 320 acres. This property was the SE of Section 11 and the SW of Section 12—Township 25—Range 11. In the spring of 1917, Number 8 changed the world for Frank Phillips.[13]

There was a flurry of new oil activity in the erstwhile chain-bankers' business plans. While the Phillips' Lewcinda crew continued their successful drilling season in Osage County, John H. Kane, a Bartlesville attorney whose father had been an early Pennsylvania wildcatter, was preparing articles of incorporation in the State of Delaware for the new Phillips Petroleum Company. The papers were signed 13 June 1917. Frank became the president of the new corporation and brother L. E. Phillips became the vice president. Henry E. Koopman, Frank's personal secretary, a business college graduate with early experience in oil field supply, was elected secretary-treasurer. Another key man was Clyde H. Alexander, a Pennsylvanian who had worked for Frank in the early days. He became superintendent of production. Frank Phillips was putting together the first Phillips team.

Well Number 8 in Lot 185 was in the southwest part of Section 12—Township 25—Range 11, that is, in the eastern part of the township. The adjacent Lot 186 extended to the west near to the present site of the Woolaroc Lodge. Foster's sublease lots were all about one-half of a mile wide, north to south, and three and three-fourths mile long, east to west, stacked in tiers which began at the Washington-Osage County line. Because the original well was in Lot 185, the entire field, though it was mostly in Lot 186, was named Lot 185. In 1917 this land was remote and inaccessible. Frank's teamsters spent an entire day delivering pipe and supplies by wagon up the rugged dirt roads that meandered into the Osage Camp at Lot 185. Frank himself drove a buckboard on his rounds between leases. Creeks, steep ravines, shaley banks, and the iron grip of the blackjack oaks are what made this land inaccessible; outlaw hideouts in the hills around nearby Okesa added an aura of the Wild West.[14]

Frank Phillips was now keenly interested in this part of the Osage. On 12 July 1917, he bought the NE ¼ of Section 11 from Fred Horton for $2500, a price that was well above the going rate. At that early stage, the company was a shell corporation, but soon the Phillips brothers began to transfer property into the company. Frank transferred the Horton property to Phillips Petroleum Company on 17 August.[15] This property included Number 8 and was soon to be the site of Phillips Petroleum Company's second gasoline plant, the Osage Plant. The Osage Plant was on line by the summer of 1918. The plant, an associated settlement of lease houses, a two-room school (where the church and Sunday School also met), a boarding house, and a grocery store eventually became informally known as Phillipsburg to the Lot 185 workers who lived there.

This is a grey-tone replication of a section of map showing Woolaroc and Lot 185. The elevations of the rugged Osage where outlaws once hid, and where Frank Phillips first struck oil and then built his showpiece ranch and museum, can easily be seen. The watershed and the many springs, as well as the lakes built by Frank Phillips will help in orientation as the story of Woolaroc unfolds. USGS, State of Oklahoma, Woolaroc Quadrangle, Township 25 North.

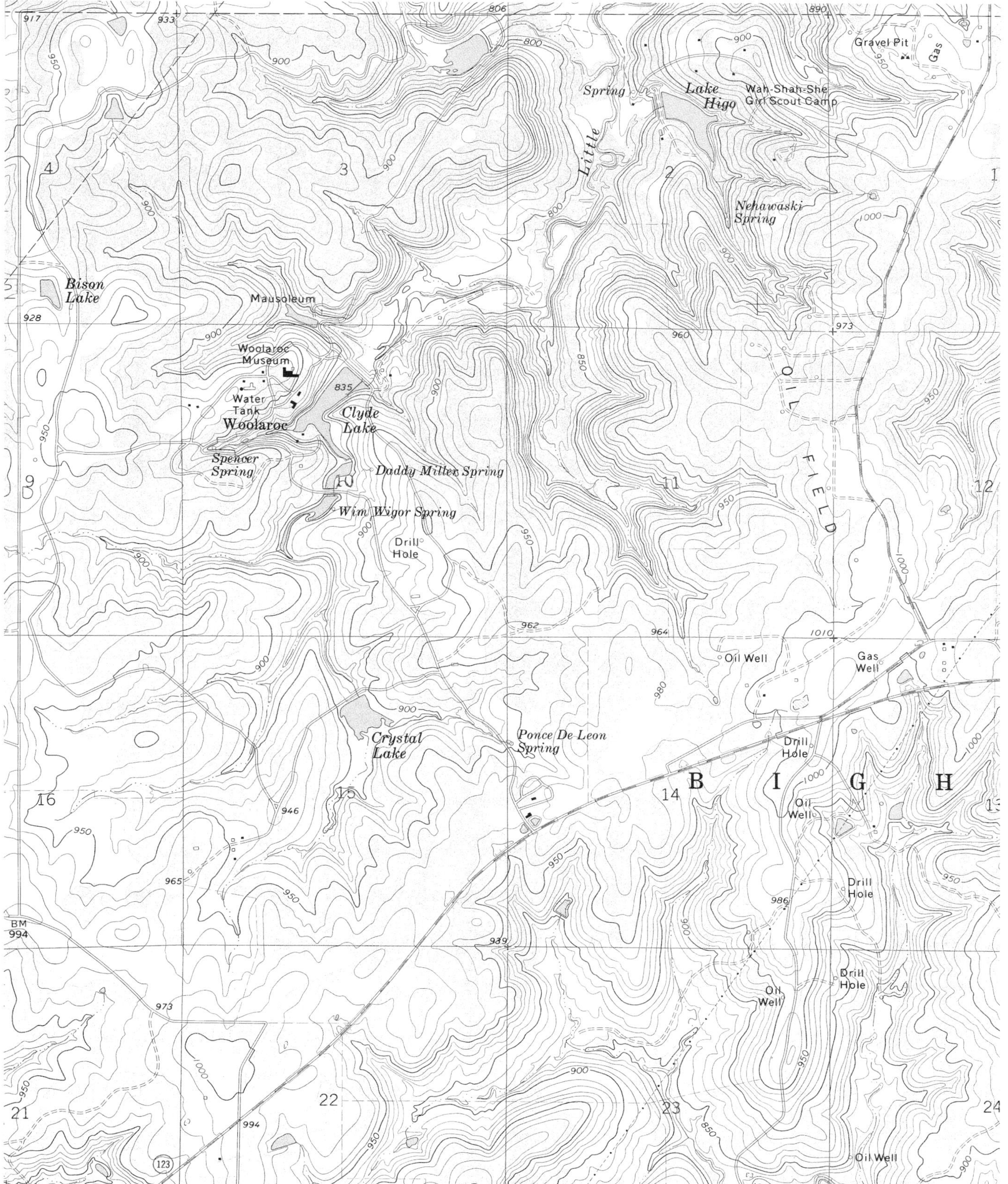
Bison Lake
Mausoleum
Woolaroc Museum
Water Tank
Woolaroc
Clyde Lake
Spencer Spring
Daddy Miller Spring
Wim Wigor Spring
Drill Hole
Spring
Little
Lake Higo
Wah-Shah-She Girl Scout Camp
Gravel Pit
Gas
Nehawaski Spring
OIL FIELD
Oil Well
Gas Well
Crystal Lake
Ponce De Leon Spring
B I G H
BM 994
123

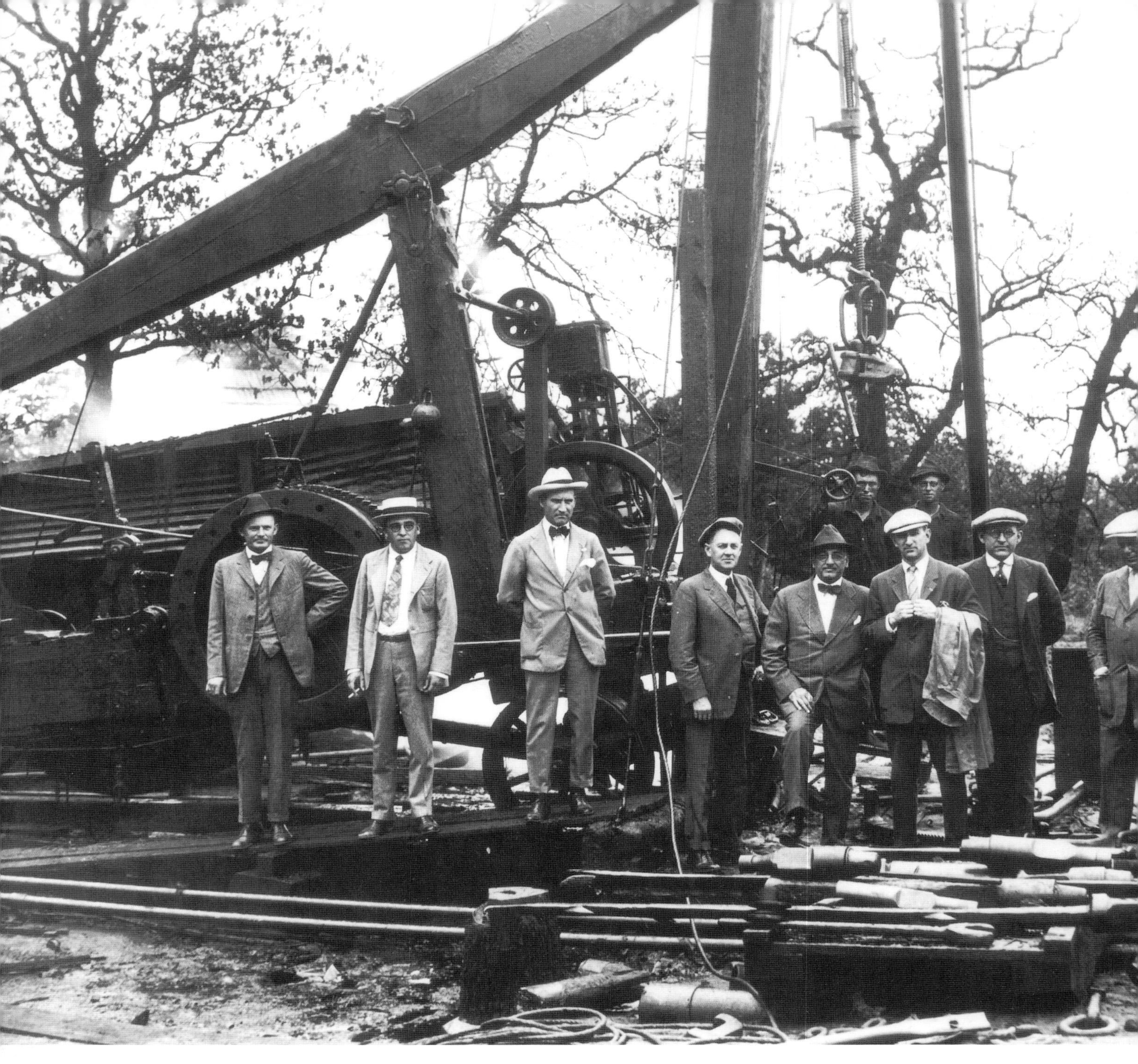

Below: Old time Bartlesville photographer Frank Griggs took a series of panoramic photographs at Phillipsburg on Lot 185 in 1920. The photo below faces north, showing the Osage Plant, the last company plant that used the old compression process to make gasoline from the natural gas. The little settlement for oil field workers included a grocery store, a boarding house, and a school (where church and Sunday School also met). The company-owned houses had a bedroom, sitting room, kitchen, and a path out back. There was no electricity or running water. In 1922 the plant burned after an explosion and was not rebuilt, but the settlement persisted for several years. In the photograph blackjack oaks encroach beneath the crest of the hill; today the concrete ruins of the plant can be seen amidst blackjack and sumac thickets. Courtesy Woolaroc.

Left: In the early days there was little to do for entertainment during the annual directors meetings but go out to the Osage and ogle oil wells. In fact, a trip to Lot 185 was pretty heady stuff in those days when big gushers and free-flowing wells were frequent features. In 1919, directors of Phillips Petroleum Company journeyed from Bartlesville out to inspect Lot 185. Shown posed in front of a cable tool rig are (left to right) Clyde Alexander, John G. Phillips, George S. Marshall, John H. Kane, Richard H. Higgins, B. S. Prentice, L. T. Crutcher, Arthur Stickney, and L. E. Phillips. Two oil-begrimed roughnecks join the picture in the background. Courtesy Woolaroc.

A person can still drive by the old Phillipsburg site. Bartlesville people know this road heading north off of the Barnsdall Road as the road to Girl Scout Camp Wah-Sha-She. The ruins of the Osage Plant are readily seen from the dirt road, with concrete foundations overgrown with thickets of sumac and tall bluestem. The old photographs show a fairly open acreage, but today the blackjack oak is encroaching. There is a taut five-strand barbed wire fence with new red t-posts on both sides of the road. Local folks know that the owner, Curt Ballew, does not allow trespassing and is a crack shot. There is an interesting recent story in that regard.

Below: The Osage lease auctions were held under a large elm tree in front of the Osage Council House in Pawhuska. After the discovery of the Burbank Field, leases sold for such large sums that the tree was dubbed the "million dollar elm." For years, huge crowds gathered to bid on the leases and to watch the excitement. It was here that Frank bid the million dollars that he and John Kane raised in Kansas City in February 1920, opening the field for Phillips Petroleum Company. Courtesy Woolaroc.

One of Frank's most important social contact points in New York, and an early source of influence on his artistic interests, was the Lotos Club, a very exclusive New York social club which was organized in 1870 for the promotion of American arts and letters. When Frank joined in 1923, it was located at 110 West 57 Street, shown in this photograph. On the wall are framed menus from Lotos Club's elegant state dinners, featuring the most important people of the era as honored guests. The club manager, J. Steinfeld, was very enthusiastic about Woolaroc. He gave Frank some early gifts for the lodge and sold Jane some paintings for the mansion. Courtesy Lotos Club, New York.

On that particular day, Ballew had been working cattle in the morning and came home for lunch. When he got out of his truck, his stock dog was acting strangely, so Ballew picked up his gun from the rack in his truck. At that moment a rough-looking stranger came out the door carrying a pillowcase loaded with Ballew's belongings. Ballew leveled his gun on the culprit and ordered him to put his hands up—just as an old beat-up car with Tulsa license plates pulled into the drive, looking for his associate. Ballew got the drop on the second man too, and made both malefactors follow him to the house while he called the sheriff. Then, he took them back out into the yard where he held them at gunpoint, on their knees, with hands behind them, weeping and begging for their lives for 45 minutes, waiting on the sheriff who never came. Finally Ballew told them to get on out of there and got a shot off in the air as they roared out of the drive. It was then that he realized he only had one bullet. He was man of the Osage and trespassers are not welcome on his land.

Ballew's friends and neighbors know him to be open, generous, and a loyal man to have as friend. Ballews have lived in these parts since the old days when outlaws lived in these hills. Curt's father bought this property in 1943 from Frank Phillips. Stripper wells now dot his acres that were once part of old Lot 185. On down the county road, a little way from his Phillipsburg property, is the entry to the Girl Scout Camp. From the road into the camp you can see the museum and lodge at Woolaroc, just above Clyde Lake.

The site for the Osage Plant was chosen because of the proximity of a good spring-fed water source at Rock Creek which could run the steam engines used in the compression processing of the natural gas that was being produced at Lot 185. The natural gas from this sand is what oil men call "wet," that is, it contains higher molecular weight hydrocarbons, especially ethylene, in addition to the methane. These heavier hydrocarbons were the fraction condensed out in the compression process, and naptha was added to make gasoline.[16] The method was soon abandoned because it produced an inferior gasoline product, so that the Osage Plant was the last of its kind built by the company. Frank Phillips was probably familiar with the good-sized pond in the northwest quadrant of Section 10 from the time of Lewcinda's 1914 drilling in that section. It may have been Clyde Alexander who suggested using the lake that now carries his name, Clyde Lake, as a water source for the plant.

On September 24, 1917, Frank bought the SW ¼ of Section 10 from Julia A. Labadie for $1200.[17] In 1914 this quarter section had been drilled, yielding three dry holes, but this is in the section that today contains Woolaroc's lakes, lodge, and museum in its northwest quarter. On January 7, 1918, Frank Phillips bought the SW ¼ of Section 1 from Joseph Daniels for $1,200.[18] It was part of the Lot 185 land drilled in 1917 for oil, and again in 1928 for both gas and oil.

It appears that in 1917 and 1918, when Frank purchased land in Township 25, his main interest was this oil field that established Phillips Petroleum Company. In Osage County only the surface can be purchased, for all mineral rights belong to the Osage Tribe who collect royalties on the gas and oil.[19] Owning the surface would allow Frank to utilize the land for his own purposes without landowner's complaints of rutted up pastures, saltwater spills, or noisy machinery.

It is probable that he was aware of this picturesque section from a very early date. For many years before Frank Phillips owned the Woolaroc land, locals drove buggies out from Bartlesville for all-day picnics at Crystal Springs, and young men favored the romantic spot for pitching a little woo to their sweethearts.[20] Frank may only have had eyes for oil wells in 1917, but he could not have missed the potential of the appealing, remote place.

The increasing demands of business soon took Frank away from rounds on his oil fields. He characteristically worked grueling days. It was typical for him to arrive at his office about 9:00 or 9:30 A.M., take a working business lunch from noon to about 1:30 P.M., return to the office until about 4:00 or 5:00, have a dinner business meeting until about 7:00, then return to the office until 10:00 or 11:00 P.M. This was frequently the pattern seven days a week. His appointment calendars sometimes even show he was in the office on Christmas or Thanksgiving. The social life that was interspersed usually had a business character to it. Business was increasingly requiring that he travel to the East to make the contacts and find the financing for the growth of the company he envisioned. Paul Endacott said that in the past he had seen appointment calendars for the earlier years, but existent calendars begin in 1920.[21] In that year, Phillips Petroleum Company opened a small New York office. Frank Phillips spent only 163 days in Bartlesville in 1920.[22]

That was the same year as the opening of the Burbank Field in northwestern Osage County. In 1963, Milton McGreevy, then vice chairman of Harris Upham, in Kansas City, told Robert M. Kane, who was a summer intern, an interesting old story. He told of the day when Frank Phillips and John H. Kane came to town looking for money. Kane had practiced law in Kansas City before 1904, and his brother-in-law was Kansas City developer J. C. Nichols. McGreevy sat in on a meeting in his father's office when Phillips and Kane told their tale, extolling the promised treasures of the Burbank Field. He reminisced that the men were so convincing about the riches of the field that the senior McGreevy loaned them one million dollars at ten percent interest, due in one year. Frank Phillips' appointment calendar for January 14, 1920 shows stockholders' and a directors' meeting, then afterwards a conference with Fernando P. Neal of the National Bank of Commerce in Kansas City.[23] One week later it shows that Frank left for Kansas City and spent two days. Frank was at the Osage Sale on February 3, 1920. Likely, this is the episode that McGreevy remembered. Phillips Petroleum Company entered heavily into the bidding at the Million Dollar Elm and was always one of the most successful bidders at the sales.[24]

It was the Burbank Field that thrust Phillips into the big time, and it was the insatiable need for growth financing that thrust Frank into the Eastern social scene. How does a farm boy from Iowa, who knew what it was to be showered by Oklahoma crude, break into the social world of high finance? All the people who knew him agree, if anything, Frank Phillips was a salesman. All the old company biographical sketches relate the story of Frank Phillips' career as a barber in Creston, Iowa. He learned the trade at 13 and had a string of shops, with barbers working for him on commission. Frank, whose hairline was seriously receding by that time, successfully sold a home-brewed tonic hair-restorer. In New York City, Frank would successfully sell Phillips Petroleum Company to wary big investors during the years of the Roaring Twenties and the grim years of the Great Depression. In an evaluation of Phillips' personality, Paul Endacott said he was "a super-salesman and negotiator, but not tricky or unscrupulous, because he said he wanted to lay the groundwork for some unknown future deal." He "worked incessantly to develop acquaintanceships with, and confidence of influential people who might have potential value in behalf of the Company."[25]

Men's associations and professional clubs were some of the principal places where business social networks were formed in those days. Of course, Frank had numerous business appointments in his office, or in the offices of people he was working with, but the luncheons and dinners where men smoked a few cigars, told jokes, and talked business were where those contacts were developed into real relationships. In the 1920 appointment book, the New York part of the records began in September. Phillips' new 115 Broadway office was opened Wednesday, September 29, 1920. Sure enough, Frank went to the Bankers Club for a luncheon meeting for the first time in the calendar on October 2, though he had probably been a member there for some time before the record begins.[26]

The Bankers Club must have been his point of entry, and it was a club that continued to enjoy his favor over the years. E. P. Earle, a Phillips director, took him to lunch at the Railroad Club in New York on October 5. This was an important contact because Phillips would be shipping large quantities of crude by the railroads.

Bartlesville's antecedent country club was Oak Hill, just west of the airport where the Osage Hills abruptly rise beyond the old meadow that was then the airfield. The old clubhouse was a two-story frame structure. The club boasted a nine-hole golf course with sand greens, tennis courts, and an unfiltered swimming pool. In this 1919 photo, Dick Kane plays with a cat on the first tee. The wooden box in the background held sand to make tees. Courtesy Richard Kane.

The Spanish Colonial-style clubhouse of the new Hillcrest Country Club was designed by Frank's hand-picked Kansas City architect, Edward Buehler Delk. Delk also designed the John H. Kane house, the Paul Dahlgren house, and H. V. Foster's La Quinta in Bartlesville, as well as Philbrook and Philmont for Waite Phillips. The new emerging star, Perry Maxwell, designed the golf course. Maxwell went on to design Colonial Country Club golf course at Ft. Worth, Texas; Southern Hills in Tulsa; Oklahoma City Golf and Country Club; and Prairie Dunes at Hutchinson, Kansas. The country club was the centerpiece in the Phillips-Foster initiative of community improvement and provided a ritzy focal point for Bartlesville social activities. Courtesy Edgar Weston.

Shortly, B. S. Prentice, another director, took Frank Phillips to the Lawyers Club for lunch; then Prentice and A. C. Earnst took him again the next day, probably to propose him for membership. He went to the Bankers Club with Dr. H. B. Baruch, and John Markle took him to the Union League Club. Frank Phillips was racking up social obligations rapidly, as he also rapidly developed the business contacts he needed in New York.[27]

By the end of the year, his favored New York luncheon site was the Lawyers Club. He ate lunch there most days. The Eastern directors meeting was held at the Lawyers Club the next spring. When the directors were in Bartlesville for the annual stockholders meeting, it was in Frank Phillips' office, and dinner was at his home. The annual company picnic was held at Pershing, Oklahoma, that summer. At this point, the social needs of Frank and his company remained relatively modest.[28]

Modestly, Frank "motored with various officers and employees of Phillips Petroleum Company to the Osage Sale" on June 14, 1921. That sale made it clear to Frank Phillips that he was in immediate need of a great deal more financing. On June 21, Frank and John Kane made another trip to Kansas City. In July there were a series of meetings with Guaranty Trust in New York. In Bartlesville on August 15, "Mr. Lewis of Strandberg McGreevy" was in the office late in the afternoon, then only two days later "Mr. Phillips was in Chicago on several matters principally in regard to proposed note issue of Phillips Petroleum Company." Kansas City was not able to come through with all the financing Frank needed so Phillips additionally turned to Chicago and the Big Apple. Frank rode to New York from Chicago in Harry Sinclair's private car.[29]

That summer the character of the Phillips' social involvement in New York City began to intensify. On July 24, 1921, Frank and Jane spent the day at John Markle's country home. Mary Markle was the daughter of a partner in Drexel, Morgan & Company, and John was the director of George B. Markle and Company, an anthracite company. He was an important member of Frank's board and grew to become a very good friend. The Phillipses had other invitations to homes and parties—the kind of activities that had not appeared on the last year's calendar. And the Phillipses began to invite dinner guests to their Ambassador Hotel apartment for evenings and holidays. They went to a Mr. Perry's residence at Great Neck for the day, and when there again two weeks later, they took a dip in the ocean. They motored to Long Island with Mr. and Mrs. C. E. Crawley.[30] Frank also began to broaden his club memberships in the city. He went to the Recess Club more frequently over the next couple of years and visited several new clubs with friends. One of his most significant affiliations began in 1923. On May 1, Colonel Lindsley and J. F. Allen took Frank to dinner at the Lotos

Club. By the end of that year, Frank joined a party of friends at the Lotos Club on a free evening.[31] This old social club has an intellectual mission and has been the site of many important art shows and lectures, among other things, over the years.[32] This club had many impressive national and international reciprocity contacts. It was a particular favorite of H. V. Foster, too, where he bought some of his fine academic painting collection. Membership added a dimension of urbane sophistication to Frank's New York social life which he enjoyed the rest of his life.

Frank was beginning to become aware that he was in need of better means of entertaining his business acquaintances. There are signs in the record that he was beginning actively to arrange means to improve his social resources. He played golf with John Kane in Bartlesville on June 4. He played in New York with John Phillips at Apawamus Country Club on June 29, 1921.[33] Frank played golf with Higgins at Blind Brook Country Club on September 10. John Kane played with Frank at Rockaway Country Club on September 25. Finally, for three successive days in November in Bartlesville, Frank played golf with John Phillips and John Kane. Mind you, Frank Phillips was not a particularly good golfer, nor did he especially enjoy the game. It must have been a warm winter because he played golf with John Kane at Oak Hill on the day after Christmas.[34]

The old Oak Hill Club in Bartlesville was just west of the present airport. It had an attractive two-storey, homey clubhouse, a tennis court, and a concrete, unfiltered swimming pool. The dining room was only open on advance notice. The golf course was not up to Eastern standards, having only nine holes with sand greens. There were sandboxes by the tees for scooping up a pinch of sand, used for teeing up the balls.[35] On December 30 Frank met with H. V. Foster in Foster's office before they went to the annual country club stockholders meeting.[36] Frank and H. V. were probably discussing a plan for upgrading the Bartlesville club to a more sophisticated standard. Frank was moving to enhance Bartlesville.

Frank was trying to entertain business guests in Bartlesville. When bankers and directors came to town there was little to do but head out to the Osage to ogle oil wells and then eat dinner and spend the night at the house. In the years of 1923, 1924, and 1925 the growth of Phillips Petroleum Company was nothing short of explosive. Its net worth went from \$3,000,000 in 1917, to \$103,000,000 in 1924, and to \$130,000,000 in 1925.[37] For a while the Phillips brothers seriously considered moving the company to New York City.[38] On March

26, 1922 Frank and John Phillips motored to Great Neck, New York, to see a house.[39] They wavered in their decision and Frank decided to fix up the Bartlesville house. In those days, his mansion was the most formidable house in town whose only rival was the Belle Meade estate just southwest of the city. When he built it in 1909, it was the height of fashion, but it must have been looking a little dated as the Phillips financial dynamo gathered steam. On April 7 the calendar says furniture men were there from Kansas City; a Mr. Boghasiar, a Lebanese rug dealer, was there from Wichita, Kansas, on June 2; Fred Beecroft, who later owned Beecroft Decorating, a painting firm, called in Phillips office on June 12 and 22.[40] Frank went to the company picnic, this year at L. E.'s new farm south of town, a pleasant improvement from past years.[41] By fall Frank was entertaining the American Legion officers in his newly redecorated home during their convention. Only a few weeks later he had a big dinner party for Senator Harreld at the house.[42]

The country club pot continued to simmer on the back burner. Frank was at the annual stockholders meeting in Foster's office again in December 1922. Winter dances became important enough to be mentioned in the diaries from 1922 through 1925. On March 25, 1925, Frank conferred with John Phillips, H. V. Foster, and Dr. Howard Weber in his office. Later the same day, Reverend O. B. Morris of the Methodist Church and W. W. Jones were in the office. Finally, Dana Reynolds came by. The last notation said "office conferences," so it can be presumed that the foregoing was not company business.[43] Two weeks later Frank played golf again, for the first time in several months, at Apawamus Country Club with R. H. Higgins and Charles Ellis.[44]

In the summer of 1925, John G. Phillips and W. D. Reynolds began buying up land in Section 30—Township 26—Range 13 of Washington County. Then, on December 9, John Phillips and Dana Reynolds sold the property to Hillcrest Country Club.[45] On October 19, Frank was in Kansas City and made a point of going to

Top: A 1922 wide-angle photograph of Waite Phillips' elegant new estate at 1621 S. Owasso in Tulsa. In April 1923, Waite hosted Frank's directors for dinner on their annual tour, stopping as they made their way by private rail car from the Burbank Field to Bristow. As the directors enjoyed the hospitality of the elegant home, Waite's old time cabin in the backyard sparked Frank's interest and gave him some ideas of his own. Courtesy Waite Phillips Collection, The Philbrook Museum of Art Archives.

the Kansas City Country Club.[46] On November 24, the calendar specifically says, "conference with Wing, John, and executive committee on country club matter."[47] The charter membership list of the club closed a week earlier with 177 new members.[48] Key names of old members were conspicuous in the fact of their absence from the press release: Foster, Dahlgren, Phillips, Kane, Koopman, Alexander, Straight, Weber, Reynolds, Blue, etc. The club continued to lease and buy land for several years, but they now had the needed nucleus of land.

Frank's fingerprints are all over the maneuver. The first club president was F. L. Dunn, Vice President of First National Bank. When he took a job as President of Tulsa's First National Bank a year later, W. D. Reynolds, John's best friend and President of First Investment Corp., became the new club president. Acclaimed golf course architect Perry Maxwell designed the new eighteen-hole course.[49] Edward Beuhler Delk, already designer of J. C. Nichol's Country Club Plaza and the Kansas City Country Club, was brought in as architect for the stylish Spanish colonial clubhouse at the suggestion of John H. Kane. With this flurry of golf club activity in Bartlesville, Frank's appointment books mention only an occasional purposeful golf game after the Foster meeting of December 30, 1921.[50]

The watershed year for Bartlesville was 1923. On February 15, Clarence Burlingame came over to talk to Frank after dinner about building an office building. Burlingame and Maire owned the property that was eventually purchased for the Phillips Building in 1925.[51] Thereafter Frank began walking home after work with John Kane who lived three doors north on Cherokee. On March 2, Frank, Fred Dunn, H. J. Holm, John H. Kane, Clyde Alexander, and A. H. Riney met with an architect, and a week later they met with Philip Thomas, a landscape architect from Tulsa. On April 16 Phillips met with

About the time that Frank quietly began his purchases of land adjacent to Lot 185, which would become Woolaroc, he made his first call on his future ranch manager, Grif Graham on 11 April 1922. Bartlesville Chief of Police Wines took Frank Phillips to visit Grif and Orpha Graham's Bartlesville home, shown here. Judging from the photograph, Grif's collection of horns must have been quite a sight. Four years later, ranch manager Grif Graham wrote Frank that he was hanging these very horns in the new lodge, only days before its debut for the annual directors meeting. Courtesy Bartlesville Area History Museum.

a Mr. Palmer of the fire department, ostensibly about educational issues. A few days later Palmer and John Kane bid on a building at Fourth Street and Johnstone Avenue but did not succeed in buying it.[52]

While these things were transpiring, Frank Phillips put on a real show for the annual meeting. Directors from Tulsa, New York, Kansas City, and St. Louis arrived in Bartlesville by special car on April 3, 1923. The stockholders meeting was in his office, with a luncheon at the Maire Hotel downtown, followed by a directors meeting in Frank's office and a dinner and reception at his home. That night all retired to the special car which carried them, while they slept, to Pawhuska, in neighboring Osage County. The next day they motored to Pershing, Foraker, and Burbank and returned again to spend the night in the special car. On April 5, the Osage sale was being held. The directors were there to experience the thrill, when a nod or a slightly raised hand purchased a million-dollar lease. After the sale, the private car carried them to Tulsa to be entertained by Waite Phillips at his beautiful new home on South Owasso, and on to Bristow, Oklahoma that night. On the 6th they motored over to Bristow, then returned to Tulsa to leave for the East.[53] The tour was such a success that it was repeated and embellished over the next few years, growing to "an early modern safari-extravaganza" by 1925.[54]

By April it seems the decision to stay in Bartlesville was mostly settled. Back on October 28, 1922, Chief Gaston had called in Frank's office the day after A.G. and Ruby Williams notarized a deed selling ranch land in the Osage to Frank Phillips.[55] L. U. Gaston was the Chief of the Bartlesville Police Department in those days, but he also kept several fine riding horses, which he stabled at a public livery.[56] On April 7, the day after the annual meeting, Frank went to Johnstone Park where he bought some of Gaston's horses.[57] These two horses were transferred to the Woolaroc account books in 1927. Home movies taken about 1928 of horseback riders at Woolaroc show these two, gaited horses that look like Saddlebreds and some Pintos. All of the horses were exceptionally fine animals.

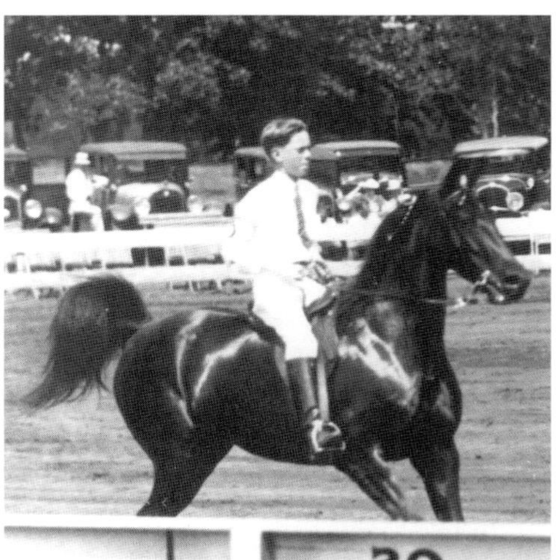

Center: Fine, gated riding and show horses were popular with the Bartlesville social set in those days. Hillcrest Country Club even had riding stables on the grounds to the southwest. In 1934 and 1935 the community hosted the first and second annual Bartlesville National Horse Shows which were the social events of the season. Here Dick Kane rides his Saddlebred mare, Nancy, in the 1934 show. Courtesy Richard Kane.

The elegant smooth action of the two Saddlebreds is obvious.[58] It seems probable that in October Frank discussed with Gaston the quality of animals he wanted, but it was not until April that the chief found appropriate horses. Before Woolaroc was built, Frank Phillips liveried his horses at Almeda Boarding Barn in downtown Bartlesville. Reminiscent of the golf club flurry, over the next several months, with increasing frequency, Frank Phillips went horseback riding evenings when he was in Bartlesville.[59] For Frank, riding was a personal pleasure that persisted for many years. Old employees at Woolaroc still remember they were expected to have Phillips' horse saddled and waiting at the lodge at 4:30 every afternoon.

On cue, horsy enthusiasm swept Bartlesville. The Belle Meade estate had a popular racetrack for many years.[60] Now Bartlesville society took up blooded pleasure horses. The new country club even sported a Spanish Colonial-style riding stable and rings. Hugh Dempsey, a retired United States Cavalry sergeant, became trainer for several show-horses around town. In 1934, the town even hosted its First (there were only two) Bartlesville National Horse Show, though the purse needed to be awfully hefty to attract participants. While Bartlesville emulated the Eastern country squires, Frank kept fine Western-type horses for his ranch guests. Mindful of the fashion trends, he kept Pintos in the early days and Palominos in later years.

On the weekend of February 29, 1923, Frank and Clyde Alexander motored to Pawhuska for lunch, then up to Burbank, and over to Ponca City that evening for a party given by oilman Lew Wentz. They stayed on the 101 Ranch at the Miller Brothers White House.[61] Frank

Watch Hill was the Foster family estate in Rhode Island. When Frank and Bill Skelly visited H. V. Foster at his home in 1922, it was clear that H. V. enjoyed the social heritage of an Eastern aristocrat. A week later Ernest W. Marland took Frank on a cruise up to Rhode Island on his yacht, and they made another call on their Bartlesville friend at Watch Hill. Foster's Eastern lifestyle probably helped Frank come to grips with the probability that he could not maximize his own potential in that rarified social atmosphere and ought to exploit possibilities on his own turf. Courtesy Ami Preston.

had been there many times, but this must have been a thought-provoking interlude, if not an actual fact-finding trip. On April 9, Clyde Alexander and Frank motored out to Lot 185.[62] It may have been some time since Frank had visited the site of his big strike, for his calendars do not mention a trip there. In the interim, Number 8 had gone dry and was plugged in 1922.[63] Only a year before, on April 5, 1922, the Osage Plant had exploded when some methane had gotten lose and drifted into an open flame. This may have been partly a business inspection, but with Frank clearly thinking about parlaying his property in Section 10 into a country estate; the picturesque potential of the site must have inspired excitement. Frank made sure no one would ever want to drill on this property. His geologists assured him there was no oil, which has proved to be the case.

Another important character was one of the local law enforcement officers. On April 11, Mr. Wines took Frank to see Grif Graham's collection of horns and relics.[64] Grif was the sheriff of Washington County from 1914 to 1918. He was a popular man around the area and a very colorful caricature of the Old West. Befitting his Woolaroc role, the highlight of his tenure as sheriff was when he shot a horse from under Henry Wells during a 1915 bank robbery. His collection of horns was certainly interesting to Frank and possibly so was the interview with Grif. He would become the first manager of the Frank Phillips Ranch in August of 1925. Many of the horns in Grif's collection are now part of the Woolaroc collection.

Only two weeks later, April 29, 1922 in New York, R. H. Higgins, a company director, took Frank to look over a Connecticut home. This was the first in a rapid series of estates and homes that Frank visited over the next several months. It seems he was again considering an Eastern estate where he could do the kind of extravagant entertaining that was becoming imperative and was so hard to do in Oklahoma. A month later, the weekend of May 29, the Phillips family went to Director E. P. Earle's country home at Monticello, New Jersey. Over the weekend, they looked over the area for a possible country estate. They looked at a city house at 5th Avenue and 90th Street on June 4. On the weekend of August 11, Bill Skelly and Frank went to H. V. Foster's Rhode Island ocean shore estate, Watch Hill. Foster's estate had been in the family for generations. The following weekend Frank spent on E. W. Marland's yacht. They cruised by Watch Hill to call on Foster and take another dip in the ocean.

On the first weekend of September the Phillipses were playing golf and horseback riding at George V. Coe's Red

Bank, New Jersey estate. A few days later he went to see the Isaac Guggenheim estate. He went to Long Island with a realtor on September 9, and to a house on West 53rd Street on 17 November. E. P. Earle entertained them at Montclair, New Jersey, for another golf weekend on October 22. The social whirl must have been very informative to Frank's critical intuition and helpful toward stimulating his imagination. He was working overtime to come up with just the right estate for an oil tycoon. Frank and Jane continued similar visits over the next year or so, probably still considering an Eastern estate, but by the spring of 1923 Frank was already moving on his initial plan for a ranch in the Osage.[65]

The national economy had taken a post-war dip in 1922 and was on the road to recovery by the spring of 1923. But, in the Plains States there was a serious drought in 1922, and the agriculture continued in a slump, lagging behind the general economy. As usual in drought years, there was a cattle sell-off to relieve the grass, and cattle prices dropped. These were hard years for ranchers because they had not gotten a chance to enjoy the recovering economy. In Osage County, a young ranching couple named A. G. and Ruby Williams had leased about 2,000 acres in Sections 3, 4, 10, and 15 of Township 25—Range 11 right after the war, then purchased the land from Ed L. Kennedy in 1920. Strapped financially, the drought was ruinous to them. They were a well-liked local ranching family for many years. Old timers in Osage County say Ruby was sort of a character. They remember a local joke from a time when Ruby wrote a check at the Piggly Wiggly grocery, addressing the check "Piggly" and signing "Wiggly." In 1922 and 23, Frank Phillips gave them a second chance. The deed record shows that they signed deeds, selling the NW ¼ and W ½ of the NE ¼ of Section 10, the site where the lodge and museum now stand, to Phillips Petroleum Company November 8, 1922.[66] They sold more pieces of their Township 25 ranch to the company on May 22-23, 1923. Other deeds followed on August 7, September 15 and 27; and in the summer of 1924 on June 15 and 28.[67] Additional deeds from other landholders would soon follow, but by the fall of 1924, Frank had the nucleus of his ranch. John Kane filed all the Williams' deeds for Phillips Petroleum Company on October 27, 1924.[68] The Williamses were able to start over. The young couple had two daughters who eventually married and moved back East. A. G. and Ruby did finally lose their ranch in the 1930s.

Frank wavered one more time in his resolution to keep the company in Bartlesville. Waite Phillips suddenly sold his interests to Blair & Co. in the summer of 1925. Blair wanted Waite to "contact Frank because he wanted the Phillips Petroleum Company to join in the big merger of oil companies."[69] On August 5, 1925 Waite Phillips came up to Bartlesville to spend the afternoon before Frank and Jane left for New York. On August 8 Harry Lockhart of Blair & Company came to the office and left with Frank for lunch at the Racquet Club. Frank had nearly daily meetings with Lockhart for the next two or three weeks. In the midst of these, Frank and Jane spent the weekend of August 16 at Bridgeport, Connecticut, with the H. L. Joneses and E. E. Stetsons. On 21 August Frank was back in Bartlesville. That day there were a series of executive committee meetings, and a Mr. DeGroyler was there as an appraiser. DeGroyler was in the office again on the 24th and 27th. In the midst of the Blair negotiations, on August 27, 1925, Frank drove out to the Osage Lodge (evidently the cabin that preceded the Woolaroc Lodge) with Grif Graham for the first time. L. E. Phillips and John Kane spent the day of September 15 in conference with Frank on the appraisal matter. Then, Kane and Alexander went with Frank to New York to meet with directors, with Frank making several calls over the next few days at Blair & Company. All the directors seemed to be in town by October 1, and thereafter no more mention of Blair & Company was made in the calendars. Waite later said, "when I talked with him in Bartlesville about it he was in another periodical mood to sell but after negotiating with Lockhart in New York something happened to cause him to change his mind."[70]

Shortly after the Blair & Company deal fell apart, Frank began work on an office building for Phillips Petroleum Company in Bartlesville. They had been searching for a downtown site and finally settled on Fourth and Keeler, the site owned by Burlingame and Maire. A. S. Keene of Keene & Simpson in Kansas City met with Frank for the first time on October 23.[71] This firm collaborated with Edward Buehler Delk to design the Philtower for Waite Phillips in 1927. In 1925, they began plans for the Phillips Building in Bartlesville. The pieces of the grand plan suddenly began to come together. Within weeks, Delk and Perry Maxwell were selected to start the country club. Frank already had a special vision for the Rock Creek Ranch, as Woolaroc was called early in 1925.

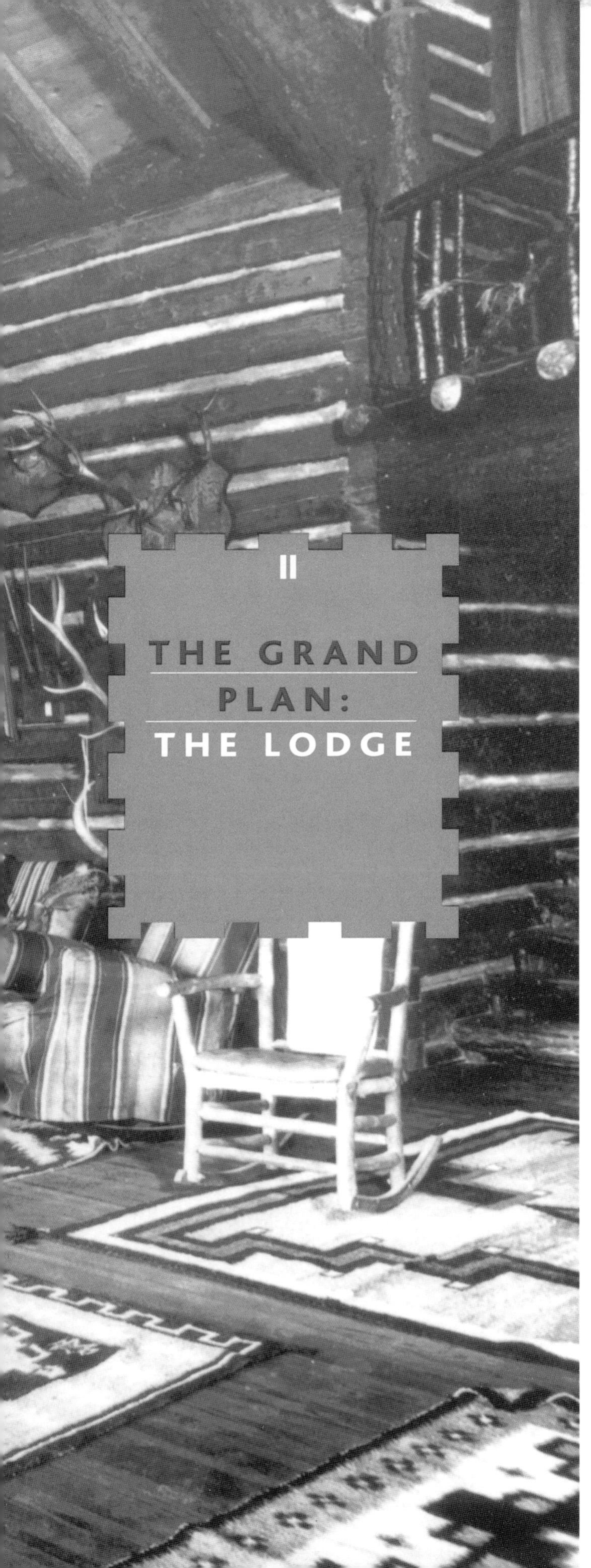

II

THE GRAND PLAN: THE LODGE

BY THE TIME THAT FRANK FINALLY decided not to sell out in 1925, he had already begun work on his new game preserve in Osage County. For the first time, the calendar of August 27, 1925 shows that Frank went out to the Osage Lodge with Grif Graham. The site of an old cabin above the Rock Creek Lake was an ideal place to enjoy a little relaxation on the front porch and a retreat from town—and no doubt, the happy put-put-put-put, squeak-clank of his oil field carried on easterly breezes. Paul Endacott said there was an earlier cabin at the site before the lodge was built. Though no one thought to ask him the character of the cabin that was there, the general impression is that it was a place where Endacott stayed when he was working at Lot 185 as a young engineer. Considering the earlier history of Crystal Springs, it probably was a small ranch house or farm home that had been there many years. Whether this cabin is the same as the Osage Lodge mentioned in the August 15, 1925 diary is not clear. It is possible that Frank put management of this proto-lodge under the responsibility of Pop Shirley as early as 1922.[72]

Jean Campbell Brown and Gladys Campbell Atkins were small children on a farm just north of Woolaroc on Rock Creek at Campbell Field, and they remember the neighborhood at the time. Though they have no recollection of the original cabin in question, Jean does have a photograph of her family's log house which may also give us a good idea of the sort of early structure that was at Rock Creek Lake. She says their house was very old at the time her family was living there.[73] Gladys remembers a few other houses in the neighborhood also being similar log structures.[74]

Left: In this very early photo of the lodge living room the only painting in evidence is *The Homeseekers* by Robert Lindneux. There were lots of horns hanging, but no animal heads. The Indian rugs were there on the floors, but very little furniture was yet in place. Courtesy Woolaroc.

When Frank purchased the ranch property there were some tenant families farming the good arable land in the creek bottoms. The C. J. Campbell family was the tenant in this log house. Jean Campbell Brown is the child in the photo, watching her father hitch the team to the buckboard. She says the log house was already quite old when they lived there. Before all the new construction began on the ranch, an abandoned cabin on the hill occupying the lodge site probably looked something like this early house. Courtesy Woolaroc.

A 1925 blueprint shows that Phillips Petroleum Company fenced a little more than the SW ¼ of Section 2; all of Sections 3 and 10; E ½ of Sections 4, 9, and 16; N ¼ of Section 15; NW ¼ of Section 14; and a little more than the W of Section 11. They used six foot no-climb woven wire, topped with five strands of barbed wire around Rock Creek Game Preserve.[75] This fence can be seen, aged like the rest of the ranch, around the thirteen-mile perimeter of Woolaroc. Ranch Manager Glen Miller told Joe Williams in 1991, "It's one of the best fencing jobs I've seen. The wire is still tight and the amazing thing is they never tied it off."[76] The high fence is an indication that Frank intended to keep deer inside the fence of this property that was already labeled game preserve, and the strength of the fence gives the impression that from the first Frank intended to run buffalo.

By September, plans were prepared for a floodgate across Rock Creek at Phillips Osage Park.[77] This was the first of a series of dams and flood control efforts across the creek. The old Pennsylvanian sandstone has worn deep ravines as the sands of millennia erode with the run-off of the rocky terrain. Rock Creek and its little tributaries are prone to flash flood. The eroded sands rapidly fill the dammed creek bed, contributing to the ferocity of the floods that regularly sweep over the dam.

On April 28, 1999, passing heavy rains on a Monday morning washed trees and limbs, fallen after a couple of wind storms and last summer's drought stress, down the creek with the torrent. Because the lakes were again in need of periodic dredging, the reservoir was too shallow to retain the water, which slammed logs into the heavy stone uprights and top rails of the sides of the low-water Stone Lake Bridge. Many of the uprights were actually broken off, and all the rock, dirt, and limbs were deposited below the spillway. The asphalt paving across the lower

Right: The plat map is from the lower right hand corner of the blueprint for the fencing of Rock Creek Game Preserve, as Woolaroc was called at its earliest stage. The map shows the sections of Township 25 brought under fence in 1925. Though Frank added a great deal of ranch land both on the north and south, the perimeters of Woolaroc, then and now, were within this fence. The lodge and museum are in Section 10. Courtesy Woolaroc.

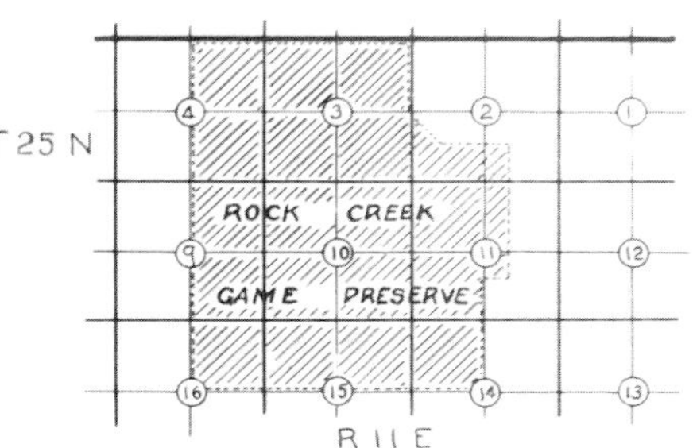

Below: The roads and dams at Woolaroc were built through the rocky hills and blackjack timber with hand labor and teams of mules to pull the grades. This 1918 work crew built what was initially an oil road in Lot 185, through the red sandstone of the ancient river delta. One wonders if any of them reflected on the passage of aeons, the fossils, the Indian hunters, the traders, the outlaws—all the elements of the mystique of the Osage that would become Woolaroc. Courtesy Phillips Petroleum Company Archives.

Left: Flash floods are a frequent occurrence in the watershed draws of Woolaroc. In 1927 a huge overnight downpour first flooded the lake, then took out the Clyde Lake dam. The bath house showed wet lines of a sudden water drop of 30 inches. Afterward Grif and Orpha Graham surveyed the damage between Stone and Swan lakes. The rock railing had been swept over the edge and piled up with brush and logs below the washed out spillway. Courtesy Woolaroc.

Below: After the 1927 flood, Frank ordered a clean-up crew and the dam was fixed right away. But when he inspected the dam repairs, he angrily declared, "I want to go on record in advance that something will happen unless some restoration work is done." The Clyde Lake Dam was re-engineered by the Phillips engineering department and properly built in 1928. Courtesy Woolaroc.

bridge was chewed up so that the drive through the water felt like a Caterpillar tractor ride. As had happened so many times before, expensive repairs will be needed. Frank's beautiful master plan of cascading lakes and spillways is an artificial contrivance that militates with nature and often loses.

Jean Campbell Brown remembers her father, C. J. Campbell, working on the original dam in 1925. He had a slip with his team of mules for the work. Though she was only 10 years old, she remembers her father bringing his team home one day and saying he was not going back—that dam was not going to hold.[78] He was right. It washed out and was repaired in 1926 when Bartlesville had a one hundred year flood.[79]

Then, after a sixteen-inch rain in May 1927, Grif and Orpha Graham inspected the damage in the bathhouse and found the water had dropped suddenly after reaching a height of 30 inches. Upon checking, they found the big dam broken.

> The dam is a wreck. The water came with such force and in such a solid wall down Copper Head Gulch and down the little creek running into Rock Creek at the west water hole that it flowed over the top of the dam; the spillway was unable to carry the water and, of course, when it went over the top of the dam it undermined the back side and the dam collapsed.[80]

Bison Lake also washed out that day. The fence was so badly broken that the ranch cowboys kept a fire going all night to keep animals from getting out at that spot. Mrs. Brown still remembers that morning. When her family got up, their flooded meadow was like a mirror in the morning light, and her mother, Melia Campbell, declared the dam must have broken.[81] Only weeks before Tom Latta of the *Tulsa World* had written a glowing piece about Woolaroc for his paper, now Frank wrote him, "I have certainly had some damn bad luck and some bad dam luck."[82]

In February 1928, the new Clyde Lake Dam was completed, but Frank was still nervous. "I want to go on record in advance that something would happen unless some restoration work is done."[83] Blueprints, dated March 19, 1928, show that he must have put some fear into his engineers. This time they constructed the dam that is still in place.[84]

It was a good thing, for on April 29, 1930, there was another damaging flood. "About 120 feet of the railing on Stone Lake Bridge was washed away. The flood gates on two lakes were completely washed out."[85] Frank instructed the staff to put everything back in even more substantial construction, and this time he wanted them to use red-tinted mortar between the stones.

Richard Kane remembers well the evening of another flood in 1933 because he was a young driver behind the wheel on the way to Woolaroc through the terrible storm on that night. When they arrived at the lodge, the agitated guests were very relieved because they had gotten word that there had been a tornado in which someone was killed on the Barnsdall Road. The guests knew the Kanes were on the way and feared they were the ones caught by the storm. That night the dam again sustained severe damage. Clyde Lake, Swan Lake, and Stone Lake needed $1,630 worth of repairs, a pattern repeated many times over the years.[86]

The construction of the fence and the lakes were the initial stages of the real beginning of Woolaroc. No doubt, unconsciously Frank had been collecting ideas for his master plan for many years, but recently the vision coalesced with his natural inclinations. The part of Frank that appreciated creature comforts had been sorely tempted at the Eastern estates he had visited. Possibly he realized that in the East he was nouveau riche who could never have the sort of social ease that generations had bequeathed H. V. Foster. Likewise, the great houses of the West, such as the 101 Ranch White House which was a copy of the family's Kentucky plantation house, never quite fit into the robust ambience of the Oklahoma landscape.

Center: Arthur J. Gorman was Frank's choice for architect and contractor at Woolaroc. His father, Felix Gorman, had been the contractor who built the mansion in town. Arthur designed and constructed the lodge, the museum, and many of the barns and outbuildings through the 1930s. Gorman Construction worked on Woolaroc projects through the 1940s. It was Arthur Gorman's barbecue hobby that put Woolaroc on the culinary map. Courtesy Arthur P. Gorman.

Back in 1918, while summering in Denver, Colorado, Waite Philips had taken L. E. and Node Phillips to Estes Park, Colorado.[87] The John Kane family had a long tradition of spending the hottest summer months in Estes Park at the Elkhorn Lodge. It is one of those magnificent rustic log-construction lodges from the turn of the century, when those who were able, fled the prairies to the cool of the mountains during the summer months. No doubt Frank was familiar with that vigorous style of the Theodore Roosevelt era Western guest lodge from similar trips and summer visits with friends. For years Frank's family had been going to the Broadmoor in Colorado Springs to escape the summer heat.

Upon returning to Oklahoma in 1918, Waite's family moved into a new house at 1621 South Owasso in Tulsa. His summer of camping and fishing in Colorado seems to have stirred a sentimental spirit, for he built a log cabin in the backyard of the Owasso home and decorated it with Western furnishings and memorabilia.[88]

Frank would have had the opportunity to observe the effect of Waite's log cabin on his Eastern stockholders and directors on April 5, 1923 when Waite Phillips entertained them all at his home during Frank's first big extravaganza tour for the annual meeting. Frank also knew how to provide plenty of rough and ready entertainment. A lengthy article about the 1925 tour of the Mid-Continent oil fields includes an enthusiastic tale of the badger fight

By the time Frank visited Fish Camp, also known as Rayado Lodge, at Waite Phillips' newly-acquired Cimmaron, New Mexico ranch in July of 1925, he had already begun fencing his Osage County ranch. He may have been on an idea-gathering mission while he vacationed in New Mexico, not far from Taos. Fish Camp probably inspired the kind of complex he envisioned for his ranch retreat. This photograph shows Fish Camp in the 1950s. Courtesy Philmont Museum and Seton Memorial Library, Philmont Scout Ranch.

Frank staged for the breathless greenhorns. It was a hilarious oil field come-on.

> The dog growled and leaped into the middle of the ring, expecting to land on the unwary badger. Imagine the surprise when, instead of pouncing on a hereditary foe, he landed with one foot inside an empty "thunder mug!" The face of the tenderfoot "judge" was a veritable study in disappointment—but there is nothing with which one can compare the baffled expression of the dog![89]

The Eastern dignitaries ate it all up as fast as he dished it out. Frank's agile mind began to formulate a grand plan for a dude ranch and Wild West Show all rolled into one. But a cabin was not sufficient for his needs—he needed a lodge that would lend a level of elegance and comfort to the kind of entertaining he envisioned at that place.

Again, his brother Waite already had an fine model to launch his imagination. Waite Phillips purchased his Cimarron, New Mexico ranch in 1922. He named the ranch "Philmont" in 1925, and eventually employed Frank's Hillcrest Country Club architect, Edward Beuhler Delk, to design the magnificent ranch house, as well as his lavish Philbrook estate in Tulsa. The brothers clearly influenced each other and, over the years, were information resources for each other. In July of 1925 Frank and L. E. vacationed at the Fish Camp Lodge at Philmont.[90] Whether Frank was again on a fact-finding mission or the lodge was a new inspiration, those two weeks came at the precise time when Frank was considering the plans for his new lodge at the Frank Phillips Game Preserve. The ambience of Waite's Fish Camp lay-out was just what Frank had in mind. He might dicker with size and arrangement, but the style was just right.

Dicker with the plan he did. Woolaroc tradition is

Left: This snapshot shows Waite Phillips' daughter Helen Jane, and the family dog, near the corner of Phillips' cabin in the backyard of his elegant Owasso Street home. Waite built the cabin and decorated it with Western furnishings and memorabilia as a nostalgic retreat and private study. The visit of the directors meeting there in 1923 may have started Frank thinking about a rustic retreat at his ranch. Courtesy Waite Phillips Collection, The Philbrook Museum of Art Archives.

Right: An early March snow lingers around the unfinished lodge in 1926. The porch was not yet built, the roof was not on, the windows were open and there was no door. Notice the detached cabin to the left. There was no fill between the logs in either the main lodge, or the cabin to the left. If Woolaroc legend is correct, this chinking wasn't a part of the original plan, until Jane was frightened by a squirrel in the lodge. Courtesy Woolaroc.

that he built the lodge in two stages. By the late fall of 1925 the first stage of the new lodge was probably underway and finished in January. This was a capacious one-room cabin. Early accounts declare that Frank's mother suggested he build a replica of the Nebraska cabin where he was born.[91] This could be Woolaroc mythology. But an undated composition by Frank refers to the cabin being separate from the main building and to his mother's visit.[92] A photograph of the partially finished lodge, taken after a light snow, shows a corner of the dining room, which shows an unattached, finished cabin just to the left of the construction.

Today, this room is the dining room of the lodge. The old front porch was enclosed with window walls and sliding glass doors in 1960 when the entire structure underwent considerable restoration, but it is essentially the same as in the days when Frank Phillips used this dining area. By January 1926, Arthur Gorman had completed elevations for the lodge.[93] It is very reminiscent of Fish Camp.

Gorman's father, Felix, was the contractor of the Frank Phillips Mansion in Bartlesville that was built in 1909. He died in 1916, but his oldest son, Arthur, was the architect Frank used on all of his ranch projects. Arthur

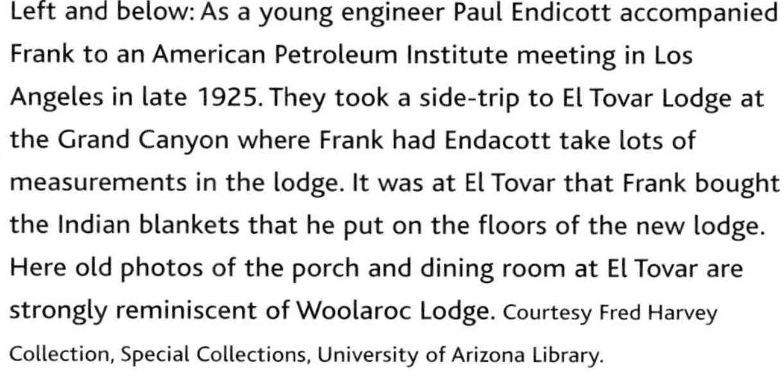

Left and below: As a young engineer Paul Endicott accompanied Frank to an American Petroleum Institute meeting in Los Angeles in late 1925. They took a side-trip to El Tovar Lodge at the Grand Canyon where Frank had Endacott take lots of measurements in the lodge. It was at El Tovar that Frank bought the Indian blankets that he put on the floors of the new lodge. Here old photos of the porch and dining room at El Tovar are strongly reminiscent of Woolaroc Lodge. Courtesy Fred Harvey Collection, Special Collections, University of Arizona Library.

had submitted plans for the country club in November, but the fix was already in. Frank chose Delk for the town project. He was keeping Gorman for himself, at his ranch. The initial meeting with Gorman seems to have been September 16, 1925. That day Gorman went to the ranch with Clyde Alexander, general superintendent of the company, and with Frank. A week later, Frank talked with Gorman and Littlejohn Plumbing. Thereafter, Gorman came in to Frank's office about once a month.[94]

Paul Endacott happened to be on one of Frank's fact-finding trips early in 1926. He was called to come along in Frank's private car as an engineer to do some map work for some of the meetings at the American Petroleum Institute Convention in Los Angeles. The appointment calendar says they were at the Grand Canyon January 15, 1926.

When we got to Williams, Arizona, the train stopped and they took the private car off and went to the Grand Canyon and went up to the El Tovar Hotel—about 30 or 40 miles up the line. Why did they go up there? Well, they went there because they were then starting to build this part of the lodge. The El Tovar Hotel is built of logs, like this, and it had a balcony inside the big lobby room and he wanted to get some ideas about how to build this room in here with this lobby thing. . . I made some notes of measurements and things inside there.[95]

How quickly the lodge was built is not exactly known. In mid-December, Grif Graham wrote Frank that he was ready to make tables for the cabin but could not because the cabin was not completed.[96] Blueprints were finally prepared by January 12 while Frank was still taking measurements at El Tovar. It seems to have been "a work in progress." The day of his return from California, Grif Graham and Gorman both came into the office, and the next day they all went to the lodge.

A group sings around the bark veneer piano in the lodge on the evening of Frank Phillips' 66th birthday party in 1939. The man behind the piano, holding a cigarette, was Frank's secretary, Bill Angel. John Phillips, Jr. is in the right foreground and the others are unidentified. From the beginning, singing around the piano was the focal point of evening entertainment at more intimate parties in the lodge. Frank ordered the piano of unfinished walnut in 1926 and had his shop apply the veneer. Courtesy Woolaroc.

This photo was taken about the time of the April 1926 directors meeting. It is an imposing picture of the grand new lodge among the small blackjacks on the hill. Saplings in Happy Hollow were not yet in leaf and the bathhouse was still incomplete. On that windy day, two canoes and a row boat were pulled up on a sandy beach. This picture is the one that was used in the first newspaper article about Woolaroc that appeared in the *Tulsa Daily World* in May 1926. Courtesy Woolaroc.

The cabin must have been nearing completion by then, for Grif wrote that he was talking to Gorman about spraying the logs.[97] A month later he wrote, "We will first spray basement and then spray logs with government mixture for killing bugs, worms, etc. We are preparing to clean house as soon as Mr. Gorman completes spraying and will put horns up on the walls immediately."[98] No doubt those horns were Grif's own collection which he showed to Frank that day back in 1923.

Meanwhile work was moving on for the main part of the lodge. Gorman was purchasing logs for the buildings in Arkansas and Southwest Missouri. Grif wrote, "Mr. Gorman has his sawmill in operation and is now sawing logs for the new building."[99] A week later construction was fully underway. "Mr. Gorman has a good start on the new lodge and is getting along splendidly. The sawmill is running fine and the logs certainly look well when laid up."[100] Bringing logs from Arkansas, spraying them, and building an on-site sawmill isn't the modern standard of efficiency, but the results are magnificent.

On the weekend of 13 and 14 November 1926 the Phillips family held a reunion at the Ranch. Frank's mother, Lewcinda Phillips, is said to have affirmed that the lodge dining room was a good replica of the Phillips cabin in Nebraska. It was chilly and some of the women were wrapped in Indian blankets. Frank sports a flashy pair of cowboy boots, with both pants legs tucked in (a signal that he was a cowman). Lewcinda was seated between Waite and Frank with L. E. and Fred Phillips to Frank's right. Courtesy Woolaroc.

It sounds as if the manager's house had probably been completed for a little while. They sprayed for bugs and Grif reported, "I had to take my wife and family out in the hills for a few nights."[101] Woolaroc tradition is that before his house was built, the Grahams lived in a tent near the entrance. Grif said that the bathhouse construction was coming along and that Charles Gray, a construction engineer for the company, was working on the roads and had the beach constructed. The barn was nearing completion and Gorman was spraying the interior white.

By the time Frank returned from New York on March 15, things were far enough along that Frank spent the next afternoon supervising his project. The appointment calendar refers to his ranch, instead of the lodge, for the first time. The day after the Osage Sale, E. W. Lenders made his first call in the office, and three days later Frank talked with Gorman and a Mr. Bachrach, a Kansas City decorator. Lenders came in that afternoon again and the next day went to the ranch with Frank and Gorman.[102] A few days later, Lenders wrote from the Mayo Hotel in Tulsa, "According to my promise I send you enclosed some suggestions, of which you might decide to use some and I shall send you more material when I come home end of next week, also a list of suitable Indian beadwork, etc. for decorations."[103] He sent two pages of suggestions—some are crossed out. Of those scratched out, some were already in the works, such as "Lots of Navajo and fur rugs on floor and furniture." Others probably were not appealing to Frank, such as "an old time dugout built somewhere in the side of a hill." True to his word, when Lenders returned he had some more suggestions. "I am getting out some pictures out of magazines which might interest you. . . rock gardens, rustic work, etc."[104] He also had some Indian artifacts that he thought might interest Frank, and he had some paintings of his own that he hoped to sell.

Emil W. Lenders was a German-born artist who was also a performer in Wild West shows. He was associated with Buffalo Bill, and it may have been he who persuaded Lenders to come to Oklahoma. Pawnee Bill thought Lender's paintings of buffalo were exceptional. The Miller brothers granted a mortgage to Lenders for forty acres at Marland, which Lenders called his Thunderbird Ranch. He was an extraordinary amateur ethnologist who produced important sketches and made a very large collection of important artifacts. Though never classified with Western artists such as Russell or Leigh, in his lifetime Lenders was one of Oklahoma's most pre-eminent artists. He had a special appeal to Frank Phillips. *Gilcrease Journal* says, "The Old West that Lenders knew was the West of the shows and films of Buffalo Bill, Pawnee Bill, and the Miller Brothers."[105] With an artist's eye, Lenders could envision the showmanship that Frank needed at Woolaroc. His paintings were also much less expensive than the big names in New York and California.

Because Lenders was suggesting that Frank use Navajo rugs, we can deduce that on March 23 there was not yet furniture in the lodge, for we know from Paul Endacott that on the Grand Canyon trip Frank bought lots of rugs.

> I was strolling around by myself and there was a little building out in the yard, you might say, of the hotel was a trading post there. The Navajos had been given a little building there. I went over there and went inside. They were selling Navajo blankets and rugs. And who was in there? Only one person beside the Indian clerk—Frank Phillips. He was saying, "Give me this one and that one," etc. He was buying Navajo blankets and rugs. Well, he says, "How much?" They said, "$1400.00." So he pulled out his roll and gave him $1400.00, and I was getting $190.00 a month. So it seemed like a lot of money to squander off on things like blankets that I didn't know what he was going to do with them.[106]

The lodge must have been very close to completion. Frank was anxious to get things into presentable shape for the Annual Directors and Stockholders Meeting on April 18. Woolaroc tradition is that originally the logs were not chinked with mortar, but one day Jane found a varmint (either a squirrel or a rattlesnake, depending on who tells the story) in the house, and the next day the work crew began chinking the mortar in the cracks.

J. H. Haeske of Haeske Music Company in Bartlesville came by to talk to Frank about his idea for the Steinway player piano on March 26.[107] It was not until August 10 that Frank placed the actual order with Jenkins Music Company in Kansas City, Missouri, through their agent, Haeske. Frank ordered very light colored unfinished walnut.[108] The piano is the subject of another good Woolaroc story from an evening that Richard Kane remembers. That night while everyone stood around the piano, singing, Frank struck a match, with a flourish, across the pale, flawless surface of the expensive new piano. The ladies gasped. He could afford to be so cavalier, though nobody else knew, for they would be covering the piano with Woolaroc bark veneer in a few days.[109] The pine bark veneer is also used on the picture frames at Woolaroc. It is a process that Arthur Gorman developed and later patented in 1939.

M. C. Findlay of the Findlay Galleries in Kansas City called in the office on March 27, and artist, Robert Lindneux, made his first call on April 2. Though he had bought a few paintings before, Frank was now really embarking on his long, growing interest in Western art. Still, at this early stage, Frank was decorating a cabin, not collecting.

The Annual Directors and Stockholders Meeting was getting close, and Frank was planning on opening his new ranch in style. The calendars show a flurry of activity as Frank planned his own Wild West Show. Joe Bartles, son of Bartlesville's founder, who was the honcho of the Dewey Roundup, and Buck Boren, a big rancher from Caney, Kansas, came into Frank's office on April 9, and then they all went out to the ranch.[110] Probably these men were recruited to secure some rodeo stock and some cowboys for Frank's show. The New York crowd all arrived at 8:00 A.M. on a chilly April 18, and the calendar says Phillips entertained his guests at a barbecue at the ranch. State Senator Gid Graham wrote an article for the *Tulsa World* that describes the rest of the shindig.

> After the barbecue the company motored to a beautiful natural prairie park surrounded with oaks where a few wild steers were corralled, the rider mounted on this rode past automobiles containing the company. The riding of a wild steer minus the saddle is always a grotesque performance, as he bounds along, wringing his tail, mouth open, head lowered and kicking for dear life. The easterners were immensely interested and pleased at this performance, and the veterans Maj. Gordon Lillie and George Miller, were kept busy explaining the 'technique' of riding to the distinguished New Yorkers. At the mean time several riders were bringing up a herd of buffaloes and Alaskan reindeer to be viewed by the company. The caribou and the buffaloes refused to herd together and a stampede ensued in which the hard-riding punchers were defeated by the escape. . . It was a scene never to be forgotten, as caribou and buffalo, all badly scared, ran like the devil, straight for the horsemen who were yelling and striving to hold them.[111]

With this sort of afternoon entertainment, the guests were back in town for a sedate buffet supper at the Phillips mansion that evening. Bartlesville had it all. What a show! The newspaper photograph with the Gid Graham article was taken across Clyde Lake, showing a completed-looking lodge atop the hill. The spindly oak trees were not yet in leaf. There was an inviting sand beach with some canoes pulled up, but the bathhouse did not yet have a roof.

By May 19 Frank definitely entertained E. J. Henry at the ranch for the evening.[112] This is the first record of a simple evening entertainment. It seems the lodge was finally open. The next day Frank wrote a thank you to Amon Carter for a gift of unusually fine longhorns for his cabin, evidently inspired by Carter's visit during the directors meeting. "My cabin and ranch are gradually assuming definite form and I think will be ready for another party in a few weeks."[113] The draperies were being hung and wall work was being completed on the first week in June. Two sofas and two chairs were being moved from town and fitted with new slipcovers. Jane ordered lots of new throw pillows. Two tables with an umbrella and some chairs were being shipped for the terrace, all pressing to having the place in order by June 15.[114] The lodge was about ready for guests. The completed lodge had a dining room with two fireplaces; a great room with two more fireplaces; ten bedrooms, each with a private bathroom and a cedar closet; screened balcony porches; and a kitchen wing with servants' quarters. Frank established a pattern that continued the rest of his life. Most days when he was in town, Frank drove to the ranch in the late afternoon, often returning to town for dinner and evening appointments.

The barrenness of the hill in the *Tulsa World* photograph explains the importance of the many visits by W. R. Scholl of Wichita Nurseries, beginning January 6, 1926, and continuing regularly throughout the 1926 growing season. Correspondence shows Frank ordered evergreens such as cedar, arborvita, and pine in January. A visit by Schell in July elicited complaints that the ranch crew was not adequately watering the new plantings. Frank ordered Grif to water twice a week but also canceled part of the nursery order. "Of course, I will need a lot of replacements this fall and possibly we can find other places for additional trees but there is no use replacing all those that the animals have killed."[115] In the meantime Frank hired the Davey Tree Company of Kent, an Ohio tree surgery

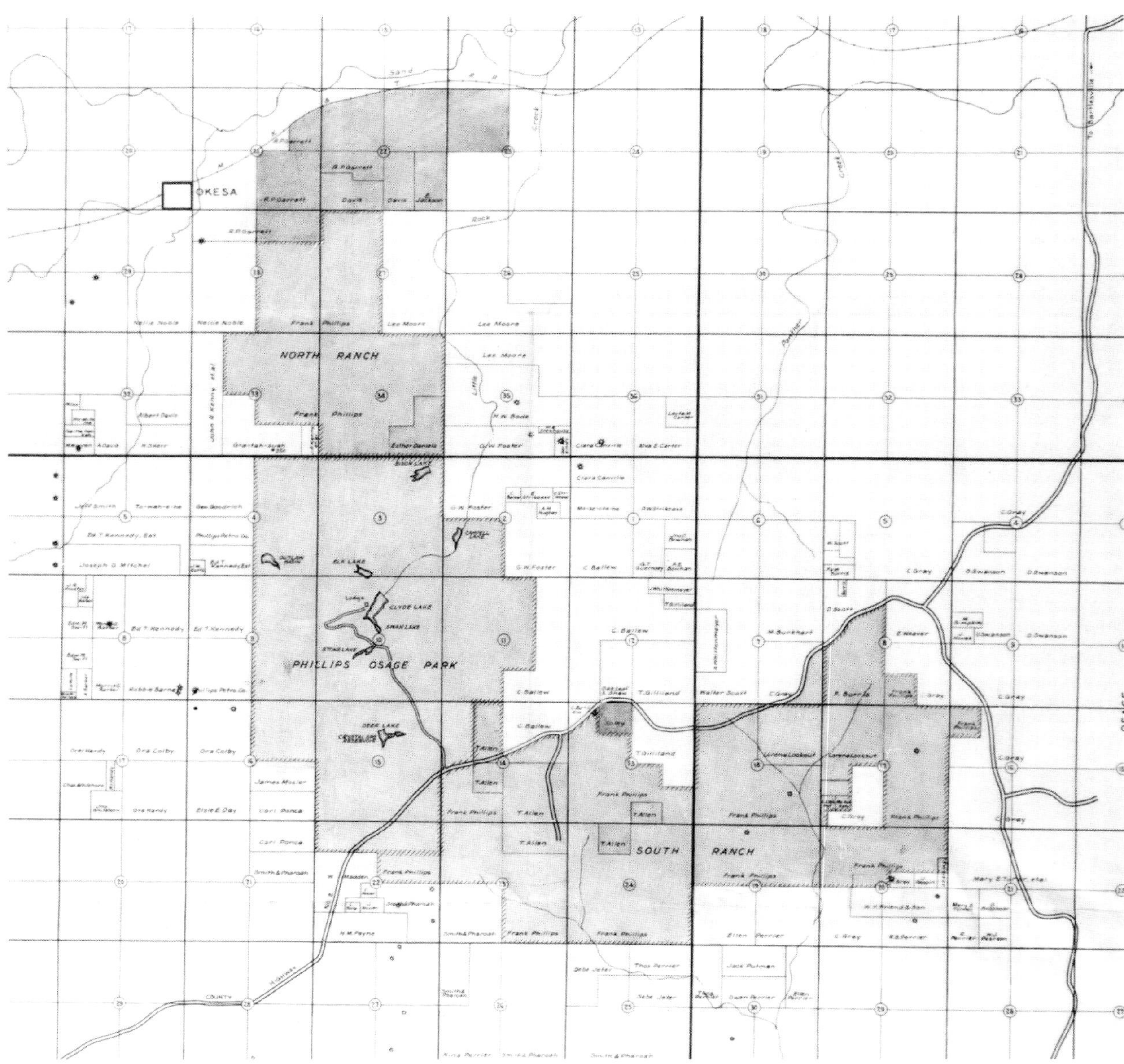

company with a Kansas City office, probably J. C. Nichols' recommendation, to prune up the native trees around the lodge. All the results may have been unsatisfactory, for the work endured the criticism of J. C. Nichols early in November.

Nichols' favorite landscapers, Hare & Hare of Kansas City, had already been called in on the first of September. The proposal from S. Hubert Hare was way beyond the plans Frank had in mind, even though over the years, much of the proposed planting eventually appeared near the lodge and around Clyde Lake. Probably as a result, on December 11, Philip W. Thomas, a Tulsa landscape architect who Frank had used before, made his first call in the office. Frank wrote W. R. Schell, who by now had a Tulsa office, "My last fence will be completed next week at which time I will be ready to complete my landscape work on the hillside."[116] But two weeks later, Frank hired Thomas to do $2500 worth of work on his hillside and around the bathhouse.[117] A year later, Frank blasted Thomas for failure to complete his contracted work and for his exorbitant prices.[118]

By 1930, landscaping was taking a settled pattern.

Schell continued to oversee the new plantings and tree trimming. The ranch employed a gardener full time who was living in a building that was a converted chicken house. Evans commented about hail damage to the flowers and new transplants after the big flood that year.[119] The old home movies have lengthy shots of prize roses and peonies near the lodge. A 1935 article in *Southern Florist* talked about the recent rock gardens and described the many varieties of flowers that bloomed in the beds and on the hillside around the lodge. Frank ordered the whole hillside sown with petunia seed in 1936. They probably never had a chance in the terrible heat that summer. In 1939, a plan for changes in the cactus garden drew Frank's most withering fire. "I can't conceive of artificial rock being suitable in that location. . . I have a feeling I will want to tear down this cactus bed when I get home and put in a new one of natural rock, such as I wanted."[120]

On November 6, 1926, Frank had a group of Kansas City friends down for the weekend.[121] Of course, J. C. Nichols was the life of the party. Frank was as strongly influenced by J. C. Nichols as he was by Waite. Nichols had been a good friend for many years, and doubtless had been very helpful in the years of the early growth of the business. He was a visionary man with an irrepressible entrepreneurial spirit and a will as strong as horseradish. He had a track record of selecting the very best consultants. J. C. could work Frank like no one else. In a series of 1943 letters, J. C. wrung a $250 personal donation out of Frank for the Kansas City Symphony, even though Frank protested he preferred "Arkansas hill-billy fiddlers."[122] A *Kansas City Star* article tells of J. C.'s visit on that first November weekend.

> Some time ago J. C. Nichols of Kansas City was a guest at Woolaroc Lodge with a group of Kansas Citians. Mr. Nichols suggested a rock and gravel drive, which Mr. Phillips had built through the ranch, was not properly constructed to conform to the general landscaping. So, Mr. Phillips had workmen busy early next day taking up the road and getting ready to resod the place. Mr. Nichols also made several suggestions for the layout of the yard around the lodge, including the landscaping in front of the garage and servants quarters.[123]

Sure enough, the appointment calendars show a Dr. Allen Miller was there for two days about the grass at the ranch—but that was three days before the Kansas City party. The reporter, a Mr. Hartley, was not there until November 12.[124] Frank had been planning the grass job all along and probably just pitched a good story for the Kansas City paper.

Frank had a family reunion at his ranch on November 13-14, 1926. All five Phillips sons, their sister, their families, and their mother were there. The *Kansas City Star* published a picture of the family gathered on the front porch of the lodge, Lewcinda Phillips wrapped in an Indian blanket and Frank in his cowboy boots and hat. It was on this weekend that Frank showed his mother the cabin/dining room and asked if it was not a good replica of their homested cabin in Nebraska, to which she is said to have agreed.[125]

By the end of the year of building, Frank's grand vision had emerged in the Osage Hills. For an insurance request, Gorman reported the following buildings on the ranch: Graham's house, including tables, farm house, horse barn, house and garage at gate, lodge, garage, blacksmith shop, chicken house, animal sheds, barn at Crystal Springs, house, and Prairie House. There was also the bathhouse, spring house, building at the well, and the driveways.[126] Building at the ranch was not completed then—and it continues to this day. Hardley, the Kansas City reporter, characterized the enterprise well, "There is no telling how much more will be spent or how much more work Philips will have done on the estate, because he is his own architect and works out the details as he gets the inspirations for plans."[127]

Opposite: This is Frank Phillips' own 1943 desk copy of the map of his Osage County ranches, including Woolaroc. The original map measures 27 $^3/_4$ X 21 $^3/_8$" and is mounted on chartex. This is a map of the ranch at its height, before the north and south ranch additions were sold. Frank raised cattle on the north and south ranches. Though adjoining, they were never a part of Woolaroc *per se*. Courtesy Woolaroc.

The buffalo from the Scotty Phillip herd, Fort Pierce, South Dakota, were delivered to the Okesa railhead just a few miles from Woolaroc in January 1926. The 101 Ranch sent over their best buffalo hand to help the local cowboys move the herd to the ranch. Amidst high excitement, the South Dakota animals proved to be quite tame and the transfer came off without incident. In a stroke, Frank became the owner of one of the largest buffalo herds in the country. This photo is reproduced from old 16mm movies, the only photographic record of the delivery. Courtesy Frank Phillips Home.

III

THE PERILS OF PAULINE: FRANK'S ANIMALS

IN FRONTIER TIMES the natural fauna of eastern Oklahoma was very rich. Besides prolific small game such as rabbits, squirrels, foxes, coyote, raccoons, skunks, and opossums, big game was very plentiful. Buffalo and herds of mustangs ranged the tall grass prairies; white-tail deer and elk browsed the Cross Timbers and river bottoms. Black bear—and some say, long ago, grizzly bears—once lumbered through the forests. Cougars, wildcats, and timber wolves were predators of the big game. Wild turkey, quail, and waterfowl were abundant. There were great flocks of passenger pigeons and Carolina parakeets.[128] But by the fall of 1832, Washington Irving's party found that already the Osage were having to range far to the west on their annual hunt because buffalo were becoming scarce in eastern Oklahoma.[129]

Slowly the pressures of population, fences, and farms squeezed the large herds into more remote regions, exterminating the large predators, passenger pigeons and parakeets, and hunted out the deer and game birds in eastern Oklahoma. Amazing to us, who now have deer eating our petunias in suburbia and Canada geese elbowing out domestic ducks from the city ponds, by Frank Phillips' time the national buffalo herd had barely survived extinction, and there were virtually no deer in the wilds of Osage County.

Fortunately for the nation, William "Buffalo Bill" Cody and the other Wild West shows romanticized and popularized the longhorns, wild mustangs, and especially the buffalo as symbols of the Old West. Theodore Roosevelt championed the Conservation Movement that took hold early in the century. A few wealthy and appreciative patrons began to keep small herds of the endangered game on their ranches and estates. Frank's friends, the Miller Brothers—Joe, Zack, and George—and

Inset: The first zebras on the ranch came halter-broke and were a delight to guests and the Phillips children alike. But there were troubles with the next zebras that arrived from Africa in 1928. They were not in good health and added significantly to the complexity of the puzzle of animal deaths at the ranch. Eventually zebras became successfully established and were quite popular for many years. Courtesy Woolaroc.

William G. "Pawnee Bill" Lilly, were among the early conservator-showmen who rescued the buffalo and longhorns from extinction. Frank's plan for a game preserve on his ranch was just natural. It fit well with progressive ideas of conservation and public spirit that were current and with old Romantic ideals and sentiments that still hung about. His was a true selling of a vision of the West, and Frank was one of the best salesmen of his time.

The Game Preserve

Evidently Frank's general plans were no secret. In 1924, *Game Breeder* had an article about his planned preserve.[130] As the fence was going up around his ranch, in the fall of 1925, Frank wrote the Oklahoma Department of Fish and Game to ask about the procedure for officially establishing a private game preserve. There was none, and the warden advised that the county clerk should publish it in the local paper to establish the desired protection.[131] In due time, Grif Graham journeyed to Pawhuska to get the county attorney to prepare the prescribed notice.[132] Frank was interested in protecting his animals, but he was also interested in establishing a tax shelter. and this public notice was an important step.

The first animals on the Rock Creek Game Preserve were a consignment of Mexican brush goats which were shipped from Eden, Texas, July 25, 1925, almost exactly coincident with the beginning of the fencing. From the shipping weight, there were probably around 200 animals in the first shipment.[133] Goats were a proven way to open

Grif Graham is surrounded by some newly-arrived pronghorn antelope in a Woolaroc receiving pen. Frank tried to buy antelope from several sources. They were both scarce and temperamental. He even tried to air freight a few from Wyoming in 1927. Pronghorn antelope were an abject failure at Woolaroc. Courtesy Woolaroc.

up brushy land for grass because they browse brush and lower branches of trees but do not eat much grass. Ideally they are brought in on a rotation in early spring to intensively browse the new buds, but they need to be pulled off the land by summer because, if they have done their job, they will simply run out of food. The proper stocking rate for this work is about six goats per acre. Though goats are very useful in this way, there is almost no market to subsequently sell them. By October, Frank was trying to sell 623 of his goats through the Kansas City Stockyards. They finally sold by early November for $1.50 per hundred pounds. The agent remarked that the goats were very thin. Frank lost money on his first goat venture. Ranch accounts show that in 1925 Frank also managed to sell 200 goats to H. D. Cannon and 22 more to J. L. Overlees of Bartlesville. The Tamblyn Commission at the Kansas City Stockyards must have liked the deal they made for they wrote looking for some more bargain goats, and Grif responded, "Am glad to say we have no more goats."[134]

This was not, in fact, the end of goats at the Frank Phillips Ranch. The inventories of 1926, 1927, and 1928 list 197 goats. Evidently the goats still proved to be useful in the fight against blackjack so Frank brought in some more. They must have been very frustrating. During the first summer growing season for the new landscaping, Grif wrote, "The goats made a raid on us night before last and destroyed some of our evergreens on the hillside."[135] Frank postponed further landscaping until the internal fences could be completed in December. It was eventually learned these brush goats were the source of intestinal parasites that killed many animals on the ranch in 1927 and 1928. Afterward, United States Department of Agriculture (USDA) veterinarians advised destroying all the goats.[136]

Late in 1932, Waite sent Frank some Angora goats.[137] Now Frank had animals that should turn a profit. But, in Oklahoma mohair is usually of poorer quality because of higher humidity than in the Southwest. Likewise because there are not many commercial sheep and goats in Oklahoma, it is difficult to find skilled shearing crews. Frank quickly ran into these troubles. The Chatham Manufacturing Company, a manufacturer of blankets, was unwilling to work with the wool, even on a private contract.[138] Frank was in desperate straights. He had 1,500 pounds of mohair in storage with no market. The drought was beginning to cut into his forage at the ranch, and the lake was almost dry. In a plaintive note at the end of the day's schedule on August 12, 1934, his secretary wrote, "117° today."[139] At the end of July Frank thought he had worked a deal at one dollar a head but was glad eventually to sell 400 goats for only fifty cents apiece.[140]

In the fall of 1925, Frank toyed with the idea of stocking his ranch with some bred whiteface heifers and talked to W. T. Leahy of the First National Bank in Pawhuska about getting together an order. It was a bad time of year to be buying cows, but Leahy found some good cows and heifers after the first of the year. Frank responded, "Since talking to you I have about decided to go into the buffalo business and am now negotiating for quite a herd, and if I close this deal I will not be in the market for any cattle."[141]

Frank had already managed to buy a dozen buffalo, along with a few elk and white-tail deer, from the Wichita National Wildlife Preserve at Cache, Oklahoma.[142] Though the entire order did not materialize for three months, some of the first elk escaped just before Christmas, and the men working at Lot 185 rounded them up—to Frank's immense gratitude.[143] That December, Frank had his big coup. The Scotty Philip Buffalo Herd at Fort Pierre, South Dakota, was in financial difficulties after the death of the founder. The sons were dispersing the herd—a hundred to William Randolph Hearst, a hundred to the 101 Ranch, and now another 100 to 120 shipped to Okesa, Oklahoma.[144] Frank planned to divide his order with Waite and the 101 Ranch.

It appears that George Miller was Frank's contact person, for the first telegrams to Fort Pierre were from Miller. The Miller brothers had been good Phillips family friends for many years. The 101 Ranch was clearly an influence on Frank's imagery for his ranch program. From their buffalo herd to the exotic animals, from the Wild West showmanship to the Old West memorabilia, and from their registered herds to the self-sufficient farm produce, the 101 Ranch had already forged the public notion of the real Wild West. It is logical that Frank would have looked to the 101 Ranch for help in acquiring his buffalo herd. The 101 Ranch herd was beginning to show signs of needing a little out-crossing so that sharing Frank's large purchase was very convenient for the Millers.

Frank asked for 120 young buffalo between two and ten years of age, and only a few bulls, at $100 a head. After dividing with his partners, he ended up keeping 98 head at $115 each. Telegrams flew back and forth; the office typed up an exact schedule; at each train stop, the Scotty Philip manager, A. H. Leonard, telegraphed their progress; and Frank made plans to have feed and water ready. He originally planned to unload and drive the herd to Woolaroc at night to avoid a possible crowd of onlookers, but the buffalo did not like all the lights when they arrived so it was decided to do the drive in the morning. The 101 Ranch sent over E. M. Botsford, who was their best buffalo hand, to help Grif and his local cowboys move the animals from Okesa to the ranch. The South Dakota buffalo proved to be quite tame and herded easily over the six chilly miles through the Osage and in the gates of the Frank Phillips Ranch. Only one heifer was lost, evidently not as a result of any shipping complications but just an accident at the ranch.[145]

Frank was in Los Angeles, California, when the buffalo arrived. In one stroke, he owned one of the largest buffalo herds in the United States. He could hardly contain his delight. Ed Botsford would not accept payment for his service, so Frank sent him a letter of authority to buy any hat he wanted. He bought a $36 Stetson at the Miller Brothers' 101 Ranch store. A similar letter was written for Scott Bruner. Lon Carpenter and Jay Keefer redeemed their authorities for hats at May Brothers in Bartlesville.[146] Botsford sent a thank you from Louisiana where he was buying stockers for 101 Ranch and included some advice on buffalo culture and compliments on the fine stock.[147]

Just at the time that Gorman's finish carpenters were working on the interior of the lodge and the directors meeting was eminent, the Scotty Philip manager wrote a note that was music to Frank's ears.

> You are to be congratulated on building such a wonderful place as you have and such a nice park for these buffalo to roam in. I have seen a good many parks and privately owned estates but none will compare with the one you have built.[148]

Frank enthusiastically chose the buffalo as the emblem for his ranch. He said it was in tribute to Buffalo Bill.

From then to now, buffalo have been Frank Phillips' most successful animal venture at Woolaroc. By May of 1926, there were seven calves, and by fall Frank wrote to Leonard that they had thirty calves that year. That is not to say it has not been without its difficulties. In the summer of 1927, Grif wrote he was doctoring a buffalo bull for screw worm, if they could get him roped and thrown.[149] That was routine, but only a few months later Frank began to lose scores of his animal acquisitions. In 1927, 16 buffalo died and in 1928 60 died.[150] Eventually it was determined that the losses were from a combination of parasites and epidemic hemorrhagic septicemia.

Waite helped Frank locate some buffalo from the Bell Ranch at Tucumcari, New Mexico in 1930, to replenish his losses and provide a new blood strain. By the early 1930s, the herd was again prospering, though the nation was on hard times. Awash with buffalo, and with an Internal Revenue Service investigation of his ranch deductions just completed, Frank was trying to establish a market value for his animals. Animal dealer John T. Benson wrote,

> After calling your butcher and asking him what he will give you for the lot, that means all your buffalo and all your cattle, then that is what they are worth. I think you will find he will offer you about 2¢ per pound and possibly a little less. This figure is dressed, not live weight. The value of these animals for zoological purposes is nothing. The Government is giving away buffalo.[151]

By December the value was down to zero.

Better times returned only a few years later. A neighbor asked to run his buffalo cow with Frank's herd to get her bred. Frank said she needed to be branded and he would charge $1.00 per month for pasture.[152] A year later, one of Frank's Osage friends wanted to buy a buffalo. Frank responded he would like to give him one but did not want to establish a precedent, and he did not have any to sell. He offered a half-buffalo.[153] Frank was being consistent. Amon Carter tried to get Frank to loan Fort Worth, Texas, 50 or 60 head for their centennial Wild West Show in 1936. Frank responded, "I would walk from here to there, if necessary, for you or Ft. Worth, especially in view of the fact I have a deed to the entire city."[154] But he still turned him down. The Woolaroc buffalo herd eventually provided animals for stocking other important herds. It has been a foundation herd for the rebuilding of our national heritage.

Frank had been writing letters since his fence was finished in the fall of 1925, looking for sources of game animals. He wrote Warden Reeves of the State Department of Fish and Game near the end of December, "I am trying to get 75 to 100 deer this spring; have already obtained a dozen elk and 11 buffalo and have them on the place."[155] The warden responded that the state was also trying to buy deer and could not find them either. From October through December, Frank wrote the states of Texas, New Mexico, Arkansas, Colorado, Arizona, and Kansas, looking for deer, elk, and wild turkey. Early on, Kansas suggested he write to Snake King at Brownville, Texas, an importer of game from Mexico. W. A. King quoted him a price of $70 a pair or $35 for males and $42.50 for does, cash with the order. On November 30, Frank ordered 35 white-tail deer, on December 7, he changed the order to 35 does and another 15 bucks and sent a check. On December 25, he ordered another 24 deer. These were relatively big shipments. Most of the small dealers that Frank found would only sell pairs, generally only two or three at a time. Normally they arrived in satisfactory condition and losses were minimal. He worried a great deal about dipping the animals from Texas and Louisiana upon receipt, presumably because of ticks.[156]

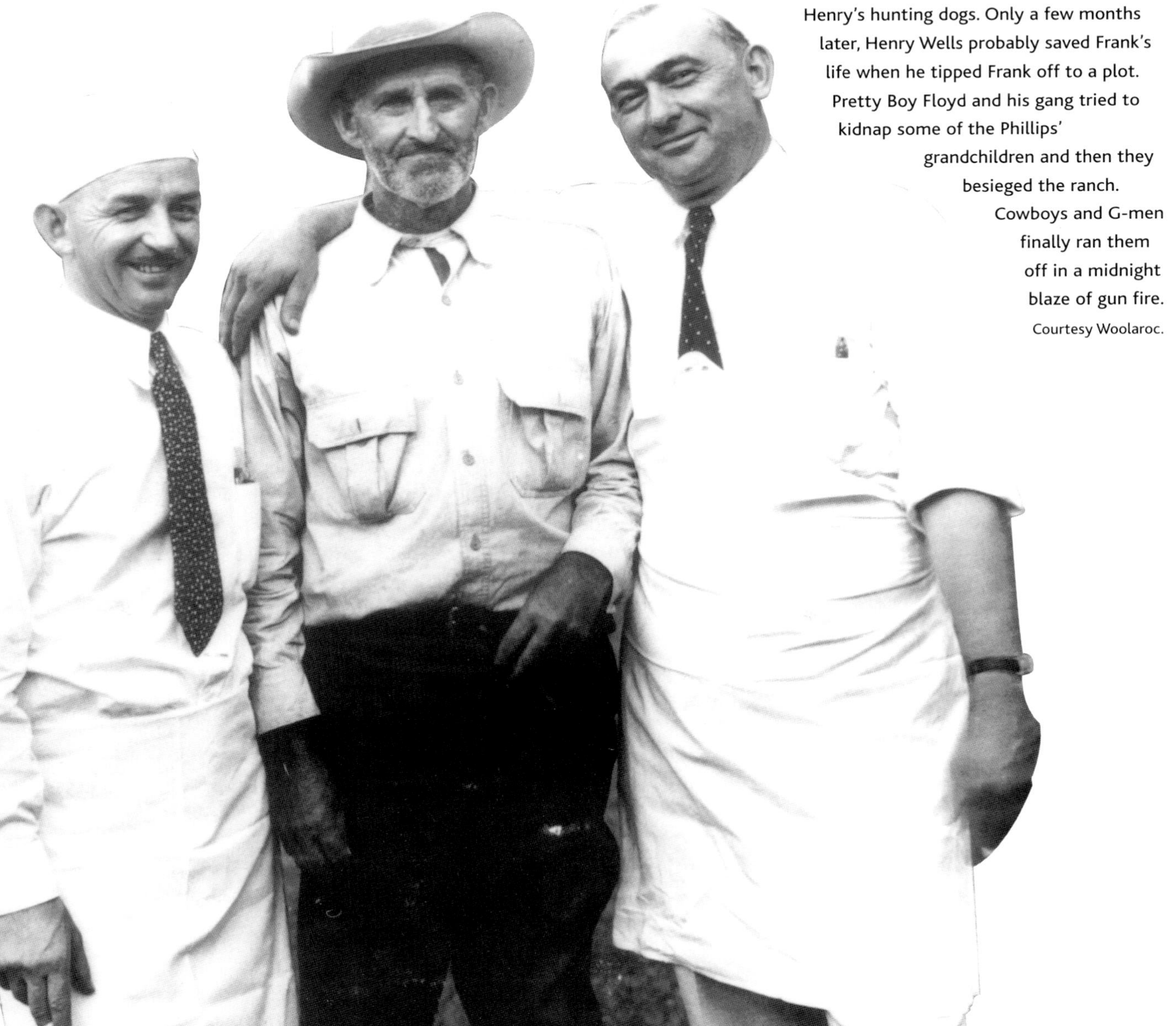

Frank took pains to cultivate Okesa neighbor, and honest-to-goodness train robber, Henry Wells. He became a fixture at Woolaroc barbecues and poker games. (left to right) Here are C. W. Hammonds (Frank's osteopath), Henry Wells, and Bert Gaddis (local Ford dealer) at the 1930 Cow Thieves and Outlaws Reunion. In 1934 Frank had to mediate a dispute with the ranch manager over some of Henry's hunting dogs. Only a few months later, Henry Wells probably saved Frank's life when he tipped Frank off to a plot. Pretty Boy Floyd and his gang tried to kidnap some of the Phillips' grandchildren and then they besieged the ranch. Cowboys and G-men finally ran them off in a midnight blaze of gun fire. Courtesy Woolaroc.

Frank soon learned that ordering animals was not like dealing with railroads and oil field supplies. Throughout December and January, letters were exchanged about the details of shipment, and Frank even added orders for quail and wild turkeys. In February, Snake King still had Frank's money, but no deer had been shipped. Nevertheless, Frank inquired about buying some "old time coaster cattle," and Snake King quoted a price of $75 per head. By the end of the month, Frank was growing impatient and admonished Snake King to get the shipments of deer and quail together before March. Finally, with the directors meeting growing close, Frank sent a telegram, "What kind of a fellow are you either send me the deer or return my check with interest." Snake King responded that he had a shipment ready twice, and they had broken out of the corral during the night. "I regret very much our inability to fill same at this time." Frank never again paid cash up front for animals.[157]

Early in the school year of 1926 one of Frank's deer provided a day's diversion for the Phillipsburg kids.

> One of our white Tail deer escaped in some manner along the first of the week and wandered over near the schoolhouse at 185; it was surrounded and driven into a small garage by the school children and I sent a truck over to bring it back to the reserve where it belonged. I thanked the children for their kindness and bought them a football with the compliments of F. P. Ranch. Also invited them over to see the animals and they came yesterday afternoon, accompanied by their parents. They certainly had a good time looking around. I thanked them again in your name.[158]

This is, doubtless, the first school tour at the Frank Phillips Ranch. They continue to this day.

Frank located Otto Martin Locke of New Braunfels, Texas, who supplied him with very small shipments of tame deer, and a few other small dealers. He subsequently found suppliers in the North. When he found that Cleveland-Cliffs Iron Company Game Preserve at Grand Island, Michigan, was able to ship larger animals at a competitive price and more reliably, he decided to confine his purchases to northern deer. Most of his white-tail deer came from this source between 1927 and 1929, until he became more interested in the exotic deer species.

Grif was in contact with a man in Alberta, Canada, in early October of 1925, looking for pronghorn antelope. Possibly the Millers were the source of the information about this dealer because this was also about the time Frank probably began talking with them about the buffalo deal. It was good information. C. J. Blazier turned out to be one of the few successful suppliers and the man that Horne used. Blazier wrote that another man had already bought all of his available antelope. Because he said the animals went to California, it was probably Horne, working for William Randolph Hearst, who made the purchase. Frank extended his order to the next year.[159]

Blazier's tame antelope were $300 a pair, and it was very disappointing to have to wait a whole year. Evidently, while on business in Amarillo, Texas, L. E. visited about the antelope problem with W. H. Fuqua who was President of First National Bank there. Fuqua had a very large ranch with wild antelope that he thought might be caught. He wrote Frank, proposing a gentleman's sporting trip at his ranch in which his cowboys would endeavor to get a loop over the neck of a running antelope from the hood of a pursuing car. The best part was stated in Fuqua's note, ". . . of course, a part of the consideration for our doing this aside from the pleasure that we might derive, would be for you to promise to refrain from trying to pay anything."[160] Frank was not much interested in the sport, but he did like the price. Fuqua was never successful in catching an antelope. Meanwhile Blazier kept promising a shipment in the fall, then selling to another person with readier cash. Frank did manage to get a shipment of 20 pronghorns from I. S. Horne in Kansas City on September 6, 1926. Difficulty with the delicate animals developed early in 1927. Grif received a letter from the New York Zoological Park, advising him of proper feeding, but saying they, in fact, had never had success with pronghorns.[161]

Frank had one more inspiration. Someone read in the newspaper that the Chicago Zoo had air-freighted in some animals. This was shortly after the time that Phillips had successfully sponsored the *Woolaroc* airplane flight in the Dole Pineapple Race from California to Hawaii. Frank was riding high on his success and on the publicity that Phillips aviation fuel was receiving. Shipping animals by air was a perfect publicity opportunity for Phillips' aviation gasoline, the promotion of aviation, and Woolaroc.

He also hoped it might be a way to reduce shipping stress that it was suspected might be the source of his antelope problems. Frank had been negotiating for some antelope with an animal raiser in Pitchfork, Wyoming, who was willing to give it a try. Charles J. Belden shipped Frank seven pronghorns on September 23, 1927 from Cody, Wyoming. They arrived in shipping crates in good condition, amidst big fanfare at the Phillips' airfield. It was quite a slick piece of flying.[162] Despite everything, the inventory at the end of 1927 shows that all the antelope died that year.

In the earliest months, Frank began to purchase first wild turkeys, then quail. He quickly passed on to peacocks, guineas, swans, geese, and ducks. Then, as he developed contacts with the exotic animal dealers, he bought exotic birds such as demoiselle cranes, sarus cranes, ostriches, and rheas. With the birds and small deer on his ranch, a war quickly developed with the predators. Frank wanted quick results getting rid of coyotes and hawks even before there were many game birds on the ranch.[163] Grif gave Tom Miller, an old trapper of 40 years' experience, trapping privileges on the ranch right away. He wrote they had suspended using poisoned bait because Frank had been warned that he would be liable if they accidentally killed a neighbor's dog. In the same letter, Grif reported that dogs had killed three of their deer.

> The last one killed crawled out beneath the fence through a hole made by dogs and was killed by Mr. Cook's dog last Thursday. Mr. Cook borrowed a horse from Alec Gay and followed the dog and deer in an effort to save the deer, but the dog had killed the deer when Mr. Cook arrived. Mr. Cook said the deer was still kicking when he arrived. We skinned and dressed this deer and expressed the hide to Jonas Bros.[164]

Theodore Roosevelt-style "wolf hunts" were one of the earliest efforts to eliminate coyotes. On February 7, they had a coyote drive. Alexander and Byron mounted horses, and the ranch cowboys rode through the hollows to drive out the wolves for Alexander and Byron to shoot at them. They probably were awful shots, because Grif said the next week they would have some good marksmen. Meanwhile Miller was putting out fresh meat for the coyotes.[165] A week later they had a bigger hunt. Everybody there: Lon Carpenter, Mert and Jay Keefer who had helped on the buffalo drive, neighbors Alec Gay, Pearl Mickels, Ed Anderson, and old Daddy Miller, Tom Miller the trapper, Arthur Gorman, Bert Gaddis, Dr. Weber, Joe Bartles, and Hamp Scudder. They saw four coyotes, and did not get a single one.[166]

When a buffalo heifer died a few days later, Grif cut up the carcass and scattered some of the meat around the ranch. He slyly remarked, ". . . do not believe buffalo meat will agree with dogs or coyotes."[167]

Tom Miller kept a sharp watch when he was about and riding fence. They had 32 riders the last Sunday in February. They must have had a high old time. Grif said they were old hardened riders. They managed to kill two coyotes, for a total of three killed and three dug out. Miller thought there was only one coyote left for the drive on the next Sunday.[168]

The trouble persisted. On April 5, Grif left a pass for William Painter and John Griggs to come in to trap. Then on May11, Frank got a telegram, "Caught wolf last night have him on collar and chain this morning will try to keep him alive until your return."[169]

There was nothing more about coyotes for months. Finally, a telegram in February stating, "Trapper began work yesterday morning caught one coyote one bobcat and one possum last night," is a reminder the coyote problem would persist.[170] General quarters predator alarm at the ranch was sometimes enough to warrant a small article in the Tulsa paper.[171] Arthur Gorman took a pack of hounds after a lynx that was preying on the birds and had eluded the trappers.[172] Even from New York, Frank expressed worry about his birds, "I have cautioned West a good many times about the wire around the bird pens. Some calamity will overtake us there, unless greater precautions are exercised."[173] In the fall, Evans wrote Frank that they had seen a coyote, and there were quite a few skunks and opossums around. He thought they needed to hire another trapper.[174]

By the middle of the decade there was a USDA program for predator control. Frank and H. V. Foster had complained about coyote and bobcat predation on their land and a hunter was sent to the area. H. V. Foster and Frank began to lobby to get a resident hunter in the area.[175] Finally, a government trapper moved to live at the Mullendore Ranch in Osage County where he would be permanently stationed in the area by 1937.[176]

The struggle against predators took many forms. Frank ordered turtle traps in 1931 to protect his baby ducks and geese.[177] Even then, if they strayed too far from the water, skunks and opossums made short work of them.[178] Rats even, somehow, got into the parakeet cage and killed them all.[179]

Except for predation of birds, dogs were always a much worse problem. Ranch manager Kerr killed some hounds belonging to C. B. Tibbett, in 1934. Mrs. Tibbett and Henry Wells visited in Frank's office on April 13 when evidently Frank told Tibbett to talk to Kerr.[180] Kerr wrote Tibbett, "On several occasions, while riding the fence, I have found the flood gates blocked open from the outside, which could indicate that they were opened for the purpose of permitting dogs to hunt within the boundaries of the ranch."[181] Tibbitt was furious, demanding $30 apiece for the dogs and threatening to see a lawyer.[182] Kerr advised, ". . . in his opinion Tibbitt can do us no harm in a revengeful way and that by threats and false accusations he is attempting to bluff us."[183]

Another dog incident a few years later was more serious. It involved Frank's friend, Henry Wells, a man whom Frank may have owed thanks for saving his life. The typewritten letter is transcribed exactly:

> On the request of Henry I wrote you some time ago about our dog,s that was killed over at your ranch. Henry and I are trying mighty hard to get in the hound business in a big way. So far we have been successful, We just returned from a hunt not so long ago. We did good over there won in field and bench also:
>
> Mr. Phillips when I tell you that those were two mighty vablue hound,s that was killed I mean they were broke All those two hound,s knew was follow a wolf where ever he went. Henry has told you how they got on the inside, Henry was the one who found them killed. He had some of the boy,s come and see the hole, Where they got on the inside.
>
> You perhaps fell like Henry & I are sore at you, But we are not but I will admit I was at the time. For that is our living mostly we are breeding dog,s and did intend to place one of those hound,s in the stud. I guess all hound men are crazy but a full sister to one of those hound,s sold for two hundred and fifty dollars.
>
> We at ant time could have sold eather one of two for One hundred dollars a-pice. But we could have easily made that in a few months by stud fees. I do not want to bore you with this matter Mr. Phillips but I would like to have pay for my dog,s. I feel like two hundred dollars would be a cheap price for those two dog,s. I only won't be fair with every one and I feel like we our neighbors, And I will repeat again, At any time you need Henry or I eather to help you to do anything at the ranch, Just feel free to call on us.
>
> We both be only glad to help you out, We are going to keep trying to get you out to one of our hunts. And I will have you saying you will never miss nother. I do wont to be friends with you, and all your employes I realize what you have did in devlping our county, and how you have, so freely helped evry one. Mr. Phillips when I say you have been a Santa to people in this section of the country, I get plenty backing up on that subject. I personally do not like to see a man like you get old.
>
> I only hope you live to a ripe old age and enjoy, Perfect health You made us Osage boy,s a nice dividend, It is not your fault we did not preserve it. Henry said tell you to come out and see him. Said he would like to show you how far an old man could follow a wold trail.
>
> Just call on us any time for a little ranch work.
>
> Your frinds, Henry Wells, and Dave Ware[184]

Frank did not pass this letter off to his managers. He answered personally, not once, but in two letters. "I appreciate your complaint and the value of the dogs to you but you must remember that my zebras alone are worth from $800 to $1,000 apiece." He even asked Grif Graham, who was no longer the manager but who had real credibility with the Osage cowboys, to walk the fence and check for the opening.[185] The same day his manager, Don Zühlke, wrote a resignation. "I have reached this decision particularly in view of the fact that you deem it advisable to hire employees at the ranch to act as spies."[186] Two weeks later Frank, managed to smooth over the riffle, and Zühlke retracted his resignation. But, the episode was not over. When Zühlke asked Grif to haul water, as usual, for summer watering of the flowers, Grif flatly refused.[187] By the end of the year, Grif and Orpha had resigned and moved from the gatehouse.

Zühlke reported various troubles with some of the animals and attached a veterinarian's report. He even went to the trouble of contacting George Vierhaller of the St. Louis Zoo about a paralyzed camel. He must have known trouble was brewing. It sure was. Grif wrote a long letter to Frank, venting accusations about the loss of every animal that had died over the last several months. "The Shetland ponies were confined last winter in the little trap just below Elk Lake. Four or five of them died of starvation; they actually gnawed the rocks." The central accusation surrounded a camel.

> The old big camel that I mentioned to you had his hind leg broken. I passed the camel pasture in the afternoon with some visitors and Mr. Zühlke had his rope on the old camel, around his neck, and he would run his horse, get the camel to running and he would just speed and swing his horse out to the side and whip the camel around like cracking a whip. At times the old camel's neck was just as long as a clothes line.[188]

The Osage County Attorney, S. T. Carmen, informally filed a memorandum listing several acts of cruelty to animals alleged to have been committed by Zühlke at Woolaroc. Though he never filed formal charges, the company took this very seriously and asked Maxwell M. Mahany, a Bartlesville attorney, to investigate. Mahaney requested that E. E. Hansen, state president of the Society for the Prevention of Cruelty to Animals, assist in the investigation. They found no basis for the charges. In fact, they learned that Henry Wells and Dave Ware were at the bottom of the controversy. The episode cost Grif his job, was the beginning of the end for Zühlke, and cost the company a great deal of money to investigate. It might have been prudent to pay Henry for his dogs.[189]

The Exotic Animals

During the first winter, the Miller brothers were probably responsible for recommending that Frank contact I. S. Horne, owner of Horne's Zoological Arena Company of Kansas City, in his search for animals. Frank wrote Horne in January of 1926, chiefly interested in stocking his game preserve with deer, elk, and buffalo. Horne's response was masterful, "I have been stocking the enormous game preserve of William Randolph Hearst (for nearly three years) in Central California."[190] Horne mentioned the varieties of animals he had supplied Hearst; in addition, he mentioned that he could get "moose, oriental birds, and. . . reindeer,. . . they are a feature and outside of Mr. Wm. Randolph Hearst, no other private individual in the United States owns any reindeer."[191] With that, Frank was on the hook.

A notation in a letter says Frank received two male and five female reindeer on March 30, 1926.[192] The same letter recorded an extensive order of exotic birds as well as white fallow deer and zebras. A February letter asked Frank—how about a couple of zebras? Then April 12, Horne began reeling in the line. "You and Mr. Hearst are the only private owners of zebras on the American continent, you and he are the only private owners of Antelope and Reindeer."[193] Within two months, Frank placed orders for pronghorn antelope, beaver, wild turkeys, elk, mule deer, black swans, sarus cranes, demoiselle cranes, peacocks, Canada geese, and guineas. The animals began arriving promptly and usually in good condition. Though Frank complained in an occasional letter about the prices being "out of line," he kept ordering more and more exotic animals and birds.

About the first of June, Frank ordered 100 reindeer from Horne. Horne negotiated a large consignment to be imported in October, but Frank haggled over the price. In a July 3 letter Horne confirmed the order of 100 reindeer at $250 a head and then put a hard sell on Frank for some ostriches. In his letters, Horne included regular progress reports on the reindeer shipment coming from Alaska, along with correspondence about various other shipments and sales propositions. As it neared, the reindeer shipment was the source of intense drama in the Horne correspondence. Finally, on October 14, a telegram announced two railroad carloads of reindeer would arrive Saturday morning.[194] Grif said that Horne accompanied the shipment and rode with the trucks to the ranch. Grif and Horne were satisfied that the shipment went well.[195] On Monday, Marjorie Loos mailed a check for $16,379, deducting $250 for a reindeer that was down on arrival and had since died. A note in Loos' handwriting at the bottom of the page says, "2 more died of pneumonia fever."[196] Three days later Grif Graham wired Horne, "Our Reindeer are dying of pneumonia fever have lost and more are affected wire instructions care Frank Phillips."[197] By November 13, pneumonia had claimed 25 reindeer. Horne's office feared the malady might be contagious. Frank responded, "this disturbs me very much and I am fearful the disease may spread to other animals. Am going out to the ranch this afternoon and have the reindeer all rounded up, if possible; which, by the way, is a difficult thing to do on account of my forests being so dense."[198]

The tragedy that struck Frank's animals was appalling. He canceled the purchase of 20 additional reindeer. "We undertook to round up the reindeer, but found the few left so widely scattered that we had to give it up although we had forty horsemen in the round-up. My reindeer are practically all gone. We also discovered that the seven, which I purchased last spring, died during the summer."[199]

Horne was struck. "I am unable to figure out, to save my life, how you could have had such an enormous loss."[200] He suggested that he would shoulder part of the loss. Frank was somewhat pacified, but believed he had been sold animals that could not survive the climate.

Will Rogers had some fun at Frank's expense in his syndicated column.

> EL RENO, Okla., Sept. 22.—When you are visiting the beauty spots of this country, don't overlook Frank Phillips' ranch and game preserve at Bartlesville, Okla. It's the most unique place in the country. Got everything but reindeer. He shipped fifty down from Alaska at a thousand dollars a piece. They stood the summer fine and all froze to death in the winter.[201]

If the reindeer were an immediate disaster, Frank's exotic birds were a headache. Over time, the birds seem to have given him as much pleasure as any of the creatures he brought into Woolaroc. Gradually he began to accumulate the wild turkeys he wanted for his game preserve. It was not easy. He had difficulty finding turkeys at all. He complained of a turkey order from Horne, ". . . my ranch foreman insists that these are not wild turkeys; they play around in the barnyard with the other turkeys and you can't tell them apart."[202]

Horne tempted Frank with black swans quite early in their correspondence. True to form, it was not long before Frank had placed a sizeable order for them. Horne purchased the Australian imports from an established collector, and it was assumed they were already pinioned. Upon arrival they were turned lose to swim on the lake, and they promptly flew off. Imagine Frank's rage as he sat at the head of the directors' table on the sixth floor of his brand new office building. . . "Yesterday while I was holding a directors meeting on the sixth floor of this building one of them flew past my window."[203]

That afternoon he wrote another letter. Another of the swans lit in a farmer's yard and died during the night. They found that she had been shot. Emil Lenders wrote that he had seen them flying over his ranch in Kay County.[204] By May 7, most had been caught and pinioned, but they were still four short. It was such a disappointment that in 1939, when animal dealer John Benson offered some black swans, Frank said he did not believe they were suited for the climate.[205]

Frank bought seven supposedly acclimated reindeer from a Kansas City zoo animal dealer in March 1926. They were probably part of the unruly herd of animals that thrilled the guests at the director's meeting in April. Another two carloads of reindeer came in from Alaska in October, amidst great excitement. Within days they began to die. Not a single one survived to the end of the year. The demise of the reindeer was the beginning of the terrible death loss that struck Frank's exotic animals in 1927 and 1928. Courtesy Woolaroc.

Above: Frank bought his first goats in from South Texas for brush control in 1925. This is the only picture of his original Spanish goats. Courtesy Woolaroc.

Right: Frank bought ostriches in his very first order from zoo animal dealer I. S. Horne in 1926. The early ostriches ranged free, and as a consequence, fell victim to all sorts of silly calamities. Despite all, ostriches were an early success and still thrive at Woolaroc. Courtesy Woolaroc.

Frank bought an ostrich from Horne in his very first purchase. In all he bought five in 1926 and five in 1927. Horne envisioned giving them free range. They fell victim to all kinds of stupid ostrich accidents. The *Kansas City Star* article recorded one calamity. "Incidentally, one of Phillips' ostriches ate some fresh cement from a workman's cement mixture recently. The cement hardened in the bird's neck and that was the end of Mr. Ostrich."[206] At the end of the disastrous year of 1927, Frank had four ostriches remaining. Nevertheless, Ostriches have been another Woolaroc success. During the ostrich-farming craze of the last several years, Woolaroc very profitably supplied birds and fertile eggs for the boom market. Frank would be proud. Because then there was been a predictable bust, but the Woolaroc office has blown ostrich eggs for sale for $10 apiece. Three aggressive female birds and an ill-tempered male pace up and down in their run, displaying their plumes, as carloads of visitors creep slowly by each day.[207]

Frank knew virtually nothing about most of the animals he was buying. He was relying on the animal acumen of old-time cowboys to manage his ranch. He assumed that surely an eland was not really different from a longhorn. Grif Graham tried to clarify Frank's goals as be began to deal with Horne. "As I understand your ideas, you would not care for foreign birds or animals as I think your ideas and intentions are to preserve the animals of North America and keep our reserve as near to nature as possible."[208] Within days of this letter, Frank was already negotiating purchase of exotic animals. By summer, Frank wrote, "have been disappointed in some things purchased because I didn't know what they were like not [sic] interested in any animals except game animals which could be turned loose."[209] Again and again Frank ordered animals only to send a telegram as they were being unloaded: what do I feed these? Do they require special shelter in winter?

Horne shipped the first zebras late in July of 1926 and more in September. The first zebras were young animals that had been handled enough since their capture that they were halter broke. That fall all of the reindeer died, and by spring the antelope were suffering some sort of fatal indigestion. A bull elk and buck deer had killed some of the pinioned waterfowl. Accidents with the ostriches, cranes, and swans had been very discouraging. The flood that washed out the dams had reduced the cowboys to seining the water holes, trying to recover some of the fish the government had stocked in Frank's lakes. One of the new kangaroos died, and the other escaped. In June of 1927, Frank complained of his terrible losses, "I am beginning to think it is a mistake to buy animals or birds from foreign countries."[210] He was exasperated.

> I find that out of 219 head of stock which we have purchased from you to date at a total cost, including express of $42,551.16, we have lost 143 head at a total loss of $28,833,58; this leaves on hand only 25 animals and 51 fowls, or 76 head of your stock which we have purchased from you.[211]

A shipment of zebras directly from Africa ratcheted up the troubles to disaster. Horne claimed they had been inoculated and vermifuged, but on June 30, 1928, Frank's veterinarian said they were very wormy, and on July 9, an autopsy yielded a graphic listing of deadly worms—everything from African filaria to common ascarids, and plenty in between. Zebras continued to die, and Frank called in the government. W. E. West, then the county agent, and

Water buffalo just appeared, without explanation, on the animal inventories in 1930. They adapted well, evidently without incident. One of the pair in this photo, Uncle Ed, became a pet of the Phillips daughters. He could be ridden just like the animals in Southeast Asia. Recently Woolaroc has acquired new water buffalo stock. Courtesy Woolaroc.

The trials of the early years, and the financial crisis early in the Depression, at first dashed any hopes of making any profit from the animals. But by the late 1930s Frank was at last profitably raising exotic stock for sale and trade. Frank really enjoyed being a big shot in the exotic animal set. This picture is from a series taken of a cute young camel and llama in 1936.
Courtesy Woolaroc.

C. C. Nichol, the government veterinarian, sent Frank a copy of their reports. The zebras had a parasite load that was sufficient to kill them. Dr. Nickel wrote, ". . . it is very unfortunate indeed that these animals were brought onto the ranch in this condition as I feel that the loss of two zebras to date is but a small item as compared to the contamination of the premises with such a broad variety of intestinal and gastric parasites."[212]

The first large losses were among the reindeer in 1926, due to hemorrhagic septicemia. The stress of shipping and incompatibility with the climate made them vulnerable to this scourge. Shipping fever continued to be a serious problem at the ranch until Frank began to insist on vaccination of his purchases before shipping. The antelope were similarly unsuited for the climate and also died of pneumonia. Half the buffalo succumbed to parasite contamination. Almost all of the mule deer and a large portion of his white-tail deer were also lost to climate, parasites, and pneumonia. It was probably John T. Benson, American agent for Hagenbeck Brothers, who suggested that Frank bring in the USDA veterinarian who finally untangled all the troubles. The USDa veterinarian, Dr. C. H. Fauks, recommended the destruction of the entire herd of brush goats and several other remedial measures. The underlying culprit was cyst tapeworm, brought in by the goats.[213] The beginning inventory for 1929 showed that 387 animals and only 22 birds remained, but the problems were under control as they entered the new year.[214]

Horne sensed that his prize client was slipping away. He made a bold proposal that if Frank would vaccinate his entire herd against hemorrhagic septicemia, and promise to buy $250,000 worth of animals over two years, he would guarantee them all.[215] But Frank was already asking his friends about other dealers. On July 6, 1927, John Benson wrote Frank, soliciting business, and used John Ringling's name as a reference.[216] John Ringling called on Frank in New York on July 25.[217] A few days later, Frank got a letter from Carl Hagenbeck himself, of Hamberg, Germany, saying Ringling had talked to him of Frank's special interest in antelope and birds and advertising his firm as "the leading house in the new idea of showing animals in their natural surroundings and in their natural state."[218] Despite his troubles, Frank was, as usual, on the cutting edge. Shortly, Frank heard from Hagenbeck's American agent, John T. Benson. Benson's words must have been music to Frank's beleaguered ears, and Frank responded that it was refreshing to note there was an opportunity to raise wild game animals for profit. He wrote Hagenbeck that he was becoming interested in foreign animals but wanted consultation on their care before going ahead. At about the time that Horne was making his proposition, Frank was inviting Benson to visit the ranch, looking to begin his restocking in the spring.[219]

The government veterinarians were still working with Frank's herd in the summer of 1928, and Frank was discouraged, when Heinrich Hagenbeck visited Woolaroc on July 25.[220] Frank wrote, "Your trip here was a real inspiration to me as you aroused new interest in my ranch."[221] In that letter Frank placed a hefty order for fallow deer. He was back on the hook. But, he had learned some things. A letter from Benson mentioned that Hearst was buying a lot of elands, but Frank wrote in the margin, "Ask Ringling."[222] Frank had also made the acquaintance of George P. Vierheller, the father of the St. Louis Zoo. His advice and guidance gave Frank's program a new rationality that was invaluable. Over the years, the Vierheller family became close friends with Frank and Jane. Jane often stopped at St. Louis to visit Mrs. Vierheller when coming and going to and from the East. They were frequent visitors at the ranch. Vierheller introduced Frank to another important importer, Herman Ruhe. Frank liked his birds.

Frank did not altogether quit buying animals from Horne. In a terse letter in 1929, he complained of a sick cassowary that Vierheller examined and another shipment of deer with hemorrhagic septicemia. "In my dealings with you in the future we must have an understanding that you will guarantee healthy animals."[223] He continued to do business with Horne but bought much less from him. Meanwhile, Frank's animals began to prosper, and Vierheller and Benson began to buy some of his surplus animals. Business continued to be brisk through 1930, buying and selling quite a few animals.

At mid-year 1930, Frank's inventory shows he had no antelope, reindeer, or wallabies. Those efforts had been dismal failures. He had 37 buffalo remaining on the ranch, 8 zebras, 41 white-tail deer, and 2 mule deer among the animals that had taken the brunt of the epidemic. Japanese sika, black and white fallow deer, and elk had prospered. He also had a few aoudad, blackbuck, blesbok, water buffalo, camels, Barasinga deer, red deer, a monkey, gnus, guanacos, llamas, kangaroos, peccaries, and tahrs, a total of 504 mammals. He had 364 birds. There were several varieties of ducks, geese, pheasants, peafowl, swans, and quail. He also had a few cassowaries, demoiselle cranes, sarus cranes, a golden eagle, flamingoes, ostriches, rheas, and a stork.

In 1931, the economy began to pinch tightly. An exchange with Horne reveals the pressure. Frank wrote in February, "I am pretty well stocked up and under present conditions am not figuring on adding anything whatever to my ranch."[224] Frank's orders for the year were very spare indeed. He bought some fancy bantam chickens, a few Holsteins, and picked up some bargains: two kangaroos, a llama, and a blesbok. Horne tried temptation, "One of our shippers in Europe is extremely hard up. He needs money very badly, and he is offering us swans at a ridiculously low price the lowest price at which they have ever been quoted to us."[225] He cajoled, "Depressions come and go so often and we all dislike them, but we do not help bring back normal times if we fail to buy everything we want as we did before old man depression hit us."[226]

Frank had plenty of problems of his own. By the end of 1930 oil prices were dropping precipitously, falling to a low of 22 cents a barrel. Phillips stock sank with oil prices from a little over $16 a share to a little more than $3. For the first, time Phillips Petroleum Company lost money and was not able to pay dividends. Frank's banking creditors were peering over his shoulder. He managed to get the financing he needed, but it was 1934 before the company paid dividends again, and during the darkest days there were times when it was questionable whether they would be able to make payroll. Typical of Frank Phillips' business practice, he aggressively met this challenge. Rather than conservatively circumscribing expenditures, Frank raised the money to build a pipeline to be ready for better business times. He continued some extravagant entertaining at the ranch, but drastically cut back on buying, building, and hiring until about 1935.

Frank emerged from the depths of the Depression a more thoughtful and purposeful collector. His animal debacles were largely behind him. He mostly bought, sold, and traded the animals he had learned did well at Woolaroc. He made improvements such as a climbing mountain in 1939 for his mountain goats, similar to Hagenbeck's in Germany, and he indulged some enthusiasms such as a monkey house, modeled on the one at the Independence, Kansas, zoo. He had carved out a reputation as a gentleman with an exotic game preserve par excellence.

In 1940, John Seward, the ranch manager, wrote an essay for a new Woolaroc brochure. It was never used, but it beautifully captures an essence that still hangs among the woods, lakes, and rocks.

> A heavy mist came in the night—the early morning hours brought the cold—every bit of moisture crystallized. Each blade of grass is an upstanding icicle, the roads covered with a sheet of glass.
>
> We can hardly expect the animals to break this film of ice and obtain nourishment from the bluestem grass, nor get through to the acorns on which they have been feeding.
>
> So out roll the heavy trucks to the store barns for cake, the inch cube pellets of cotton seed cake and minerals, and the great hay shed, where there are hundreds of tons of prairie hay and sudan grass. Then thru [sic] the woods, horns blowing, and here come the range animals.
>
> First, always, the buffalo, heads and shoulders a mass of tiny spears of ice. Then the brahmas and their tones of discontent over the weather. Small wonder, when we remember that their sires came from the lowlands of India. The zebras, from the veldts of Africa, join the buffalo. Holding a little to the side, but still not too wary, are the elk, and beyond them, always a bit cautious about approaching too close, are the deer. The native whitetails, strangely enough are the most shy. The white fallows and the black fallow, now a far cry from their Siberian home, are a bit more willing to come near to the feeding trucks. The Barasinghas, far from the swamps of India, the largest of the known deer, mingle with the elk, but are easily distinguishable by the golden color of the fur and the peculiar face markings. And the little Japanese Sikas join the strange procession thru [sic] the woods. Suddenly the Angora goats appear—not shy at all if the truck stops for even a moment—they manage to climb aboard and nose the bags of cake.
>
> The bales of hay are broken and scattered—one man sits at the rear of the truck and lets the 'cake' dribble from the open sacks. A mile thru [sic] the woods we go, and behind a scene that few are privileged to view. Animals from the four corners of the earth, most of them, and yet living safely . . . [227]

Crystal Springs Farm

If Frank's exotic animals were his joy, his pride was his farm and its domestic stock. The farm was a part of his original grand vision for a gentleman's estate. Not many men had a game preserve or exotic animals at large on their estates; but, well, everybody who was anybody had prestigious registered stock. It was a manifestation of their progressive era to employ scientific methods and diversified farming to illuminate their true status as country squires. At the time that Frank bought the ranch, there were already 200 acres of farmland near the Crystal Springs and Campbell Field. By the first of 1926, Frank had given notice to the tenants: the Gentzel family, living in the small red house near Crystal Spring, and the Campbells, living along Rock Creek to the northeast of the lodge.[228] A Mr. Gray had his crew removing the old houses and cleaning up around the springs within days.

One of Grif Graham's first ranch reports says, "Have not been able to buy any hogs as yet; haven't been able to steal one. Am still trying. Have bought a plow and harrow and have a man whom I think can handle the farming situation for us. Also have a pair of young mules which I am considering."[229] Frank instructed Graham to buy 100 Hampshire or Duroc sows. Frank hired W. E. Miller from Tulsa to farm for $75 per month and gave him a house near the barn with water and gas and pasture for a cow. He was anxious to see preparations for spring planting.

> I want that land gotten in shape at the earliest moment for seeding. The two west plots of ground are to be put in oats and seeded with alfalfa at the same time. The pieces in the bottom farthest east are to be put in kaffir corn, as is also the Crystal Springs farm to be put in kaffir. I want the ground all put in first class condition, especially the portion which we are to put in oats and alfalfa. Clyde Alexander can give you information regarding where to get alfalfa seed, how to sow it and how much seed to use.[230]

Miller arrived for work a few days after the big buffalo shipment. He was just in time to pitch in on winter feeding during several days of stormy weather. He was able to begin preparing the fields by the first week in February. They planted potatoes and made garden in March. By May they had also hired a Mr. Larrimore in time to plant the kaffir corn.[231]

Technically, the brush goats were the first domestic animals on the ranch. Grif was reporting inquiries about hogs, turkeys, chickens, and work and riding horses during the first spring. On March 8, 1926, L. E. sent Frank one of his good milk cows.[232] The inventories at the end of 1926 still showed only 1 cow, 9 horses, and 65 chickens. Frank had a fine little family farm, capable of augmenting his table.

Late in 1926, John A. Bell of Pittsburgh, wrote Frank that he was asking O. B. Toalson to send over a Holstein cow.[233] Bell was one of Frank's business acquaintances who had recently been entertained at Woolaroc. He was a breeder of registered Holsteins and knew of Toalson's fine Holstein dairy herd.[234] The inventory at the end of 1927 included 1 Jersey cow, 3 Holsteins, and 2 mixed Holstein and Jersey. Bell's gift was the beginning of Frank's registered dairy herd. In the next year Bell sold Frank some good cows and three bulls. Throughout the years Bell supplied Frank with exceptional bulls. Holstein bulls can be particularly nasty-tempered and, in 1929, Bell negotiated a trade between Frank and J. Reynolds Waite, Bell's son-in-law, who was willing to take one of the Bell-bred bulls, owned by Frank, that had become irascible, in trade for *King Romeo Advocate*.[235] Bell sent out a young bull registered *Oklahoma Chief of Woolaroc.* Frank was sometimes generous too. In 1933, he exchanged young bulls with G. A. Gerken, Bishop of Amarillo, Texas, to help out his breeding program.

Frank's friends sometimes sent him extravagant gifts from their registered stock, and Frank, likewise, sent animals to some of his friends. Frank and Waite did a lot of exchanging such gifts and, sometimes, purchases. The angora goats were from Waite's ranch in Cimarron, New Mexico. Frank sent three of the angoras to Sheldon Clark of Sinclair Oil and Refining Company. Waite sent Frank six beavers in 1927, but they did not make it. Frank sent a camel to Waite's thrilled son, Elliott, in 1933. One of the company directors, Arthur Hilmer, sent Frank a Saddlebred mare in 1929. A copy of the papers for *Highland Lady Lightfoot* are in the files, showing she was a granddaughter of three of the most famous foundation horses in the Saddlebred registry, and the fourth line contains, at another generation distance, one of the famous Morgan Horses in the foundation lines of the breed. This was an exceptionally well-bred horse. Frank subsequently gave her to George Miller.

Frank's personal favorite riding horses were usually Saddlebreds. But, he catered to the Wild West mystique by acquiring distinctively Western breeds for his guests to ride. In an early letter, Frank stated his intent of using only Pintos on his ranch, but by the late 1930s, he was looking for good Palominos to satisfy the new fashion in Western mounts.[236] Eventually, Fred Phillips sold Frank four Palomino mares and two horse colts of the quality he was looking for.[237] The ranch also kept some Shetland ponies after 1930. Frank bought Sardinian donkeys in 1937. The ranch had a light and a heavy draft team. In 1938, Don Zühlke made an inventory of the horses: 6 riding horses, 4 roping horses, 5 mares, a carriage team, a Palomino stallion, a small draft team, 3 large draft horses, and 6 horses under age three.

Frank's earliest venture in registered hogs appears to be a Duroc boar from his friend Charles Schwab, in 1928, as a thank you for his entertainment at the ranch.[238] The inventories show that during 1927 he had 73 hogs, apparently all but 23 butchered by the end of the year. At the end of 1928, Frank owned 111 hogs, 78 butchered for food. He got a lot of mileage from his hogs. There was a lot of banter in his thank you letters about the delicious Woolaroc Acorn Sausage his guests had eaten at the lodge. Frank competed with Amon Carter's Christmas turkeys by sending Woolaroc hams as gifts to his friends.

In October of 1930, E. W. Evans sent Frank a blueprint for the proposed layout of Crystal Springs Farm.

This barnyard photo shows some of Frank's prize Holstein cows at the dairy barn at Crystal Spring Farm. He was proud of his fine barns, out buildings, fences, and the best dairy herd, hogs, chickens and turkeys that money could buy. Frank enjoyed his image of progressive farmer and exploited it to the hilt when he entertained his Eastern guests. Courtesy Woolaroc.

This included a working plan for the slaughterhouse; the foundations were already poured. Evans wanted to know if Frank wanted to begin the hog house immediately so it would be finished in time for the spring pigs.[239] Evans said they had just finished vaccinating (he probably meant testing) the hogs for tuberculosis. Five of his sows had already farrowed, totaling 41 pigs on the farm then.

The first part of September, Pearl Mikels reported to Evans that some of the hogs on the range did not seem to be doing well. They rounded them up into a pasture at Crystal Springs and began to feed them, but they did not improve, so Evans and Cecil Hardman killed one and found what appeared to be tuberculosis lesions. On October 6, Cecil brought Dr. Nickel the viscera of the hog they had slaughtered, and Nickel confirmed the tuberculosis lesions.[240] Days later Dr. Nickel's State Report had awful news. A Jersey cow and a hog tested positive for tuberculosis.[241]

Evans wrote that two hogs were killed and burned, and the cow was killed and taken to Banfield Packing Company in Tulsa.[242] Frank was horrified. "I am surprised to note there is TB on the place, and am very surprised to note that you would sell the meat of the cow which was affected."[243] Evans replied that when tuberculosis is found the animal carcass must be burned, or if sold, the packer destroys the affected part and pays for the good meat only.

The veterinarians suspected the source of the disease was an old elk that was kept in the pig yard because she was frequently sick. They slaughtered Old Wabbly, finding actinomycosis but no tuberculosis. Meanwhile intensive testing of the swine and other animals using the same runs and pastures began to turn up about 50 percent reactors. Dr. Nickel and Dr. Ewers, of the Federal Department of Tuberculosis Eradication, set up a lab at the Frank Phillips Ranch. Evans wrote, "They report a pretty bad situation. . . "[244]

So far, another cow and 53 head of hogs were reactors. Evans took them to Banfield's. Thirty-one of the hogs were unfit for meat. Evans hoped to keep the sows with pigs until they could wean the piglets and raise them to marketable size. Old Charlie Schwab, the prize Duroc boar, was a reactor, but Evans hoped he could isolate him so he could be used for breeding for a while longer. Frank was duly alarmed. "I am afraid that the other animals including game animals and fowls on the ranch will become infected."[245]

The source of the infection was never determined. The veterinarians thought it either came from the household garbage that was fed the hogs or was residual from some of the original swine and had just flared into an active form. The veterinarians said the outbreak was very virulent and recommended the complete eradication of all the swine, chickens, and turkeys, then prescribed the very aggressive clean-up procedure for the pastures, barns, sties, pens, and houses.[246]

This was an ugly blow at the time of the low ebb of Frank's fortunes during the Depression. Frank wrote, "I certainly hope we can get this hog situation cleaned up as soon as possible, especially where feeding grain, as I do not want to maintain the expense of continuing to feed hogs corn or anything else, except such as they can find for themselves on the ranch."[247]

Frank replaced his Durocs with Hampshires. In 1932, he bought 13 and had 64 hogs at the close of the year inventory. A hog analysis early in 1932 said he had one Poland China sow with 7 mixed breed pigs. L. E. raised prize Poland Chinas and was probably the source of this replacement sow for Frank. All the remaining 73 head were Hampshires. The original 4 Hampshires were acquired in February 1931 at $20 each. His hog operation showed $114 profit that year.[248]

This is Frank's string of fine riding horses, tethered and waiting to be saddled. Frank preferred to ride a Saddlebred, but he kept Western type horses for his dude guests. In the early years he used Pintos, probably because they looked more Western to the movie-goers of the time. Later the trendy horses were Palominos and Frank switched his ranch string to that breed. Courtesy Woolaroc.

Frank began looking for a special Western breed of cattle very early. In the spring of 1926 he inquired of Snake King for "old-time coaster cattle." That order never materialized, but he did make periodic inquiries to several potential sources through 1927 and 1928, looking for longhorns. As time went by he became more particular, realizing that the horns were everything. J. M. Davis sent him a clipping from the New York Times about the USDA buying longhorns for the Wichita National Forest.[249] Frank responded, "Regarding the Longhorns, I have searched northern Mexico and southern Texas but have not been able to get the kind of cattle desired. The Government in this case beat me to it."[250] The inventories show he evidently did not find any for a few years. Through the search, he contacted an agent named Smug Byler, in El Paso, Texas, who proved very useful in some of his other searches.

Around Christmas of 1929, Amon Carter located a fine steer that interested Frank.[251] As a result, C. E. Autry of Fort Worth became a satisfactory source of some of the first longhorns. Frank also bought a horn chair from Autry. By the 1930s he had a handful of longhorns. He got a pair of oxen in 1926 that were used to pull his covered wagon.

In the spring of 1928, he hit on the idea of raising Brahmans. George Miller made inquiries with Caesar Kleberg about pure bred Brahmans and was also looking for zebus on February 13.[252] Within a week Miller had a shipment of a bull and 20 heifers on the way. Robert Kleberg wrote the provenance of the stock Frank had purchased. They were from stock that originated at Pierce Station.[253] Shanghai Pierce was the old Texas rancher who, in 1906, first imported carefully selected cattle from India for a cross-breeding program that was eventually carried out by his nephew, Able Pierce Borden, to develop the breed.[254] When the registry was formed in 1924, J. W. Sartwelle, the first breed recording secretary, suggested the name Brahman.[255] The Klebergs were the famous King Ranch family. They were instrumental in establishing the breed and eventually used Brahman stock in the development of their Santa Gertrudis breed.

A year later Zack Miller, was ordering Kleberg Brahmans again for Frank. On March 28, an order of 29 Kleberg cattle was received. Characteristically, in the interim, Frank began making inquiries among his acquaintances. Shortly after entertaining the Catholic bishops at the ranch on March 4, 1929, Frank got a nice thank you from C. E. Byrne, the Bishop of Galveston, with some information about Brahma breeders.[256] Frank went to the source, writing A. P. Borden for a bull. Borden wrote a complicated letter to say he had none for sale.[257] Finally Rev. Byrne's help led Frank to the Sartwelle herd. By then Frank had decided to breed white Brahmans. W. E. West went to Houston in June to select the animals for Frank. Frank bought 39 heifers and 2 bulls, and Sartwelle sent along the registration papers.[258] Frank's were some of the earliest registered animals of that breed. On October 21, 1930, Frank wrote the American Brahman Breeders Association, asking for a registration visit by the committee. James Sartwelle visited the herd and was very complimentary. There was some more special branding required before certificates for 68 cattle were issued March 23, 1931.[259] In 1931, Frank's herd may have been the only one outside of south Texas.[260] The Miller brothers were clearly the inspiration for the idea of raising Brahmans. Encouragement for the idea may have come from Benson. Letters as early as 1928 from Hagenbeck and Benson refer to zebus, and even later, they refer to his registered zebu herd. Zebu is a generic term for hump-backed cattle.

With cattle prices so low, the stock was not worth selling; in December of 1931 Benson bought four perfect white Brahman calves from Frank and paid big bucks. Benson had an idea for a publicity stunt with one of the calves.

> Feeling that you can keep this confidential, my intention is to shave all the hair off and tattoo the skin, which takes something like a year and a half to cover it. If it works all right and the marks can be seen you will read about the Sacred Bull of Burmah [sic] being imported and where it is being worshiped by the Hindus as their Idol.[261]

Something about the exotic-looking cattle seemed to invite stunts. A cowboy named Johnny Grimes bought one of Frank's Brahman steers, named New Deal, and trained him to jump, pull a cart, and drink beer for a an act at the Oklahoma Junior Livestock Show in 1937.

Involvement in a scheme of rustling some of Frank's Brahmans may have been the reason W. I. Compton was fired as ranch manager. An October 1932 ranch report says,

Frank bought his first zebu (Indian hump-backed) cattle from an animal dealer named Johnson. But, his interest in zebu-type cattle quickly refined. George and Zack Miller suggested that Frank might be interested in looking at a new cattle breed that was being developed on the King Ranch in Texas. Very soon Frank was buying Brahman breeding stock from the Klebergs. His fancy Brahmans were a source of pride, and often a source of fun. He probably had the first herd of registered Brahmans outside of South Texas. Here is a prize bull. Courtesy Woolaroc.

> On the calves (Brahmas) sold to Dyer, Bill was offered $20 per head in the pasture. We received $12.50 per head. states two of these calves were weighed and they averaged 475lbs. each.
>
> During the recent round-up for branding the Brahma calves, two men made the statement that they were having another round-up out here and they had better go out and buy some more; another fellow said 'Buy hell; you mean steal.' These two fellows came out to the Ranch one day. and his men attempted to watch the Okesa gate and did so three nights, but saw nothing.[262]

Frank must have suspected something before the investigation, for he chided Compton for incomplete reports on February 24.[263] But nothing must have been proven. The hard times caused Frank to sometimes be parsimonious, which may have been part of the reason he had some troubles with his employees.

> I want to gradually cut down on the expenditures at the ranch in every respect. I dislike very much to have to discharge any men, but these are such bad times everywhere that from my standpoint it seems foolish to be spending money for anything except necessary repairs and improvements... all men must be kept busy and do a day's work.[264]

Frank was sometimes irritable, firing employees on the spot, then hiring them back a few days later. The wife of a discharged farmer wrote to plead their desperation. Frank responded,

> My report is that Wesley became indolent and seemed to lose interest in his work; however, Mr. Zühlke was no doubt right in stating that he was no longer needed after the grasshoppers ate up the garden.[265]

In some sort of altercation in December of 1930, he fired W. E. West and placed E. W. Evans in the position of ranch manager. West tried desperately to stay on, and Evans, who actually was hired as a secretary, strongly disliked his new position—for lower pay. Frank told him that "under the present depressed conditions" he should be grateful. In February of 1931, Evans, the man who had handled the tuberculosis crisis so ably, resigned.

> And since you now insist on my moving to the ranch and living in the garage, paying me through the ranch payroll, which would deprive me of my insurance and stock rights, and a possible cut in salary, when I am already working for a great deal less than you have ever paid, I feel that you are just naturally trying to see how far you can go.[266]

The belt-tightening persisted despite the troubles with his good employees. Frank rebuked Compton for paying a new farmer too much. "I notice that you hired a farmer for $60.00. He may be worth that under normal times, and probably is worth more, but under existing conditions I told you not to pay more that $50.00."[267] A week later, Frank reduced Compton's salary from $100 to $85.

Frank had chickens and turkeys on the ranch early in the first year. Over the years his ranch records mention Rhode Island red and buff orpington or standard chickens. These are both dual-purpose breeds, the kind of birds a farmer would chose for his own use, but neither were really efficient as layers or as broilers. Later ranch records frankly state that they had never made much profit with their chickens, and a 1941 analysis of Crystal Springs Farm chicken operations show a loss of $1,014.57.[268] Frank's friends evidently enjoyed chickens, for they sometimes gave him some fancy bantams as gifts. Frank Buck gave him rosecombs and helped him find some good specimens on occasion. Seabrights were a gift from General Hoffman. The inventories show he kept some interesting breeds of bantams: white and black rosecombs, silkies, frizzles, turkens, seabrights, buff cochin, and brown leghorn bantams.

A fire in the blacksmith shop in January 1936 nearly spelled disaster for Frank's fancy chickens. A blowtorch exploded in M. Marshal's hands, while he was working in the shop. Before some water buckets could be brought the fire was out of control. The horse barn and chicken house were threatened by the flames, so the animals were released. Fortunately the fire was contained, and only the blacksmith shop was lost.[269] Things were not so lucky in September when the cow barn burned. The cause was evidently wiring because the blueprints for the new barn were very meticulous about the wiring.[270]

In the late 1930s, turkey prices were very good. Frank worked a deal with John Mayo, selling him 400 Thanksgiving and Christmas turkeys at 25 cents a pound dressed. [271] Frank had Don Zühlke converting some of his chicken space to turkey brooders the next year. They were greatly increasing the size of their flock from 1,000 birds to 1,500, besides 500 Rhode Island red chicks.[272] This was a far cry from the 65 chickens in 1926 or 25 domestic turkeys in 1935.

There were a number of ducks and geese on the ranch that could be called domestic varieties, though it does not appear they were raised for the table. There were even four hives of bees. Frank's Scotch Highland cattle were a domestic breed that impinged on the exotic label. He bought the first of these in 1935 and had some trouble in establishing his stock over the next few years. They have been immensely successful at Woolaroc, so that today visitors can readily see several of the wooly creatures, usually near the road in the "Scotch" pasture, looking quite at home on a wintry day but rather pitiful in the August sun.

Frank bottled water under the Woolaroc and Gingeroc labels. These were for consumption by his guests at the ranch. Gingeroc, Woolaroc, and Acorn Sausage were Frank's favors to his guests in 1930. His farms sold cattle and swine for market, as well as butchering for personal use. As already mentioned, they sold chickens, turkeys, and eggs with some success. The garden and dairy produced well for their own use. He even planted some paper shell pecans, though they are never heard of again, and a fruit orchard. The scientific and diversified nature of the farm operated in fits and starts, but it was a goal, and profitability was usually marginal at best. Frank was very proud of the fine barns, out buildings, pens, and fences that he could show his friends, and the best stock money could buy graced his pastures. In its heyday, Woolaroc fulfilled most of Frank's vision of himself as a progressive farmer, and his dreams of a game preserve for his friends to admire.

IV

ALL BALLS IN THE AIR: THE GROWTH OF THE RANCH

In 1903, Frank Phillips was engaged in the banking business in Creston, Iowa, working for his father-in-law, John Gibson. That spring, while on a business trip in St. Louis, Missouri, Frank met a Methodist minister he knew from back home, and from him first heard of the rich oil discoveries in Indian Territory. In May, John Gibson and Frank visited Bartlesville to investigate the rumors. They found that the quiet little Jake Bartles trading post on the Caney River had burgeoned into a mud-mired boomtown with as many tents as houses, sheltering a rough, tough crowd of roustabouts, wildcatters, gamblers, prostitutes, drummers, missionaries, and a smattering of ordinary citizens. It was a town with black gold flowing literally in the streets. The vision captivated the imagination of the young businessman. Returning home, Gibson agreed to finance Frank's venture, and Frank and L. E. struck out for Indian Territory, only weeks after the Wright Brothers flight at Kitty Hawk, North Carolina, in December.

The turn of the century decade was a time of explosive growth in the central plains, and oil and aviation were two industries that took root there. Oil discovered in Oklahoma, Kansas, and Texas supplied whole new industries. The central plains were a natural place for the growth of aviation. The treeless expanses provided unlimited landing strips, hot summer winds and thermals gave lift to the airfoils, and straight roads and unobstructed

How tantalizing—to capture an actual moment in aviation history in this shot, taken at 12:42 P.M. on 16 August 1927, of the Woolaroc aloft over San Francisco en route to Honolulu during the Dole Race that made the Phillips 66-sponsored Beech Travel Air one of America's historic aircraft. Courtesy Woolaroc.

views made dead-reckoning a breeze. In thousands of barns, farm boys built experimental flying machines, and fired imaginations that soared beyond the tops of the fair weather cumulus that floated above their fields. In places like Wichita, Kansas, and Oklahoma City and Dewey, Oklahoma, entrepreneurs began little manufactures of early aircraft.

Surely Frank read the newspaper accounts of the Wright Brothers flight and those of local visits of the first flying men. We are told that in the early days people used to run outside to watch when the roar of an airplane engine slowly traversed overhead. Surely Frank joined his bank patrons and employees on the sidewalk on such occasions. But there is no reason to believe that he had any special fascination with flying, even during the World War I years when the Army Air Corps had a flight training camp at Dewey's airfield.

Construction of the original hanger for the Woolaroc at the Ranch in 1929 quickly evolved into a showroom by early 1930. After they moved the airplane into the showroom, they hung a few pictures on the wall to spruce things up a bit. Then, Frank began to put some of his gifts and oddities there for a place to stash them. Unintentionally the hanger quickly became the original museum building. Courtesy Woolaroc.

From the earliest days of Phillips Petroleum Company, Frank was aggressively interested in innovation. In 1925, the company hired George Oberfell, a chemist who established one of the first hydrocarbon research laboratories in the new Phillips Office Building. Phillips' chemists and engineers developed better methods of refining and better gasoline products in rapid succession in the 1920s. One process, using polymerization, involved the company in a lawsuit with Union Carbide. John Kane was council in charge of the suit, and George Oberfell's testimony was instrumental in winning the case which put Phillips on the cutting edge of petroleum research.

Always taking advantage of innovations, Phillips was using airmail for business correspondence between Bartlesville and New York in 1926.[273] That year Phillips employed Billy Parker as their first pilot. He flew executives to the oil fields, and firefighters and nitroglycerin to put out well fires. (Yes, he flew nitroglycerin!) Phillips had one of the earliest company aviation divisions.

The Charles Lindbergh trans-Atlantic flight took place in May of 1927, at a time when Phillips was planning the opening of its first service station in Wichita, Kansas. Frank Phillips was in New York when he first read of the Lindbergh flight in the *New York Times.* Frank was as captivated by the events as most Americans, and he also

immediately appreciated the possibilities. Lindbergh's ticker-tape parade in New York, the frenzied crowds everywhere, and his Medal of Honor focused world attention on air travel. There was going to be money made now in aviation, and money in aviation fuel—and big sales and promotional opportunities for those who could hitch their wagons to that star.

Frank's singular opportunity materialized very quickly. Phillips' chemists had also developed a new, lighter fuel especially for aviation, Nu-Aviation Gasoline.[274] James Dole of the Dole Pineapple Company wished to capitalize on the Lindbergh publicity to promote commercial air travel to Hawaii by sponsoring a $25,000 prize for the winner of a race from California to Hawaii. Frank summoned Billy Parker out of the field where he was promoting the new aviation fuel. Frank wanted the company to sponsor an entry in the contest. Parker was put in charge of organizing the operation. In rapid succession, Phillips acquired sponsorship of two Beech Travel Air monoplanes: the *Oklahoma* piloted by Bennett H. Griffin and the *Woolaroc* piloted by Art Goebel.

Frank immediately began to capitalize on the publicity opportunities of such an endeavor, only weeks after the flight of the *Spirit of Saint Louis.* There was a picnic and huge rodeo at Philmont in New Mexico in honor of the Dole aviators on the Fourth of July. Bartlesville reporters got the story on July 21, and Frank had a conference with E. K. Gaylord of the *Daily Oklahoman* July 25. The story of the actual Dole Derby on August 16-17 is one of high drama and tragedy, as well as glory and victory.[275]

Frank was there, taking every promotional opportunity and hobnobbing with the heroes. There was a dinner and dance at the ranch for Goebel on September 23. Frank even managed to organize a dinner at the Tulsa Mayo Hotel to honor Art Goebel—and Charles Lindbergh himself—during the Petroleum Exposition on September 29. Phillips' aviation gasoline got valuable publicity, but more important, Phillips Petroleum Company came to prominent public attention as the producer of quality petroleum products just at the time the company was entering the retail market. Frank continued to utilize the *Woolaroc* for a long time with Goebel barnstorming in the aircraft throughout the country. Skywriting at air shows, county fairs, and football games, he wrote "PHILLIPS 66" first in white, and then in orange smoke across the sky for the delighted onlookers. By 1929, it was time to retire the airplane to a specially built hanger at Woolaroc.[276]

The 1945 expansion of the Museum added the striking rotunda with its distinctive mosaic entry designed by Winold Reiss and cut by the Fascotti firm, and the doors with medallion designs in the style of the Spiro Mound shell gorgets. On the afternoon of its grand opening, eager guests in their mink coats and business suits wend their way up the entry sidewalk to the impressive new rotunda addition. Courtesy Woolaroc.

First the *Woolaroc* went to Wichita where Travel Air restored the aircraft to its original condition; then, Goebel said, it would be sent to the Frank Phillips Ranch.[277] Paul Endacott recalled that they did not quite know what to do with the famous aircraft. Frank decided to take it to the ranch and put it on the site where the museum now stands. Initially, Frank built a pavilion similar to the dance pavilion which is at Clyde Lake, with stone pillars and a roof, to house the namesake orange and blue Travel Air. Like the other projects at his ranch, this quickly became another work in progress.[278]

THE "WOOLAROC," WINNER OF THE 1927 DOLE FLIGHT, IS COMING HOME.

THE TRUSTEES OF THE FRANK PHILLIPS FOUNDATION AND THE STAFF OF WOOLAROC CORDIALLY INVITE YOU TO JOIN IN WELCOMING THE NEWLY RESTORED AIRCRAFT TO HER NEW DISPLAY AREA.

COCKTAILS AND HORS D'OUVRES WILL BE SERVED IN THE NEWEST WING OF WOOLAROC MUSEUM.
SEPTEMBER 6, 1985.
5:30 P.M. TO 7:30 P.M.

Shown here is the invitation to the dedication of the new Museum wing, built to house the newly restored *Woolaroc* in 1985. The grand old aircraft was restored to factory specifications under the direction of Phillips Petroleum Company aviation section. Guests at the dedication included some of the aviators from that era, mingling with businessmen and political personalities. It was an evening that could have been planned by Frank Phillips himself. Courtesy Woolaroc.

On January 28, 1929, Arthur Gorman was at Frank's office discussing plans for building a pavilion for the aircraft. It was not long before Frank wanted it enclosed. By April 22, Gorman was in Frank's office again with plans for an enclosed building that was beginning to take shape.[279] In mid-July, the Bartlesville and Tulsa newspapers had several articles about the farewell tour of the *Woolaroc*. The Tulsa paper published a drawing of the "hanger" which Frank planned to construct. That article said the building would be finished in time to install the aircraft on the second anniversary of the Dole flight.[280]

Goebel left Bartlesville on July 31 on a two-week farewell tour that zigzagged through Oklahoma and Texas and back to the north through Minnesota, completing the circuit in Tulsa on August 13 amidst plenty of hoopla all along the way. Frank gave a small dinner to honor Goebel that evening. "During the dinner, it was announced that the hanger recently constructed on the Phillips estate for the *Woolaroc* will be used only temporarily; work on a larger structure will be started at once, it was said, and completed probably in October."[281]

When Lucky Lindy gave the *Spirit of St. Louis* to the Smithsonian Institution while he was still in Paris, France, in 1927, he unwittingly created the Smithsonian Air and Space Museum. The writer of an article in *U. S. Air Services* may have caught a glimpse of the workings of Frank's mind at that time. He wrote, "Frank Phillips. . . is starting a little Smithsonian on his ranch."[282]

Frank had always been nervous about his lodge built of logs. When he built the museum he bragged that it would be fireproof, all rock and steel. They re-opened the quarry where the rock for the original ranch construction had been dug. There had been dissatisfaction with some of the earlier stonemasonry, so this time Gorman hired a crew of Mexicans for the stone work. Their rock work was so satisfactory that Gorman kept a crew of Mexicans working sporadically for the next 10 years, not only working on the museum and it's additions, but also on barns and outbuildings, and rip-rap guttering. The Woolaroc Archive box M-Z for 1925-1929 is missing. One of the most important files from this box that is probably gone is the one containing blueprints and letters concerning the construction of the museum. We know that it was constructed between the July newspaper announcements and the Cow Thieves and Outlaws Picnic in October.

The original building is pictured in a Woolaroc leaflet from 1932. There were large plate glass windows on either side of the entry. The linings of draperies inside, pulled closed over the windows, may be seen. A graceful canopy over the entry was suspended from chains, reminiscent of the entry to the Phillips Building downtown. A thirty-foot door in the rear allowed the airplane to be rolled in. It appears to have been an inviting building.

Almost from the beginning, collections began to accumulate in the museum. The *U. S. Air Services* writer mused, "Few know why Frank Phillips is gathering such souvenirs at Woolaroc—the FP Ranch. There the largest single chunk of anthracite ever mined lies as a veranda ornament, decorated with a bronze plate that carried a legend. There a petrified tree it took two flat cars to transport, holds the interest of the visitor. About such souvenirs cavort the last herd of white deer, imported from Russia for Mr. Phillips by the Hagenbecks."[283]

At first a few paintings decorated the walls to keep the room from appearing barren, and a few cases held little collections of rocks or artifacts. Fairly rapidly it became the catch-all for the overflow from the lodge, and quickly enough, people began to encourage Frank to expand his wonderful museum.

The museum underwent expansion twice in the 1930s. The front windows were filled in with rock work, and rooms were added at the back. In 1945 major expansion added more rooms, work space, and the striking entry and rotunda. The brilliant entrance, designed by Winold Reiss, features a mosaic mural that depicts representative figures of the three major Amerindian cultural areas, interspersed with typical decorative motifs on a turquoise background. The mosaic was cut by the Fascotti firm. The huge double doors of brushed metal are inset with medallions of Spiro designs. Further additions, large and small, have been made every decade, and another large one is planned in the next few years.

With each addition the *Woolaroc* seemed to be moved. After being moved from the original room, for a while it rested in the third room, at the back of the museum. A little later it was moved downstairs. It was a tight fit there. Eventually it was moved to the bunkhouse next to the lodge. Its condition was becoming deteriorated. The grand old flying machine was no longer the feature of the showcase.

In 1984, the trustees for the Frank Phillips Foundation began a fifth addition to the museum and decided to have the airplane restored. Richard Kane was chairman of the trustees, and Bill Blakemore was the ranch manager at the time of the project. Restoration of the *Woolaroc* was handled by the aviation section of the Phillips Petroleum Company's corporate services. Keith Gann was in charge. The old canvas skin was replaced and painted bright as new. The engine was cleaned and rebuilt. All the cables and wires were replaced. The plane gleamed like the day it rolled out onto the runway for the first time in Wichita back in 1927. With the consultation of Beech Aircraft Company in Wichita, everything was done to exact manufacturer's specifications. The instruments and radio were enthusiastically reconditioned by their original manufacturers. While the *Woolaroc* got her facelift, a new 4,000 square foot addition to the museum was built downstairs, with a high ceiling and viewing balcony. The aircraft was suspended from the ceiling there, as if frozen in a shallow bank. Today visitors can catch the drama of a moment in aviation history.[284]

Woolaroc unveiled the restored exhibit at a cocktail party in the museum on September 6, 1985. Phillips executives, Bartlesville movers and shakers, and people interested in aviation and Oklahoma history were in attendance. A few of the big names in aviation history gathered as special guests for the celebration. Truman and Newman Wadlow and Forest Leathers were local men from those early aviation days; Anthony Bitetti from Westminster, California, came to the showing. The Smithsonian sent a representative. Clarence Clark who was the Travel Air chief test pilot from 1925 to 1930 came. Exciting to the museum staff were Torrence Parker, Billy Parker's son; the widow, two brothers, and four children of the *Woolaroc*'s navigator, William V. Davis; and Martin Jenson, the last surviving participant in the race, the man who came in second. Hors d'oeuvres and champagne, speeches, and socializing—except for the fashions, it could have been an evening planned by Frank Phillips. The old aircraft loomed over the well-wishers almost as if poised to begin skywriting just like back in the good old days. Way back in 1929 the *U. S. Air Services* writer said Woolaroc was for posterity. The Smithsonian had attempted to acquire Goebel's airplane, but Frank's little Smithsonian still persists, the beginning of the Woolaroc Museum.

State Senator Gid Graham, Pawnee Bill Lillie, George Miller, and Frank Phillips pose outside the tent in Happy Hollow during the first director's barbecue at the Ranch in April 1926. The spring afternoon was chilly and the businessmen were wrapped up in their overcoats with fedoras on their heads. Frank's premier event was a prototype in which nothing was spared—from the barbecue to the rodeo it was archetypical Woolaroc.
Courtesy Woolaroc.

The Big Bashes

In the fall of 1925, Frank was trying to learn how to have the ranch designated a private game preserve. He wrote the state Department of Fish and Game, "I am putting a lot of fine buildings on this place and making it rather a resort for my friends so you will note I am anxious to make it a nice place."[285]

He was, indeed, anxious. The first social event at Woolaroc was the annual directors meeting held April 18, 1926. On that afternoon Frank held the first picnic for his all-important visitors near Clyde Lake at Happy Hollow. The old photographs show that on that chilly afternoon the directors stood around, visiting, their overcoats buttoned up and fedoras on their heads. Frank served the first barbecued venison and buffalo. "There was dancing and music and gay pioneers mingled with austere bankers, capitalists, and railroad presidents."[286] The Easterners were entertained in the afternoon with the Wild West Show that was put on by the Osage cowboys that Joe Bartles and Buck Boren had assembled.

Frank's vision was a glorious success that he proceeded to hone to an art. Grif Graham pulled off a barbecue for Frank with clock work regularity thereafter. Grif himself was one of the attractions.

> But as picturesque as the rest of the preserve is "Grif" Graham, caretaker and superintendent. An Indian Territory pioneer, Graham still affects a colorful combination of wearing apparel, that includes a scarlet flannel shirt, open at the throat, high-heeled cowboy boots, and an eight gallon hat. Belying his soft native drawl, the giant caretaker, a former Washington County sheriff and for years a peace officer in this section of the state, can be roused to quick action, and his record as a peace officer over many years shows him an adept with the brace of .45's that formerly graced his belt. He is the finishing touch needed to make the Phillips preserve a true and lasting picture of Oklahoma frontier life.[287]

The American Institute of Banking was entertained on July 11. Two years later Frank received a formal apology in behalf of the Institute from Richard W. Hill who was then secretary. It seems some of the bankers had taken home towels as souvenirs.[288] Human nature is ever the same; the bankers just had to have a memento.

Grif was colorful and Frank was the most gracious of hosts. A Woolaroc invitation quickly became a social plum. That first year the newspapers carried accounts of the social events at Woolaroc with regularity. The annual employees picnic on July 24 was a huge success. It was originally planned as a two-day event, but Frank managed the whole crowd of 600 that afternoon with a picnic lunch, swimming, and boxing and wrestling matches.[289]

Old photographs show mobs sitting on the roof of the bathhouse and lining the platform, bobbing in the water, and milling on the beach.

The highlight of the picnic was a bathing beauty contest for "Miss Petroleum" with Frank as the chief judge and the other executives filling out the committee. A half a dozen grinning Phillips executives and Frank posed for photos with rolled up shirt sleeves and tape measures in hand, standing among sweet young things with bobbed and marcelled coiffures, daring one-piece swimming suits, garters, silk stockings, and high-heeled shoes.

Originally planned as a two-day event, Frank managed to entertain the whole crowd of 600 people in just one day at the employee's picnic 24 July 1926. There was a noon picnic supper and entertainment included boxing and wrestling matches. While many stood visiting on the landing and squeezed onto the dock at Clyde Lake, some tried out the canoes. Mobs delightedly paddled in the water and dove from the roof of the bathhouse. Courtesy Woolaroc.

The first of September was the FP Ranch Wild West Show, staged by Mary Phillips in honor of Frank Phillips. Orpha Graham made wild-colored western shirts for the guests. Everyone needed to be dressed in full Western regalia. Stewart Dewer was the master of ceremonies and Grif Graham told "whackers." Mary and her friends staged a parade, using Woolaroc mounts and riders, spoofing the 101 Wild West Show acts.[290]

By fall, the ranch entertainment facilities were purring like a well-oiled machine. Andrew Mellon visited June 30, and Senator Howe of Illinois was a guest at the lodge on September 22.[291] The Kansas City guests were at the ranch on November 7. On Thanksgiving weekend, Frank and Jane entertained a railroad carload of New Yorkers: Maybelle Manning, Helen Pusenelli, Maybelle Woolfelt, Belle Daube, Caroline Riley, Fred Landeck, Pretsy Menilleson, Dick Sheldon, and Nate Clark. They attended a dinner at the lodge and a "tea" given by Mildred Phillips.[292] Tulsa and Bartlesville guests joined them at a Thanksgiving Eve dance at the lodge. The party evidently was not as staid as it sounds.

Frank holding a measuring tape (right), and other Phillips executives grin sheepishly at the beauty contest during the employee's picnic. After the photo, Frank slipped out and left the problem of picking the winner with the other men. Courtesy Woolaroc.

Guests played a practical joke on Frank at Thanksgiving in 1926. They tinkered with his car and when it broke down, hauled him back to the lodge in an ox-drawn wagon. Courtesy Woolaroc.

> Folks out at the ranch played a trick on him and put his car out of commission. A stranger rode up at about that time and offered to haul the car back to the lodge, a distance of about two miles. When the team drove up it was one that friends had bought for Mr. Phillips from the 101 Ranch and it pulled his stalled car back to his garage. [293]

A carload of Oklahoma City guests came up for the weekend of December 18 with Major General Roy Hoffman. Governor Johnston did not make it, but Lieutenant Governor William J. Holloway and 10 others had breakfast at the townhouse, then went out to the lodge for the rest of the weekend.[294] It must have been fun, for the next year Frank reissued the invitation. "I will have a special car on the tracks which will contain six compartments and three drawing rooms available for your use leaving Oklahoma City. . . You and Mrs. Hoffman fill up this car with your friends as our guests."[295] He invited Amon and Nanetta Carter too, assuring them the guest list would be very limited for the New Year's weekend bash.[296]

The Carters could not come, but that did not prevent the New Year's revelers from playing a little joke on him that everyone enjoyed for weeks. Evidently Amon had a Sunday evening radio broadcast, using the handle, "the Hired Hand." The Bartlesville party sent a telegram to Amon at WBAP that was meant as a joke, but was inadvertantly read over the air to everyone's hilarity and feigned embarrassment.[297]

Early in 1927, the calendar shows Frank entertained New York businessmen at the ranch, and then John D. Rockefeller on January 31. The annual directors meeting was on April 17. Governor Johnston came up with Gid Graham on May 4. Entertaining was taking on a regularity and character that was truly meeting Frank's needs better than he had dreamed.

State Senator Gid Graham of Nowata worked with Frank to host the Izaak Walton League at Woolaroc on May 5. Both were important to Frank's game preserve and tax program. The Izaak Walton League was a national organization that was committed to wildlife conservation. Gid Graham, a Nowata County rancher, was an early days state senator who had been recently re-elected, and chairman of the wildlife committee in the Senate. Graham was a one-issue politician if there ever was one. He was single-minded in his devotion to wildlife conservation. Some of his writings are reminiscent of modern animal rights tracts. Frank certainly was interested in wildlife conservation, but he was really interested in personal property tax exemptions for his animals. In 1927, Gid Graham had John H. Kane reviewing some legislation to exempt game

his Manager

preserves from taxes.[298] The Izaak Walton League party was one of the big events at Woolaroc that year. It was a rainy day for a tour. Frank, wearing a black "fo' gallon" hat and yellow slicker, "made every visitor feel that he was personally glad that he had come to the ranch." Osage Chief Bacon Rind and his wife were there. The entertainment was buffalo and ostriches, the lake, boats, fly and bait casting, and the lodge. Frank provided buffalo barbecue to the wowed guests.[299]

Simpler entertaining also gained newspaper accolades. Jane Phillips entertained Miss Mabel Boe's sixth grade class from Horace Mann school, Mary and Sara Phillips' class. They had an all-day picnic and George Bullock, the Y.M.C.A. swimming instructor, was there to ensure everyone's safety.[300]

The Star Drug Store bills for August through October of 1926, for some reason, survive in the archive. The bookkeeper divided purchases into household and special supplies. Everything from pencils, to toilet water, intended as supplies for the lodge, are listed. The most constant items are large quantities of Lucky Strike and Chesterfield cigarettes, matches, mouthwash, and gum. A 1933 review of the entertainment account for 1926 shows cigarettes and cigars from Mabel Fry, tobacconist, and lots of ice cream. The tobacco bills must have impressed Fern Butler too, for there are notes in her handwriting, bringing all the tobacco and gum entries together at the bottom of the 1933 review.

FRANK PHILLIPS RANCH
WOOLAROC LODGE
BARTLESVILLE, OKLA.

Mr.________

Breakfast in honor of
CARL R. GRAY

Seminole Orange Juice

Osage Oat Meal

Bacon — Woolaroc Acorn and — Sausage

Rhode Island Red Fried Eggs

Buffalo — Venison

Brahma-Zebu

Elk

Hot Rolls — Buffalo Cream — Coffee

Jelly — Honey

Wednesday, March 12, 1930

The employee's picnic in July cost $313.62 and the New York special party car and meals in December cost $3088.32. In all they killed 1 buffalo, 2 deer, 4 wild turkeys, and 10 chickens for the entertainment that year. In 1927, some bills for the Campbell Serenaders' Orchestra survive. On September 28 a nine-piece orchestra played for five hours for the Welty-Durham party; on October 11 nine men played for four hours for the Goebel party. The famous fiddler, Henry Hall, was paid $30 for his music at the fall barbecue. A magician was paid $250 for a December 31 performance. The party for the annual directors meeting only cost $90.71, though the liquor bill was substantially more. They killed 8 buffalo, 1 cow, 16 guineas, and 7 turkeys for the parties.

In 1927, they began to ask architect Arthur J. Gorman to help with the barbecuing. Arthur P. (Art) Gorman, Arthur Gorman's nephew, remembers his delight as a little boy in frequently getting to go to the ranch with his uncle. One of the Mexican workers was always assigned to follow him around all afternoon, and he could swim or fish or skip rocks or anything a boy's heart might desire. Art Gorman relates that Arthur was an accomplished barbecue hobbyist. Uncle Arthur did this service for many years, and Art was along to observe the procedure many times. Gorman would go out and shoot the animal, and then drag it to the barbecue hut. A screened hut was built near the barbecue pits where Gorman butchered the animals himself.

Left: For months Wiley Post planned a 1934 stratospheric flight. Woolaroc files even contain a brochure for a deep-sea diving suit, that appears to have been the prototype for the pressurized flight suit that Post wore on his history-making flight in November from the Phillips airport. It was heady stuff right at the cutting edge of technology in those days. Post set an altitude record of almost 55,000 feet in the *Winnie Mae*, and discovered the jet stream. A couple of months later Frank threw a big party to honor Wiley Post and celebrate the accomplishment. In this photo R. C. Jopling (left) and Wiley Post horse around at the party in honor of Post's flight. Courtesy Woolaroc.

Center: Frank honored Carl Grey, president of the Union Pacific Railroad at a Woolaroc breakfast during the 1930 Traffic Club meeting. The list of guests that he entertained that morning was huge. True to Frank's style, the menu featured Woolaroc's best in both food and humor. Courtesy Woolaroc.

They had huge smokers where he slowly cooked the meat starting on the day before the barbecue. In 1927, Gorman worked on three barbecues: the 18 April directors' Meeting, the May 5 Izaak Walton Barbecue, and the June 2 Early Day Cowboys Picnic.

Business entertaining took on an industry-wide scope. A party of New York Central Railroad executives visited Oklahoma on a tour that was a predecessor to the Traffic Club parties at Woolaroc. They breakfasted on buffalo steak, bacon, eggs, toast, biscuits, and coffee, and toured the ranch for a couple of hours on January 19.[301] Charles Schwab came to Oklahoma to open the annual International Oil Exposition in Tulsa, and Frank entertained him at a dinner at Woolaroc where the 60 men who attended represented half the capital in the oil industry. Schwab was a gracious man who charmed the local journalists.[302] His thank you gift to Frank was the Duroc boar that was the foundation sire of all of those Woolaroc hams and sausages.

Frank entertained a number of railroad officials at a breakfast in honor of Carl R. Gray, president of the Union Pacific Railroad, during a Traffic Club meeting in 1930. The menu is a model of decorous showmanship. He featured his Woolaroc Acorn bacon and sausage, Rhode Island red eggs from the farm, buffalo, venison, Brahman beef, elk, and who could pass up "buffalo cream" for his coffee.[303] He entertained the directors and general committees of the American Petroleum Institute for the afternoon and dinner on October 3, 1930. The printed menu for the meal featured the usual barbecue. A note at the bottom stated, "Fish, meat, and vegetables on this menu raised on F. P. Ranch. Honeydew and cheese from 101 Ranch."[304]

Other 1930 parties were the Semi-Annual Convention of Sheriffs and Peace Officers at a barbecue and a group of St. Louis bankers for a luncheon, both in May. The Transcontinental Air Race had a huge barbecue in the summer of 1932. The feature of the shindig was the pilots who were celebrity idols in those days. That fall Frank gave a dinner the Eastern Bright Stock group who stopped by on their way to the American Petroleum Institute convention in Houston, Texas. Everyone was impressed when Frank had a luncheon for Amon Carter's friend, W. W. Atterbury, president of Pennsylvania Railroad, and William H. Rankin, an advertising magnate, early in 1933. It must have rubbed Frank wrong when Rankin told a reporter, "The Democrats under Mr. Roosevelt will make good for the farmer and the business men of the country."[305] Nevertheless, invitation telegrams went out to the executives of a half dozen railroads, and 56 area oil men to attend the affair.

By 1931, company picnics had gotten too big. The various divisions began to have separate picnics for their people at Woolaroc. The earliest of these seems to have been Dr. Somerville's party for the Medical Division in October. These were immensely popular, and everyone looked forward to an afternoon of cutting up. The Purchasing Department had a picnic in July of 1936 that is a good example. The program called for touring the grounds and museum, swimming, and a picnic meal. In the evening, there was a dance and program of silly homegrown acts in the dance pavilion. Nothing in the mimeographed program was serious, with lots of spoofing, ribaldry, and cartooned illustrations.

The Boy Scout Council had occasional meetings at Woolaroc. Frank footed the bill for their big dinner for the first time in 1928. He helped out the Girl Scouts in the same way two times. The Osage Agency employees had an annual picnic at Woolaroc after 1927. School groups came out frequently. After the museum was built they especially coveted invitations to tour the exhibits.

Cow Thieves and Outlaws

The Early Day Cowboys Picnic of 1927 was to become a prototype. Frank was grateful to the local cowboys and ranchers for the many times they had helped him get his show on the road over the last couple of years. He remembered the buffalo drive, the wolf hunts, and the rodeo for the first annual directors meeting at the ranch, among others. He wanted to keep the favor of the neighbors and the good esteem of the local ranchers. He hit on the idea of a party to honor the early day cowboys in the area.

On May 26, he had about 200 cowboys, their families, and some Bartlesville dignitaries out for a barbecue. Locally notable cowboys included R. B. Ledbetter who once rode up the Texas Trail; George B. Keeler of Keeler & Johnson Ranch; Mert Keefer who rode for Jake Bartles; Jimmy Rider and Bright Drake, side-kicks of Will Rogers; Blake Gore who rode for the Boggs Outfit; and W. S. Gore, another rancher. They came for noon dinner and stayed for supper. Barbecue was in abundance and iced

Invitin'
yu an yer wimmin folks to
Second Annual
Cow Thieves and Outlaws
Re-Union
at F. P. Ranch
SATURDAY, OCT. 6th, 1928

Aims to throw chuck about noon, if the Boss can borry a side of meat an some flour.

No guns er store cloze is purmitted, er no golf breeches.

Show this here invite to the Brand Inspector feller at the big gate, cause he wont pass yu thru without none.

Hopin' to meet yu all

at the F. P., we begs to remain

THE COMMITTY

P. S. The Boss wants yu all to be at the wagon at 10 o'clock forenoon.

2nd P. S. Leve yer nives an guns with the Boss at the gate, cause we aint allowin no shootin'.

Left: The invitation to the 1928 Cow Thieves and Outlaws Reunion was probably the composition of Grif Graham. The hammed-up down-home jargon set the atmosphere for the pull-out-all-the-stops party that Frank threw. All those cow thieves and outlaws were even admonished to check their knives and guns at the gate. Courtesy Woolaroc.

Below: At the 1928 Cow Thieves and Outlaws Reunion the guests presented Frank with this cowboy outfit of chaps, side-arm, and wild-rag bandana (he was wearing last year's hat in the photo). The picture is often thought of as typical of Frank Phillips at Woolaroc, but Frank actually only sported the outfit for the photographs, then took it off. The outfit is on display at the museum. Courtesy Woolaroc.

lemonade was a feature. Dancing was to the real music of famous fiddler Henry Hall—made famous because he was broadcasting his old time fiddlin' over KVOO-Radio. A kangaroo court provided entertainment and raised $55 that the cowboys used to buy Frank Phillips a 5X beaver Stetson, inscribed in the band, "with the compliments of cow-thieves and outlaws reunion, F. P. Ranch 2 June 1927."[306]

A Woolaroc tradition was established at the Early Day Cowboys Picnic. The "cow thieves and outlaws" line set off bells in Frank's mind. The next year, Frank repeated the party, grown bigger and better. The invitations went out to 125 couples for October 6, 1928, with a cover letter by Grif Graham that just simply twanged.

Pawnee Bill and George Miller came over, and Bob Ledbetter came up from Texas. Harve Freas, the Osage county sheriff was there, as promised, mingling with the Okesa crowd. Everyone had a great time gorging on barbecue, dancing to Henry Hall again, and enjoying some trick roping and riding by Ford Christian.

Above: In 1928 Frank invited 125 couples to the Cow Thieves and Outlaws Reunion. Most of the guests, then, were still Frank's Osage County neighbors, but the guest list had significantly expanded to include some of the business and political notables that Frank loved to entertain. They were invited to rub elbows with the real Wild West of the Osage. In this wide-angle group shot of all the guests that day, Frank and Pawnee Bill are front and center. Courtesy Woolaroc.

Below: During the 1930 Cow Thieves and Outlaws Reunion a shocked Frank Phillips received a bedecked Indian pony from Chief Lookout. Chief John Abbot is the man with a raised arm, standing in the foreground. The pony was a symbol of Frank's adoption into the Osage tribe. This rare honor by the Osage Tribe was a total surprise to Frank that afternoon and he was obviously completely taken aback. Courtesy Woolaroc.

Above: Here is the original entry gate and gatekeeper's cabin at Woolaroc, finished in 1926. A dirt road leads to the closed iron gates; overhead the sign says, "The Frank Phillips Ranch Home of Buffalo and Wild Game." A section of the all-important fencing can be seen in front of the cabin. A windmill brought well water to the gatekeeper family. It was here that the shoot-out with Pretty Boy Floyd's gang took place in 1934. Courtesy Woolaroc.

In 1929, the Cow Thieves and Outlaws Reunion had grown to 300 guests. The reporter waxed eloquent, "It was a genuine gala day for folks who have lived those days so soon to be gone in their entirety, and made possible only by the particular type of gathering where there is no showmanship or make believe—but merely folks living over the past."[307]

Frank invited genuine cow thieves and train robbers to his shindig. Partly, the object of the party was to thank the local cowboys and neighbors, and that included several shady characters; partly, the whole idea, suggested in the hatband inscription, had an aura of the Wild West that Frank wanted associated with his place. Frank had an easy relationship with the local outlaws and bootleggers. Stories are told about some of them being early depositors in Frank's bank in Bartlesville. In 1905 Frank's teller, Fred Spies, questioned depositing some royalty checks belonging to Ernest Lewis, an Osage bandit. Frank saw the checks were legitimate and made the deposit. Another time, L. E. inadvertently made a loan to Henry Starr, the bank robber. Frank correctly assured him Starr would repay. As time went by, it was rumored that outlaws robbed other banks and deposited in the Phillips' bank. At the same time, the Phillips' leases in the Osage put them in close contact with other desperados. Al Spencer, one of the turn-of-the-century train robbers, had his hide-out at Spencer Spring that is now part of Woolaroc.[308]

Henry Wells, a neighbor living at Lost Creek, north of the ranch, was colorful enough that Frank cultivated him, inviting him to poker games and dinner parties. For Wells' part, the man who had lent money to Henry Starr had to be all right. When Wells announced his "retirement from the banking business" in 1946, it was learned that Sheriff Grif Graham had shot the horse from under him at his first bank robbery at Avant January 30, 1915. He was released from prison after five years and one day in the early 1920s but did his last "job" in 1934. This tough customer was a loyal friend of Frank Phillips and a fixture at the Cow Thieves and Outlaws Reunions.[309]

In transparent imitation of the 101 Ranch's Cherokee Strip Cowpunchers Association, an actual association of Cow Thieves and Outlaws was formed.[310] By 1930, the party list had swollen to 1,000 guests. Eastern bankers and businessmen and Hollywood notables and their wives eagerly got themselves up in frontier regalia to rub elbows with Indians, outlaws, and oil men.

Some swore it was true that Frank had arranged for a few outlaws serving time to be released from jail for the day so that they could come to the reunion, and that Frank posted his own personal bond guaranteeing their return. More than likely that was one of the many tales cooked up and perpetuated by R. C. Jopling, called "Jop," Frank's ace public relations man. Besides insisting that all lawbreakers and law enforcers abide by his one-day moratorium, Frank left instructions at the gate to "admit any cowboy with a saddle horse, admit any American Legion boys in uniform and all Spanish-American War veterans in uniform; also any full-blooded Indians in costume."[311]

Besides the ever-present barbecue buffet, the Indian dancing, kangaroo court, roping and trick riding, there was a contest for most authentic dress, speeches and horsing around, fiddling and dancing, and plenty of whiskey. Frank came up with some special arrangements. Eastern guests took a stagecoach ride, complete with a hold-up.

As with Frank's animal purchases, the Depression began to cut deeply into Frank's entertaining expenditures by 1931. That year there were several important dinner parties, but many of the big bashes, including Cow Thieves and Outlaws, were curtailed. The big affairs were the Osage Council Picnic on June 20, the National Air Race Picnic August 27, and The Traffic Clubs of America barbecue on October 29.[312]

SECURITY

Hard times brought out desperate men. In 1932 Charles Lindbergh's son was kidnapped and murdered. Closer to home, a year later Charles F. Urschel, an Oklahoma City oil man, was playing poker in his home when George "Machine Gun" Kelly and Harvey Bailey burst in and kidnapped him at gunpoint. Wealthy people around the nation began to look over their shoulders, and the Phillips family was no exception. The road to Woolaroc was lonely and deserted; the ranch was remote. This was one of the reasons Frank cultivated his shady character neighbors and one of the motives for the Cow Thieves and Outlaws parties.

Since the beginning of the ranch, Frank had a practice of having his manager made an Osage County sheriff's deputy. The 1933 ranch investigation exposed manager Compton's questionable activities. He was fired and Frank asked Sheriff Conner to commission M. S. Kerr, the new manager. Security at the Woolaroc gate was beefed up, and Frank also had Grif Graham deputized. [313]

Charles"Pretty Boy" Floyd started hanging out in Bartlesville to case the Phillips family during September of 1934. He knew of Henry Wells through a mutual train robber acquaintance from Wells' time in prison, and because Wells lived at Woolaroc's back door, he conferred with him on Frank's vulnerability. Wells answered a few questions but did not give anything away. As soon as Floyd left, Henry headed for Woolaroc.

In the meantime, back in Bartlesville, as little Betty and Johnny Phillips were walking home from school, a black limousine pulled up and two men tried to grab Betty, who wrenched away and ran home. Mildred and Jane called Frank at the ranch, just at the moment when Henry Wells arrived there with the intelligence of his conversation with Floyd. Frank immediately sent a car to pick up the family and notified the authorities. Frank, John, and Mary Kate, John's second wife, were already at the ranch and were joined for several days by Jane, Mildred, Johnny, and Betty. Grif, Henry Wells, the ranch cowboys, and some federal agents were patrolling the perimeter and watching the gate. Johnny related the story many years later.

> We had all retired one night about midnight and everything seemed so peaceful. Then about two o'clock in the morning a big sedan pulled up at the gate and blasted its horn. There were agents in Grif Graham's gatehouse and more hiding in the brush. I understand the car tried to ram the gate and everybody opened fire and the car got out of there in a big hurry.[314]

They stayed at the ranch a few more days until Henry Wells gave the all clear. Frank's cultivation of Henry Wells probably saved his life.

Some ranch emergencies were more humorous. K. S. "Boots" Adams told of an incident when he was a young aide-de-camp in 1927.[315] He was working at the gate, checking against the guest list for a barbecue in honor of Chief Bacon Rind of the Osage. Engrossed in his assignment, he ignored a Pierce-Arrow at the back of the line of cars that were waiting to get in the gate. After some minutes, the touring car full of Indians pulled out of line and sped off, and Boots thought little about it. About an hour later, Frank was in a fret because his honorees had not arrived and began to ask questions. With a sinking realization, young Adams admitted that they had driven off. "Mr. Phillips looked at me for a moment as if he were about to take my head off. Then he growled, 'Those were my guests of honor—you idiot!'" Frank jumped into his waiting car and drove straight to Pawhuska where he personally apologized to Chief Bacon Rind. He rode back to Woolaroc with the chief, and the barbecue continued as planned. The next day young Adams escaped with his life and a formal explanation and apology to Chief Bacon Rind.[316]

THE OSAGE ADOPTION

Frank had nurtured his friendships with the Osage chiefs, and neighbors, since his earliest days in Indian Territory. Chief Bacon Rind had been at the opening day of the Phillips' bank in 1905. Fred and Julia Lookout were personal friends of Frank and Jane, as was George Labadie. There was a mutual respect between the Osage leaders and the oil tycoon. Frank always dealt honestly with the Indians. He was a pragmatist who realized he needed the long-term good will of the tribe, but he also knew the chiefs as men and leaders who deserved his deference, and he remembered that Phillips Petroleum Company's early growth was in the Osage.

The years of friendship culminated in a singular honor in 1930 and 1931, probably the highest honor of Frank's

lifetime. First, at the Cow Thieves and Outlaws Reunion, Frank was informally welcomed into the tribe. Fred Lookout presented Frank with a horse, blanket, bridle, and saddle to welcome the new tribal member.[317] Frank's reaction was expansive. He wrote his friend General Bullard a bread and butter letter:

> Senator Owens, whom you know, is a Cherokee, called upon me this afternoon and we were talking of having a conference in the near future with Will Rogers, who is also a Cherokee, and Vice-President Curtis, who is an Osage, with a view of starting a movement to take this country back. The white folks seem to be making such a mess of things that we think that we Indians should have the nation rightfully restored to us, and see if we can't do a better job in running the country.[318]

The Lodge dining room was filled to capacity 28 March 1931 for the formal ceremony for Frank's adoption as a member of the Osage Tribe. The entire tribal council was present among the guests when Chief and Mrs. Lookout and Frank Phillips entered the dining room to the cheers of the crowd. Speeches and toasts graced the evening and Chief Lookout honored Frank by giving him the Osage name of his deceased oldest son, Hulah-Kihe-Kah. Courtesy Woolaroc.

A formal adoption ceremony was celebrated at Woolaroc on March 28, 1931. About one hundred Osage and close friends of Frank Phillips attended. On that chilly day in March, toasty fires crackled in the great fireplaces at each end of the lodge. The tables in the dining room were set up and covered with red and white checked tablecloths. The whole tribal council, garbed in full Osage dress, was there. "As Chief Lookout and his wife, accom-

At the adoption dinner, The tribal council dressed Frank in Osage regalia, then Frank's friend Zack Miller got into the act. In this photograph Frank was wearing his new Osage dress clothes. The buffalo hide he was viewing was given to him by Zack Miller, from the 101 Ranch, engraved (using a new-fangled electric needle) with the adoption resolution in Osage and English.
Courtesy Woolaroc.

panied by Mr. Phillips, entered the room, the guests arose and cheered." Father Hubert from Pawhuska gave the invocation, and luncheon was served. After the meal, George Labadie, acting as toastmaster, introduced Chief Lookout. Chief Lookout spoke in Osage, and Assistant Chief Harry Kophay translated the address. He spoke of the affection the Osage felt toward Frank Phillips and of the significance of the adoption ceremony. T. J. Leahy, a Tulsa attorney who was married to an Osage woman, presented Frank with Chief's regalia, delivering an eloquent speech. Frank responded with appropriate remarks, then he was taken to another room where the council dressed him in his new finery: "an elaborate headdress with a feather train, a beaded vest, shirt, breechcloth, leggings, moccasins, arm bands, and bells." The ceremony was attended with respectful silence, but Frank's entry in his new dress was met with applause.[319]

Thirty-eight Osage dignitaries, Frank's family, and many close friends from Bartlesville and the company were at the ceremony. Zack and Virginia Miller, Pawnee Bill and Al Lillie, John Bell of Pittsburgh, H. V. and Marie Foster, Fern Butler, and Armais Arutunoff were among the delighted guests.

Unknown to anyone not Osage, Kohpay committed a faux pas at the ceremony. The Chiefs were deeply concerned that Frank might have been offended. The first thing on Monday morning, they were in George Labadie's office. He wrote a long letter of apology at the behest of Chiefs Bacon Rind and Lookout. The flap, explained by Labadie, surrounded the use of the name "Little Oil Man" in reference to Frank. Chief Bacon Rind thought Harry

Kohpay must have some grudge against him.[320] Labadie explained that English names were hard for Osage people to pronounce, and they commonly use the term "Little" as an honor, something like "Sir." They were afraid Frank would take offense at his common name in Osage. Fred Lookout's letter, as translated by Julia Lookout and transcribed by George Labadie, was very moving.

> Mr. Bacon Rind said in his speech that you have a name of your own, but as I could not pronounce the name myself, but I always called you "Little Oil Man," and then the full blood Indians know you by that name, and then since last fall I have heard what the Chief has done to you. And you white people I see everywhere on paper or anything, a bird that it seems to me you thought lots of, you have it on the money even, so that always makes me think you white people think lots of this bird, that a great bird and among our people, Osages, we are the same we think lots of this bird, and the Indians go by different animal and bird clans. Chief Lookout is the Eagle Clan, and so from now on I will not call you "Little Oil Man", but I will call you Eagle Chief.
>
> I belong to the Eagle Clan, Mr. Bacon Rind is right about his speech about me belonging to the Eagle Clan. So last fall when they wanted me to give you name, I gave you name Eagle Chief. In our clan when the first son is born, they name him Eagle Chief, the first boy born, but they have other names to, they just choose names, but that is one of the names. So our first son name was Eagle Chief. When they asked for an Indian name for you, I thought of my son, who has been dead when he just a year old, and that was his name, and so I gave my oldest son's name to you. In my speech I said to you that you have been a good help to our people, and a good friend, and my Tribe have drawd a good deal of your money.[321]

The transliteration of Frank's Osage name was Hulah-Kihe-Kah. It is a name of which Frank was very proud.

Zack Miller presented him with a buffalo hide with the adoption resolution inscribed in English and Osage with an electric needle. Telegrams and letters of congratulations poured in from such friends as Will Rogers, Amon Carter, Vice President Charles Curtis, William Allen White, and Bishop Kelley.

Special Interests

Political entertaining was an early development at Woolaroc. The Izaak Walton Picnic was probably the earliest big one, and General Hoffman brought State Senator W. J. Holloway for the weekend in May. However, in 1926, there was a short-lived effort to enlist Frank's help to get President Calvin Coolidge to Oklahoma and to Woolaroc on a trip that was planned in the West. The editor of *The Daily Oklahoman* was the source of the information, "I believe that if the proper ground work were laid in New York and Washington you could have the president as your guest in July at Willoroc [sic]."[322] Frank went right into high gear. After several letters among his influential contacts, E. P. Earle wrote that the President had decided to summer in Vermont. It was all over by February 14.[323]

John Kane brought Woolaroc a retreat for Republican oil men who were backing Charles Curtis for president. David W. Mulvane, national committeeman from Topeka, Kansas, and W. G. Skelly, national committeeman from Oklahoma were among the guests, though Frank denied the political nature of the get together. As usual, he came up with some attractive bait—this time the guests had "elk cream" for their morning coffee.[324] Curtis became Hoover's Vice President. Hoover, too, was a guest at Woolaroc.

In 1928, Frank entertained the State Highway Commission. The party included all the Washington and Osage county commissioners, and influential ranchers, and the Bartlesville movers and shakers. Getting the road to Woolaroc paved was a priority that was not achieved for many years, but this time Frank got a bridge over Sand Creek and convinced the commissioners to oil the Barnsdall Road. There was a thank you barbecue for government and state veterinarians in 1929. A Tulsa convention of the wives of the International Association of Milk Sanatarians toured the ranch in 1941. One immensely important letter was from the labor counselor of the Petroleum Administration For War. After being entertained at Woolaroc, he wrote thanks and assured Frank the War Manpower Commission was seeking a solution with the company manpower problem affecting younger technical personnel.[325]

Frank turned the 1935 Bartlesville National Horse Show into a political opportunity. Bartlesville planned a gala social whirl. The horses were stabled in tents at

Johnstone Park, and many of the exhibitors and guests stayed all over town with friends. Private parties and a formal dance and cocktail party at Hillcrest Country Club were key events. The big bash was planned at Woolaroc. Frank invited 600 exhibitors, friends, and guests to a barbecue in honor of Oklahoma Governor and Mrs. E. W. Marland and Governor and Mrs. Alf Landon of Kansas. Landon would soon announce his candidacy for President of the United States, and Frank was helping out. KVOO-Radio broadcast from the lodge, and KGGF-Radio broadcast the opening ceremonies for "Kansas Night" in honor of Landon. Frank enjoyed exhibiting his latest acquisitions, three little Sardinian donkeys, at the horse show.[326]

Frank detested the New Deal but was not above hedging his bets. Frank's good friend, Amon Carter, was a Democratic national committeeman, deeply involved with many of the key players in the New Deal. The President's son, Elliott Roosevelt, who was vice president in charge of stations for Southwest Broadcasting Company in Fort Worth, of course, was a friend of Carter. So, in December of 1935, Frank entertained Roosevelt and his entourage at Woolaroc. According to the newspaper, the menu was elk barbecue and beer. Frank had a little fun planned to make the weekend memorable. Roosevelt wanted to bag a buffalo, so Frank gave him a 30-30 rifle, then out the

Top: Presidential hopeful Alf Landon was the guest of honor at the 1935 (second) annual Bartlesville National Horse Show. His party was met at the Phillips Petroleum Company airport before a big bash for 600 guests that Frank threw at Woolaroc. (left to right) C. C. Jonas, J. C. Nichols, Alf Landon, John H. Kane, Frank Phillips, K. S. Adams. Courtesy Woolaroc.

Above: Though Frank detested the New Deal, he was not above trying his hand at cultivating the son of F.D.R., Elliott Roosevelt in 1935. The thrill of the weekend for the president's son was bagging one of Frank's buffalo. Courtesy Woolaroc.

boys went to stalk a buffalo. Elliott considered himself a crack shot but did not know the first two rounds in his rifle were blanks. Sure enough, Roosevelt fired once, twice, at his prey but the animal did not drop. Grif grabbed the gun from him, aimed, and killed the buffalo. Of course, everyone teased Elliott unmercifully all through lunch. Eventually it was admitted his rifle had been loaded with blanks. "Young Roosevelt immediately announced that he would like to see that tried on his father."[327] After lunch, Frank had to fly to Chicago to give a speech, but Elliott loaded up once again and this time bagged a big bull buffalo.

Lots of publicity shots were taken, and a joyful Roosevelt wired Frank, "We have the keys to your private stock and are going to stay at Woolaroc until it is gone. You must train another buffalo to play dead when the guests point a gun at him. This one is dead. Weighted sixteen hundred pounds and a beauty. Took only one shot after lunch. You owe me 98 shots."[328]

Frank entertained the Resettlement Administration employees at a picnic in June of 1936. One frank woman wrote a thank you that must have horrified Frank.

> I had the grandest and best time I have had in years and years. I couldn't even get mad about your speech so you would bring me home (I heard you tell another lady that you would take her home if she was mad and wanted to go)... I wish that Uncle Sam could force you to accept a place as R. A. farm supervisor for awhile...[329]

Frank entertained the Annual Conference of Governors at Woolaroc as a favor to Oklahoma Governor Marland in 1938. As usual, Frank produced in spades for his good friend. He saw to it that the governors got the chance to meet virtually every influential person between Little Rock and Denver who cared about the oil business, and Frank established new political contacts for himself. Seen in the photo (left to right) are Governors E. W. Marland, C. M. Townsend (Indiana), Leon C. Phillips (soon to be governor of Oklahoma), Frank Phillips, Walter A. Huxman (Kansas), R. L. Cochran (Nebraska), Boots Adams, Alf Landon, W. Lee O'Donneld (elect of Texas), James Alford (Texas). Courtesy Woolaroc.

Frank's speech must have been an anti-socialist stem-winder, for more than one guest wrote a lengthy apologetic along with hearty thanks for the hospitality.

The biggest political event at Woolaroc took place in 1938. Governor E. W. Marland asked Frank to entertain the Annual Conference of Governors which was in Oklahoma that year. "You are always so good in matters of this kind that I feel no hesitancy in presuming to ask you to invite us."[330] Memoranda flew back and forth. Frank was anxious for the governors to tour his museum and lodge and get a chance to ride over the ranch if possible. Marland especially requested a certain Western band from Stillwater and that Frank invite lots of oil men. R. C. Jopling and Don Zühlke had a detailed list for preparation and the program.

Frank produced in spades. He invited 600 to the Governors' Conference and Interstate Oil Compact Meeting barbecue. The 28 governors met oil men aplenty, Indian chiefs, publishers, bankers, and almost anyone else between Denver, Colorado, and Little Rock, Arkansas, who cared about the oil business. Barbecue, Indian dancing, a cowboy band, square dancing, and touring the museum and lodge were the program. Jane even put on a little act with an old fashioned buggy.[331] Frank gave a short talk about the interstate oil compact and introduced the Indian chiefs who were there.

The newspaper accounts are pretty cut and dried with lots of pictures of fat cats with cigars, slapping each other on the back. Evidently the actual party did have its modicum of jokesters. A regret from one friend betrays one agenda, "Among the governors I hope you pick out the biggest 'new dealer' in the outfit and let him have it right in the eye at your initiation ceremony at Woolaroc Lodge."[332] KVOO-Radio broadcast the exciting event from the lodge.[333]

Jopling reported to Frank about some of impromptu gifts. The Governor of Indiana admired a pistol that happened to have his name on it, hanging on the bar, so Jopling presented it to him. Jopling subsequently learned that he also wanted a big hat, so he arranged for the division manager in Indianapolis to present the governor with one. On the same day, he notified Frank that the Governor of Illinois regretted having to leave before the buffalo was served, so they were sending him some.[334] The Governor of South Carolina had to leave early because he learned a tornado had struck Charleston. In this case, the governor sent Frank a commission as lieutenant colonel in his military staff and thanks for the good time.[335] Probably one of the most important pieces of political capital was a simple thank you from Robert S. Kerr, a man who would be very important to oil and Oklahoma for many years.

Frank's ranch was sometimes a retreat where harried state executives could take a break. In 1939, Bishop Francis C. Kelley brought Governor Leon C. "Red" Phillips to the ranch. Frank was in New York, but W. C. Smoot and Marjorie Karch handled the hurried arrangements. He did not want a crowd of politicians, just a good poker game. A few Phillips, Empire, and ITIO men, John Kane, who was then retired from the company, and John Cronin came out after dinner and played until about 1:30 Sunday morning. After lunch on Sunday John Cronin and John Kane, went out again and the governor insisted on another round which continued until time to eat and head back to the capitol. "He said that he never had such a fine time since he started running for office last year. I believe he enjoyed every minute of it, and I know the Bishop did."[336] Lucille Zühlke, who had just returned from a few days of conferring with historians and archaeologists in Norman about the museum, did use the opportunity to put in a word for better support of higher education.[337]

Frank extended a similar invitation to Texas Governor Coke Stevenson, the man Lyndon Johnson defeated for the United States Senate seat in 1948. Stevenson's wife was very ill, and friends thought he needed a rest. They wrote the governor,

> Mr. Phillips is of the pioneer, rugged type of individual as yourself. He is as honest as the sunlight and just as democratic and gracious as a human being can be. . . At Woolaroc, you can sit on a big rock and fish with a pole., if you like, and really catch fish, and while it is out in the woods, yet every advantage in the way of service will be at your disposal. And it occurs to me that it will be well for you to slip up here for a few days where the office seekers and lobbyists cannot find you and at Woolaroc really relax.[338]

Private Weekends

The big parties are well documented in the Woolaroc record. But Woolaroc really shined on the weekends when small groups of close friends came to the ranch. Some of them are only hinted at in the appointment calendars, and most are unrecorded. For example, the calendar says J. M. Davis, E. M. Connelly, and J. A. Jackson were at the ranch with Frank on the weekend of January 8-10, 1927.[339] There is no other hint of what was taking place. Odds are they played poker and rode horses. A few weeks earlier, E. E. Dale spent the day at the ranch with Frank.[340] We know that Dr. Dale was working with Frank about his interest in historic preservation. About this time, Frank gave the University of Oklahoma a $10,000 grant. No doubt, that was the purpose of that day at the ranch. Mr. and Mrs. John Mayo were at the ranch in the summer of 1927, probably planning the Lindbergh/Goebel dinner that would be at the Tulsa Mayo Hotel in September.[341] On October 2, Dr. H. B. Baruch, brother of the financier and presidential economic advisor, Benjamin Baruch, was at the ranch.[342] Dr. Baruch was a close social friend of the Phillipses in New York. Following the big convention and party the previous week, it must have been a time to relax and unwind.

Jane Phillips' daily diaries for 1935 and 1936 have survived. They contain scant personal insights, but she did keep a complete list of all of her personal guests during that time. She only ate dinner alone with Frank two times in those two years. Analysis of 1935 shows that Jane Phillips was in Bartlesville 213 days, including day trips to Pawhuska, Tulsa, and Oklahoma City. That year, Jane and Frank took lengthy vacations at Boca Raton, Florida, and Lido Club, Long Island. She planned a Chicago wedding for Mary, in addition to shorter trips, and the usual time

Jane enjoyed entertaining "the young people" at a costume party 5 June 1936. The young men in this shot were C. Granville, Dean Low, Max Minnig, Marcus Low, and Walter Granville (the doctor and nurse are unidentified). Parties for the Phillips girls' friends were frequent over the years. Costume parties were always very popular. Courtesy Woolaroc.

in New York. There were 104 Woolaroc entries, indicating approximately half of her time was spent in Bartlesville. On 93 of those days, she entertained from 1 to 27 personal guests, an average of 8; there were 9 dinner parties with 9 to 22 guests, an average of 14; and 8 large social events such as a company picnic. Frequently she invited her girlfriends out for the afternoon; then the women were joined by their husbands and a few other friends for dinner. The children entertained their friends four times, including New Year's weekend.

A year of troubles continued when in 1935, a "dreadful dust storm" struck on April 10, and the company picnic was rained out on July 20. A cloud burst and flash flood caused cancellation of a dinner gathering on June 14. Obie Wing died in April. During that time of company crisis, the ranch saw heavy utilization by friends and family of the Wings. Jane Phillips' diaries reveal that the ranch had truly become the country home for Frank and Jane. It was a place where they could retire with friends and where they could comfortably and easily meet large and small social obligations.

There was only a little light on such weekends. Fortunately, Tom Latta of the *Tulsa World* left us a little peek. He was an old acquaintance of Frank's from his early days in Washington County. Latta wrote, "Frank called me on the phone and said: 'I'm going out to Woolaroc Lodge and want you to come out and spend today and tomorrow with me. . . Bring some of your pals or old friends with you. Bring Gene Lorton.' Which I did."[343] Latta was impressed by the game preserve and the collections that were already in the lodge. Absolutely everybody was. When he arrived at the lodge he was greeted by a garrulous Frank. The car left them at the door, and their luggage was immediately carried to the blue room and the green room. "What do you gentlemen prefer first, highballs or something to eat?" Frank asked. They had buffalo steaks for dinner and a roasted wild

This is a fairly late photo of the living room at the lodge in its prime. The art, horns, and animal heads collections were fairly complete. The bark veneer piano and the furniture are essentially the same as is seen in a tour of the lodge today, but the Waldorf Astoria chandeliers were not yet moved from the Museum. Blackstone's ace of spades can be seen, stuck over the door. Courtesy Woolaroc.

turkey for Sunday lunch. They sat around, smoked, and visited about old times. Latta admired Frank's expensive Dunhill pipe, and a few days later Frank sent him one as a gift.[344] Frank tactfully rebuked Latta, "I would have liked your article much better if you had not been so darned personal in your reference to my money."[345]

Though not mentioned in the Latta story, guests evidently enjoyed gathering around the piano for some singing. Frank was so impressed with one guest from Dallas, that he recommended her singing voice to Amon Carter for his radio broadcasts.[346] Of course, in good weather there was fishing, swimming, boating, and riding.

The poker games that were played at the table in the balcony, overlooking the great room were one of the favorite stag activities. Woolaroc lore says that in one high stakes game John Ringling bet the circus—and lost it to Frank. Of course, Frank gave it back the next day.

Richard Kane was one of the guests at a dinner party in the early 1930s, when one of the lodge's famous incidents occurred. That evening Harry Bouton Blackstone, Sr., the world famous magician, provided the entertainment for a fairly large crowd of friends. Blackstone stood on the second or third steps of the stairs to the balcony, so that he could be seen easily by the crowd. He preformed a series of card tricks to the delight of the guests. People laughed and clapped at each feat. Finally, Blackstone had Jane Phillips cut the cards, showing everyone a queen of spades. Then the magician shuffled them. Suddenly he threw them, hard, at the opposite wall over the front door. Cards scattered across the width of the living room, and a few hit the wall and fell at the foot of the door. To the amazement of the guests, the queen of spades was stuck on the wall above the door. It is still there, part of the narrative for every tour of the lodge.

Overnight guests frequently took part in one of Frank's on-going jokes on greenhorns and easterners. A glass of milk was set at every place at the dinner table, and the guests were told it was buffalo milk, something like the elk cream. Of course, they were amazed when they found it very agreeable. Frank then informed the wide-eyed guests that the buffalo had to be milked at midnight because they would not stand to be milked after daylight. Frank was in the habit of turning in early, but guests were regularly fooled by the joke.[347] Clyde Nichols, second son of J. C. Nichols, wrote a thank you after he was a New Year's guest of the Phillips girls in 1936.

> I understand that the young newspaper man from Tulsa that came up to the ranch that night, got up to see them milk the buffalo. Mother told me about it at the breakfast table and Dad looked up in a queer little way that makes me half believe you had him fooled. I think he had always regretted that he never got up to watch the milking process.[348]

Frank was absolutely delighted.

> We expect an abundant early crop of minces this spring at my Ranch. Bring your Dad down and we'll not only have him witness the buffalo milking but will make up some nice mince-meat for him. The spaghetti and macaroni trees will not bloom before April so it's a little early yet for me to judge the crop.[349]

Frank had a gift for making each guest feel he or she was especially welcome. By modern standards, Frank was hopelessly patronizing to his women guests. "You are a dear sweet girl to present me with the wild ducks and Japanese chickens. . . "[350] For the women who were guests at his ranch, it evoked delight.

> We just returned from Woolaroc and I don't want even a tiny minute to slip by before I tell you how I adored being with you all this week-end. It was just a bit of heaven—and my memories of it I will treasure always. I do that only with my happy ones. My only regret is—well—don't ever be a sleepy head again.
>
> Woolaroc was so delightful it captivated me. It was like a lovely dream I had come true. You were such a charming host. I think you must have given me a drink from the "Well of Happiness." I sincerely hope it won't be the last time I have that good fortune.
>
> You have a precious gift of making people contented and happy. I love to be happy—and was this week-end very, very!
>
> Thank you for letting me come to fairyland and for being so kind and very sweet.[351]

After the 1928 New Year's Party, Frank referred to Mrs. Fletcher Riley of Oklahoma City as "Little Annie Rooney." An old time song began, "Little Annie Rooney is my sweetheart." Judge Riley and his wife came down with mumps shortly after the party, and Frank wrote several solicitous letters. Mrs. Riley responded, "I have decided to pen a letter to the Prince of Hosts. . . I hope you will let us come again and will not forget."[352] Even the most serious women succumbed to his charms. As requested, Dr. Ruth Alexander dutifully reported that her very next radio broadcast was a debate with revolutionary academic, Harold Rugg, on the topic of "Does Capitalism Offer Youth Fair Opportunity." She hoped that Frank would be able to listen. Frank answered he was sorry he would miss the broadcast because he would be hosting a barbecue that evening. Dr. Alexander wrote, "Ask Node if I didn't fairly rave my head off."[353]

The only Woolaroc social bomb, of record, was the visit of Edna Ferber and William Allen White in May of 1928. Ferber was doing research for a novel that eventually became *Cimarron* and was traveling with the Whites, looking for local color. She was an acquaintance of the Phillipses from back East, and they were anxious to entertain her, along with Mr. and Mrs. White and their son on her May 12 visit. An accompanying Tulsa reporter wrote a wonder-struck story about dinner at the Lookout's and the sights of Woolaroc. Frank hit it right off with White and enjoyed a good evening's conversation on the front porch. Poor Ferber's problems started at bedtime. Jane's peacocks roosted on the roof over Edna Ferber's bedroom, and the shrieks of the birds kept her awake all night. She was so exhausted the next morning she could hardly make it through the day. She retired early to her room to try to catch up on the lost sleep, only to be tortured by more peacock screams on the second night. The next morning she fled the ranch as early as possible.[354]

There was quite a bit of official entertaining at the ranch even when Frank was out of town. Before his retirement in 1938, John Kane usually acted as host, later Paul Endacott did the duty. The ranch staff was sometimes called on in such an emergency. Frank and Jane were in Palm Springs, California, when the University of Tulsa asked if they could bring S. S. Hall, the treasurer of the Carnegie Foundation, and his wife, to the ranch. Marjorie Karch arranged a luncheon and meeting with Fred Dunn of First National Bank and Mr. and Mrs. Paul Endacott who were good friends of Dr. Clarence Pontius, University of Tulsa's president. It ended up being a very pleasant afternoon and the Halls lingered late.[355] Paul Endacott put together a small dinner at the ranch later that year in honor of some Japanese army and navy officials that Oberfell and Billy Parker thought the company needed to entertain.[356]

The visit of Aimee Semple McPherson to Bartlesville for a revival in the summer of 1934 was one of the highlights of those years for the local churches. She was an exceptionally famous Pentecostal evangelist and founder of the Foursquare Gospel Church. In the 1920s she was one of the most successful evangelists in the country, but after an alleged kidnapping incident in 1926, her mental health deteriorated.[357]

Night after night Bartlesville families, dressed in their Sunday clothes, poured into the Civic Center to hear the famous evangelist, dressed in an exquisite white gown. At each services' close she extended her arms, the wide sleeves flowing out to form a dazzling cross, as she pronounced a benediction. Frank's secretary somewhat dryly answered a request from the local committee, asking Mr. Phillips to entertain her at the ranch: arrangements would be made for a tour and lunch, if she wished. He would not permit a newsreel camera on the ranch, and he would not support the revival with a financial contribution.[358] He was always supportive of church activities, including the Pentecostal denominations, but this was one that worried him.

Frank and the Bishops

Frank Phillips was a descendant of Miles Standish on his paternal side; his maternal grandfather was a Methodist lay preacher. Frank was raised in the bosom of Protestant tradition and was a member of the Methodist Church. Despite this, Frank was not a religious man. In 1937 M. H. Aylesworth of the Scripp-Howard newspaper chain wrote him a thanks for a recent visit to Woolaroc in which he inquired about Frank being a Campbellite. Frank responded that it was L. E. he was thinking of, and besides, he had not been in church in 20 years.[359] Still, true to his rearing, Frank was exceedingly generous to all the local churches, so consistently so that his calendars show that shortly after he came home from each trip East, the local ministers usually began to show up in his office.

Among these was Father John Van den Hende of St. John Catholic Church.[360] He was a church ministry builder and must have received many donations from Frank Phillips over the years. The thing that is different about Father John from the many other ministers in Bartlesville at the time is that he also occasionally called on Frank Phillips at his New York City office. It was

Above: Frank entertained several Catholic bishops for his good friend Bishop Kelly at a Woolaroc retreat in March 1929. Here some of the delighted bishops and Frank descend the stairs from the look-out tower that was then on the horse barn. Courtesy Woolaroc.

Top left: Frank and Jane were always willing to oblige their close friend Bishop Kelly by entertaining Catholic dignitaries and groups at the ranch. The diocese didn't have retreat facilities at this early date. On the day this photograph was taken in March 1935, Jane had a luncheon for the Ursuline sisters and a few priests. Courtesy Woolaroc.

probably Frank's favorable long-term experience with this friendly man that established a positive impression of the effectiveness of Catholic charities in Frank's mind. No doubt it was Frank's growing interest in Boy Scouts that brought him in contact with Francis C. Kelley, Bishop of the Oklahoma City Diocese, for Bishop Kelley was chairman of the Bishops' Committee on Scouting. Bishop Kelley became one of Frank's closest and most enduring friends, and it was through him that Frank became acquainted with many influential Catholics of those days who became so important in Frank's network of friends.

Prelates of the Church were frequent guests at Woolaroc over the years. The first Woolaroc event where Frank's growing friendship with Bishop Kelley became evident was a ranch weekend on March 4, 1929.[361] A few weeks later Frank entertained Catholic dignitaries at a gathering of several friends of Bishop Kelley.

It was a successful retreat and all the men had a delightful weekend. Group photographs were taken of the bishops sitting on the lodge porch wrapped in Indian blankets. Frank promptly sent copies of the photos to each of them. He solicited an autographed photo from Rev. A. J. Drossaerts, the Archbishop of San Antonio, Texas. After this meeting, they enjoyed several years of mutual friendship, and Frank helped him out in everything from giving him a Holstein cow to making contributions to some ministries. Reverend C. E. Byrne, the Bishop of Galveston, Texas, helped Frank contact some of the best Brahman breeders. Reverends Byrne and Drossaerts were again among the Catholic dignitaries Frank entertained in April of 1932.

By the middle 1930s, casual and formal occasions at the ranch were frequently graced by Catholic clergy. Bishop Wise came calling on March 29, 1935. Frank and Jane hosted a luncheon for Ursuline sisters from Tulsa and Bartlesville, a group of 12 nuns, 5 priests, and some lay women on April 22.[362] Photos from that day show happy groups of nuns, in the striking, graceful black habit that was characteristic of the order, demurely walking among the trees and laughing with the priests. A few weeks later Frank's foster daughter, Mary, was married in Chicago in a Catholic ceremony.[363] Despite this relaxed cordiality, Bishop Kelley worried about his friend in a pastorly way that he expressed with a pun in a letter to W. C. Smoot, "though he seems more interested in horns than wings."[364]

Frank and some friends pose with George MacDonald, Archbishop Spellman (later Cardinal), and Bishop Kelly at a visit to Woolaroc in 1940. The archbishop teased Boots Adams, who was wearing a Wendal Wilkie campaign button, that "he might get a place in the new cabinet." The cardinal's portrait hangs in Jane's rogues gallery in the lodge. Courtesy Woolaroc.

In 1938, Bishop Kelley and Bishop Shell of Chicago held a national Catholic youth conference at the ranch. By this time, Frank was using his foundation to give large grants to Boy Scouts and to some Catholic charities in Oklahoma. Catholic scout chaplains had another retreat at the ranch in 1941.

Probably the most impressive opportunity to entertain Catholic dignitaries came in 1940 when Archbishop Francis Spellman brought a party to Oklahoma, and Frank provided a company airplane and the lodge's hospitality. The man who would become one of America's most beloved cardinals autographed a photo for Jane's gallery. He remarked on the uniqueness and friendliness of the place and teased Boots Adams, "Mr. Adams had on the first 'Wilkie for President' button that I ever saw so he might get a place in the new cabinet."[365]

The friendship between Frank and Bishop Kelley was comfortable enough that the Bishop felt free to invite Governor Phillips to the Ranch in 1939 and bring him up even though Frank was out of town. In 1946, during a time when the bishop was having health problems, Frank was so concerned about his friend that he took him to a speech pathologist in New York.[366] Both Frank Phillips and Bishop Kelley hoped to gain something from their acquaintance. Yet, out of it grew a genuine deeply felt friendship. Woolaroc was a place where it was nurtured.

An International Attraction

Occasionally Frank and Jane met European nobility and notable persons on their travels, and, like most Americans, they were always impressed. Some of these people made their way to Woolaroc once in a while and there was usually a flurry to impress the European guests.

The first of these was a visit by Henreich Hagenbeck, the world famous circus owner from Hamburg, Germany, who happened to be in the United States shortly after Frank contacted him for help with his animals. Frank gave a dinner in his honor, and the following day they all went to the 101 Ranch.[367] Later that year, on the Fourth of July, Frank entertained Viscount Alain de Leche who was on a trip to the West Coast as a special envoy for the French government. The previous November, Frank and two of his gasoline executives had gone to Paris to deliver a speech to the Chamber of Deputies. It was on this trip that Frank became acquainted with the Viscount. His visit to Woolaroc stirred the local press to predictable excitement.[368] A month later, Frank was notified he was to receive the Legion of Honor. Evidently de Leche was an enduring acquaintance, for the Viscount appeared in the appointment calendars in New York occasionally for many years. Three weeks later Heinrick Hagenbeck again visited Woolaroc. This, too, was an ongoing business and social relationship that persisted until World War II intervened. In 1933, the Count and Countess de Comminges and a Mr. Alleanne visited from Paris, and Frank threw one of his big dinners at the ranch.

By far the most elaborate effort for a foreign dignitary was the occasion of the visit of the British Ambassador and his wife, Lord and Lady Edward Wood, Earl of Halifax, to Tulsa in March of 1945. The Embassy asked for a chance to talk to some Oklahoma Indians, so the Tulsa Chamber of Commerce asked Frank to put together an event.[369] Frank's staff planned a luncheon for thirty-one, including Chief and Julia Lookout and the Labadies. They put on their best show, complete with Indian dancers. Chief Labadie gave the delighted ambassador an Osage name, and Frank presented a blanket and headdress. By the time the party left, Frank and Halifax were on a first name basis, and the young squadron leader who organized the event was on the way with his career. Never missing a trick, Frank sent "Halifax" a copy of the *Philnews* that covered his visit to Woolaroc, and the Englishman responded with thanks from San Francisco, California, where he was serving on the United Kingdom Delegation to the organizational meeting of the United Nations.[370]

Among the unnumbered visitors to Woolaroc over the years, Frank and Jane hosted thousands of the captains of industry, bankers, politicians, heroes, movie stars, artists, writers—the notables of their time. The lists of photographs on Jane's wall

Right: Will Rogers was a frequent guest at the ranch and a close friend of Frank and Jane. Whenever Will came to town it meant that there would be some fun. Here, on a weekend when Frank was not in town, Will jests with L. E. and the boys on a 1930 visit. Shown in the photo are (left to right) L. E. Phillips, W. McSpadden, W. Rider, G. Lane, Will Rogers, John G. Phillips, Frank Overlees. Courtesy Woolaroc.

Left: French Viscount Alain de Leche was an acquaintance that Frank had made at the time of his 1928 speech before the Chamber of Deputies in Paris. He visited Woolaroc the following summer on his way to California as a special envoy for the French government. It was the Viscount who secured the French Legion of Honor for Frank. Courtesy Woolaroc.

and in her album only highlight some of the famous people who visited. A. D. Mellon, Sir Thomas Lipton, Harry Truman, Mary Pickford, Herbert Hoover, Wallace Berry, Tom Mix, Rudy Vallee, Jimmy Doolittle, Frank Buck, Osa Johnson, and Clyde Beatty are a few of the other famous names that have not already been mentioned. Jane's photos do not include everyone, for one reason or another. John D. Rockefeller, Amelia Earhart, Henry Ford, Jr., and Tom Pendergast, for example, were evidently not invited to put their pictures in Jane's rogue's gallery. It is said that Jane put up the pictures of people she liked and took them down if they fell into disfavor.

Jane Phillips' diaries from 1935 and 1936 have survived with a complete listing of the social events and personal guests at Woolaroc in those years. It is evident that by that time Jane enjoyed the ranch and used it at least as heavily as Frank did. By the middle 1930s, the ranch had become a secondary home. Frank, and especially Jane, entertained informally for lunch and dinner there almost daily. Jane's constant presence at the lodge gives some credence to the Woolaroc lore that the real reason Grif Graham was moved to the gate was because Jane and Orpha had a falling out over the proper recipe for chocolate chip cookies.

This is Jane Phillips' bedroom at the ranch, with her famous "rogues gallery" arranged on the walls. It is said that Jane only asked for pictures of guests whom she liked, and should they fall from grace, their pictures were taken down. The list of photographs from her wall is a Who's Who of the era.
Courtesy Woolaroc.

THE FARE OF THE HOUSE

Woolaroc home cooking was one of the important parts of entertaining at the ranch. The recipe for the cookies has not survived, but the files do contain a few of the formulae that made meals at the ranch "so durn good." Arthur Gorman's barbecue owed its savor to slow cooking and to his special touch. Still, barbecue requires barbecue sauce, and an obliging cook left the recipe. This is the "F. P. Ranch recipe for meat sauce served, heated, with buffalo roasts and steaks":

> 1 gallon Heinz catsup
> 1 qts. Strong vinegar, or 2 qts. weak vinegar
> 2 lbs. Brown sugar
> 1 lb butter
> 3 bottles Worcestershire sauce
> 8 buttons garlic (split)
> bottle hot sauce; salt and pepper to taste
>
> Bring to boil and let simmer 2 hours.
> Makes approximately 1 gallon[371]

Frank sent his Tulsa friends a New Year's greeting at the end of 1929. His package included "Woolaroc" and "Gingeroc" his house brands of bottled water. He also sent some elk meat and some "Duroc Acorn Sausage." The sausage was persistently quite popular with the hungry men guests at breakfast, so, in 1930, Waite Phillips' manager begged the recipe from Frank's manager.

> We don't have any particular trick in making our Woolaroc Sausage. We just season it good with black pepper and salt, use a very small amount of red pepper and a strong seasoning amount of sage.[372]

Evidently, somewhere along the line, Frank began sending Woolaroc hams as gifts to his friends. The special recipe for the hams was on John G. Phillips' stationery.

> Butcher hogs and bleed well. Let hams stand in salt for six weeks first rubbing salt well into meat, joints, etc. After six weeks take out of salt and wash in hot water thoroughly, then dip hams in boiling water for one minute—first one end then the other. Wipe with dry cloth and while damp cover well with black pepper. Rub pepper in and hang up until ham get real dry (one or two days). Then wrap in paper and place in white cloth bag (Flour sack). Hang up and keep six month or longer before eating.[373]

The 1936 election inspired one mailing of hams as gifts to Frank's political friends. The enclosure letter read:

> This is a Woolaroc ham, raised and cured on F. P. Ranch. Try it and if you don't like it, feed it to the dog—pretty expensive dog meat but what do we care, the Government's going to take over everything anyhow if we don't look out; that's the reason I can afford to give my hams away. Seriously, I am disposing of everything I can so as to have a fresh start under some kind of new deal, which both candidates promise us.[374]

The hams pleased everyone and brought a bevy of happy thank you letters. E. P. Earle wrote, "Why don't you put a little arsenic in one of the hams and send it to F. D.R.? However, I hope the suggestion is not going to be needed and that next Tuesday we are going to put your friend Governor Landon, over and get rid of F. D. R. and his 'brain trusters' forever."[375] Another friend wrote, "I feel we are apt to draw a better hand with Landon dealing the cards than we have had for the past three years."[376] And Ed Loomis wrote, "I have referred the matter to our legal department for advice as to whether I shall have to include it in my tax returns."[377] J. M. Davis' enthusiastic response rounds out the Woolaroc recipes with one of his own.

> I have felt very badly for some time that I did not receive my share of the eggs produced at the ranch. I have never tasted eggs that cost $5.00 per egg, and the[y] must be different from those we use here.
>
> Seriously, I appreciate very much your thought of me; and may I suggest that you cook one of these hams at your own home, being careful to carry out the following instructions:
>
> (1) Soak the ham in cold water for 12 hours.
> (2) Boil for 6 hours.
> (3) Bake for 2 hours.
>
> Then serve hot, and place what is left in the refrigerator and try cold the following day. That is the way I have hams cooked in my own home.
>
> It is impossible to get a well-cooked ham in a hotel or cafeteria. . . [378]

The hams were immensely successful gifts in 1938. Frank generated the kind of sensation he hoped for with his buddies. "If you can handle it like Amon Carter does his turkey, watermelon, and pecan business you certainly will make a lot of real money. . . "[379]

One of Frank's first ideas was to have the springs on the ranch analyzed. Of course, he wanted to know if the water was pure and potable, and he also wanted to check for possible mineral waters.[380] The result was a comprehensive analysis of the six springs, two lakes, and a well on the ranch by the company chemists. Clyde Lake was judged pure and potable, but the pond at Stone Bridge was contaminated with salt and organic matter. All the springs were potable. Spencer Spring contained quite a bit of calcium salts and the spring at Old Pole Bridge and Alec Gay Spring were considerably mineralized, including some iron oxide. The well near the main gate was judged typical mineral well water, but contained 12.9 parts per million, 43 times average, of iron oxide.[381]

Some months later Frank asked his friend E. E. Dale, of the history department at Oklahoma University, to help his chemists get a medical opinion of the purity and therapeutic value of his spring waters. Promptly, Dr. Lloyd E. Harris and D. B. R. Johnson of the University of Oklahoma's School of Pharmacy and Dr. Ben H. Cooley of the School of Medicine obliged in time for Frank to bottle his first "Woolaroc" for some parties.[382]

When his friend Tom Latta came up from Tulsa in January of 1928, Frank greeted him with, "What do you gentlemen prefer first, highballs or something to eat?" This publication is the first positive reference to what was generally well-known, the presence of alcohol during Prohibition. Obviously, whiskey flowed freely in social circles. Latta got a teasing letter from the United States Commissioner, Northern District of Oklahoma. "You had some highballs at Frank's Woolaroc. That's in my jurisdiction and I want something done. It's a plain case of possession, transportation, and giving away. Conspiracy maybe. But you can have immunity by being a witness for the Government. . . Bribingly yours, [383]

Frank joined right in the charade, "You should get in touch with me sometime when I'm going to the Ranch and go out and try that mineral water. If Tom had anything besides our mineral water mixtures then he must have brought it with him and cheated because he didn't offer me any."[384]

The *Bartlesville Examiner* carried another public mention of the F. P. Ranch bourbon and draught beer at the second Cow Thieves and Outlaws Picnic that fall.[385] Most mention of liquor was at least a little veiled. Amon Carter sent Frank some "old-time Democratic measuring glasses" which he yarned he had gotten from a friend who was moving his business to Mexico.[386] Frank's 1929 gift of "Woolaroc" and "Gingeroc," elk, and Duroc Acorn Sausage recommended the waters be tested with "liquid corn."[387]

Records were kept of the liquor supplies 1926 through 1934. For the opening directors' party in 1926, C. M. Curry supplied 24 "cases to B'ville [sic]." In August, the same person supplied "19 G. & 14 S." There was no record for 1927, but 1928 had records for liquor, alcohol, wet goods, and S, payment to L. L. Bell and B. Waldman, and some transactions were cash. Most was purchased in Bartlesville, but the cash transactions were listed as "liquor to B'ville," and on 2 July 1929, Tony Gardella sent $205 worth of wet goods to Bartlesville. Total outlay in 1926 was $8,082, and $2,725 in 1928. The tight economy and probably law enforcement in 1932 kept expenditure to only $275.[388] After the repeal of the Eighteenth Amendment the beer dealers began to compete for the Woolaroc account. Liquor and beer quickly appeared in the budgets despite Oklahoma remaining a dry state for many years.

Evidently, Jane Phillips had limits of tolerance. On the weekend of March 28, 1935, Jane and her close friend Marcell Haskell spent the night at the ranch with a group of Oklahoma City guests. The next morning Jane was glad to wash her hands of her charges, "all three drunken bums from O. C."[389]

Managers

From the beginning, Frank recognized that the success of the ranch rested heavily on his managers. He had his eye on his first ranch manager, Grif Graham, years before the ranch became a reality. Grif was an apt choice. Tall and handsome, he was the genuine article, Frank's very own Wild West showman in the age of Tom Mix, Bill Hart, and Hoot Gibson. His big smile and red flannel shirt, his yarns and practical jokes were a burlesque of the Old West that fairly delighted the Eastern dudes and local folks alike. Grif had been a real lawman, and Frank wanted both the appearance and capability of security on his ranch. Most of all, Grif was a real cowboy. He had genuine credibility with the hands on the Ranch, and real experience managing men and cows.

Grif Graham, 1927, examining flood damage on horseback during his days as ranch manager. Grif was a handsome, jocular man with genuine credibility as an Old West character. He was a fixture at the ranch, even after he was no longer manager. Courtesy Woolaroc.

Frank's original plan was to stock the ranch with North American game and decorate the lodge with old-time Western memorabilia. Grif capably oversaw the opening of the game preserve and imaginatively managed the entertainment demands that made the Frank Phillips Ranch an immediate success. In the disastrous summer of 1927, he resigned as manager. "Owing to the conditions that have lately arisen I think it is probable that you would be better satisfied and contented with someone else running the Ranch."[390] It was almost a month before Frank responded to the resignation. "You will be relieved of any responsibility after September 1st, and Mr. Shirley will take over the management of the house. Should you desire to remain until you can conveniently make other arrangements, it will be entirely satisfactory."[391] It is evident that Frank regretted the needed change. Though relieved as manager, the Grahams continued to live on the ranch for many years, and Grif continued as an important part of the Woolaroc staff. Grif and Orpha were at the gatehouse in the middle 1930s. In those years people who lived at the ranch had to be in by 9:00 P.M.; except on Saturdays it was 11:00 P.M.[392]

Frank was especially generous and indulgent of Grif. It is easy to see why. A 1937 letter gives a flavor of the irrepressible jokester he was, "If you ever need the skin of an old broken down cowpuncher for your collection, you are more than welcome to this old skin of mine."[393] It was not until the Henry Wells' dogs incident in 1938 that Grif was actually dismissed and moved from the gatehouse to Bowring, 20 miles north. Still, as late as October of 1939, Grif was conducting regular tours of the ranch for visitors.[394] He was evidently as beloved by Frank Phillips as he was by the many guests. His photograph, a colorized portrait, still hangs in Frank Phillips' bedroom in the lodge.

Charles Opal "Pop" Shirley had been a Phillips Petroleum Company employee since 1919. He was originally employed as a roustabout, but was soon promoted to the Telephone and Telegraph Department where he developed the communications systems for the company. In 1922, Frank Phillips made him manager of the lodge, and he served in that position until 1937.[395] People who remember him say he was the sort of man who never met a stranger. He was a very competent man and a reliable organizer. He helped Jane organize Jane Phillips Sorority, was an active Mason, and was busy in civic affairs. It is not surprising that Frank would turn to him to take the interim management of the ranch.

Evidently, over the next several years, Frank endeavored to find a ranch manager who could deal with the usual ranch functions, management of personnel, livestock, and improvements, while dealing with the exotic animals, constant construction, and the demanding social functions.[396] At first he considered hiring an exotic animal man from Hearst's estate, a high-priced quick fix for his animal problems.[397] It seems that Grif continued to help out, and Shirley managed satisfactorily for several months while Frank passed up several promising-looking applicants.

By the summer of 1929, Frank had replaced Pop with W. E. West as ranch manager.[398] West was a graduate of Oklahoma State University and had been the county agent during the search for the cause of the deaths of so many of Frank's exotic animals. At that time he had shown himself to be a very capable man, and that is doubtless why Frank hired him to manage the ranch. By that time some, of the responsibilities for planning social functions had devolved to Marjorie Loos, Frank and Jane's personal secretary. Letters between Marge and Fern Butler in New York show that she had assumed oversight of some of the bookkeeping, inventory, and arrangements at the ranch at an early date. On site, West supervised the farmers, cowboys, maintenance and construction people, and the housekeeper and staff at the lodge.[399]

E. W. Evans, another secretary at Phillips Petroleum Company, was increasingly handling management and personnel matters of the ranch when Frank was out of town.[400] The winter of 1930 was very severe and was followed by flooding and twisters in the spring. West was still functioning as manager, but Evans was supervising and reporting to Frank while he was in New York. He began spending weekends at the ranch to supervise the progress of the ranch work. He was deeply involved by April when he wrote, "The old turkey hen you saw over near the Blackberry patch hatched out fourteen chicks (turkeys)."[401] This was not the detachment of a secretary who was simply making a report. Frank sent him a list of

New York purchases for the swimming facilities and wrote instructions on their placement. Meanwhile, Frank was growing dissatisfied with West's attention to detail, and Evans was filling that demand with efficiency and precision. While on company business in Boston, Massachusetts, in September, Evans made a call on Benson in Nashua, New Hampshire, and the Tilley bird farm for Woolaroc.[402]

It was probably the tuberculosis outbreak that spelled the end for W. E. West at the ranch. At any rate, Phillips was reducing salaries of its employees because of the Depression, and Frank began to reduce salaries and positions at the ranch too. West did not take the news gracefully, and Frank fired him. "Since leaving Bartlesville it has been reported to me that you have been most vicious to your associates and have threatened me in ways which leads me to say that you are hereby discharged effective January 1st and Mr. E. W. Evans. . . will succeed you."[403] He did, however, send West on with a good recommendation.[404] Evans was not happy with the new appointment, but Frank simply refused to allow Evans to return to employment at Phillips Petroleum Company. In only a month he resigned as ranch manager.[405]

Bill Compton had been an employee at the ranch for some time. West had even suggested that his wife would be a good gatekeeper. He was receiving 37¢ an hour on the construction crew for the new road in March of 1930.[406] West considered him a willing worker, and Evans and Riney moved Compton and his wife to the gate in the summer of 1930.[407] In those days, the gatekeeper went to the gate with a drawn gun before admitting guests.[408] W. I. Compton became the manager in the lurch after Evans' precipitous resignation. He was exceptionally handsome and is reputed to have been quite a ladies' man. The little correspondence from his tenure reflects constrained finances. Frank admonished Compton to give fewer chickens to the employees and rebuked Compton when he hired a farmer for $60 a month. Finally, in 1932, Frank reduced Compton's salary by 15 percent.[409]

Hard times and weak character were the end of Compton. An unsigned ranch report, with some names blacked out, refers to an investigation by Pop Shirley into allegations against Compton.

> Wes Deardorff advertised the fact that hot money could be secured two for one ████ a person giving $100 could get $200 in hot money; stated it was not hard to dispose of this hot money as Bill Compton handled it and got by. One of Shirley's men expects to see Wes when he returns from Muskogee and find out more about the money matter.[410]

The report continued on with information about Brahman rustling and kickbacks on feed purchases.

By mid-November, Compton was replaced by M. S. Kerr.[411] Evidently charges were never filed for the allegations against Compton. He left his family and was eventually divorced. A handful of inquiries about him show that he went to western Oklahoma and moved around a lot. In 1936 he was in Bartlesville while unemployed, and it was reported he had been working at the Denver, Colorado mint, a peculiar proclivity for a man that liked hot money.[412]

During the tenure of M. S. Kerr as manager, Fern Butler and Marge Loos Karch worked on developing a better accounting system for the ranch. Kerr developed a system for keeping daily records, and monthly financial reports.[413]

In 1935, M. S. Kerr listed A. Bors as ranch foreman for $85 a month.[414] Evidently the structure of the ranch organization had subtly changed. The ranch manager seems to have been an on-site superintendent of ranch and lodge, with a foreman in charge of actual ranching functions, and with Pop Shirley as something of a business manager. At any rate, Kerr was dismissed by the end of that month. Frank's landscape man, Arthur Phillips, was afraid that a complaint he made about not getting

This portrait of Grif Graham still hangs in Frank's bedroom in the lodge, a tribute to his fondness for his first manager.
Courtesy Woolaroc.

"Pop" Shirley first worked for Phillips Petroleum Company as a roustabout in 1919, but went on to develop the telephone system at the Company. He was a man that Frank relied on often as a trouble-shooter. He was probably site manager at the ranch before Grif Graham came on as ranch manager in the summer of 1925. Then, he served as interim manager after Grif resigned. Frank called him in again in the 1930s when he was reorganizing the ranch and having trouble finding reliable managers. Courtesy Phillips Petroleum Company Archive.

men to work on the landscaping when he needed them was the cause. Evidently, Kerr angrily blamed him.[415] Frank responded, "Mr. Kerr is not at the ranch any more because of a number of things similar to his action in calling you as he did."[416]

Kerr was replaced by D. C. Zühlke by January 1936. Don was married to the sister of Marjorie Karch, Lucille, who was director of the museum and lodge. Don Zühlke resumed the regular letters, reporting ranch activities that had been entirely missing since Evans' resignation, and the monthly account records continued. Zühlke arrived just in time for the terrible heat and drought of 1936. He inherited the discontent of the times but evidently did not have the gifts for working with his employees that, say, Grif Graham had enjoyed. Frank had to sort out a mutiny on the road crew that accused Zühlke of forcing them to work in the cold rain without raincoats. He created genuine enmity with faithful employees such as Grif Graham in the episode about watering the entry gate plantings. Because of his relationship with Marjorie, Frank had a great deal of motivation to tolerate more problems than he might have otherwise, and Lucille was a very valuable employee in her own right. In April of 1940, both Zühlkes resigned, effective in July, after some personal disagreement with Frank.[417]

By the summer, John N. Seward, a former military officer, was the new manager. Ranch employees remember that there was some resistance to Seward's military discipline style of leadership, but they say he was a "hard worker and a good hand." He was evidently a man of some sensitivity and reflection, for it was he who produced the thoughtful essay on winter feeding late in 1940. He resigned October 5, 1942, and returned to military service, finishing the war as a colonel. He was replaced by Joe Billam who served as ranch manager for many years.

As the financial fortunes at Phillips improved, the emphasis at the ranch was slowly turning toward the

development of the museum. Frank continued to take a great deal of pleasure in his animals, but the explosive growth of that phase of his hobby was past. New interest in the Spiro Mound excavations and opportunities to acquire the best in Western art fed a motivation to expand his museum, while his friends continued to make gifts to his various collections. During the time Zühlke served as manager, the second and third rooms were added to the museum in 1936 and 1939. Important improvements were added: such as air conditioning in 1936 and stonework for the window panels in 1937.[418] The growth of the art and collections was taking a new priority. By 1936 Lucille Zühlke was also working as director of the museum. After Lucille left, Margaret Elliott was museum curator for a short term before Pat Patterson was hired to direct the museum in 1941. The administration of Woolaroc was becoming more complex.

Frank never really differentiated between where "his" ended and "Phillips" began. This Frank Griggs portrait of Frank Phillips at Happy Hollow on the ranch beautifully captures the real lord of Woolaroc. Courtesy Woolaroc.

Frank or Phillips

The boundaries of ownership and responsibility between Frank Phillips and Phillips Petroleum Company at the Frank Phillips Ranch were blurred from the very beginning. The earliest purchases of the property that was assembled for the ranch underwent transfers from Frank to the company, sometimes within days. The company owned the Osage Park property in 1925 and transferred it to Frank after completion of the fences, roadwork, and dams late in 1926. Company engineers designed and built the dams and roads, company chemists analyzed the springs, company accountants kept the books, and company lawyers evaluated contracts. Frank paid the company only $95 for some of the buildings and improvements on the ranch.[419] Frank Phillips built the ranch to entertain business contacts, and large and small company social functions were always fixtures in the Woolaroc calendar. Frank owned the ranch, the animals, and the museum and used them for his private enjoyment on a day-to-day basis. Paul Endacott said he never really grappled with where he and his ended and the company's began.

From the beginning, Frank was attentive to any tax breaks. He needed to be. The first top marginal rate for the graduated income tax had been 6 percent in 1913, but by the end of World War I the maximum income surtax had soared to 65 percent. The Warren G. Harding Administration whittled it down to 50 percent after 1924, and Calvin Coolidge rolled back the rates more, to 20 percent in 1926. The New Deal aggressively raised taxes by 1935 to a punitive 75 percent top rate. At the end of the World War II it stood at 90 percent.

Frank had no trouble showing losses in the early years. These were helpful on his federal taxes but had no bearing on the property taxes he paid in Oklahoma. He successfully worked hand-in-hand with his friend State Senator Gid Graham to get legislation for an exemption for game and exotic animals from the personal property tax rolls. By the 1930s, "soak the rich" was the mood of the times. Starved state and federal tax collectors were eager to target the rich to squeeze out a little more revenue. In the summer of 1930, they were eyeing Frank's ranch. I. S. Horne advised Frank that Internal Revenue Service (IRS) always questioned these animal losses. He recommended Shouse, Doolittle, Morlock, and Shrader in Kansas City as the firm that did J. C. Nichols' taxes.[420] Frank's financial situation added a lot of pressure to find deductions. It was hard to separate the personal and ranch expenses, especially the groceries.[421] He did not take Horne's advice of accountants but instead employed Barrow, Wade, Guthrie & Company of New York to negotiate with the IRS concerning the 1928 losses in a case filed in 1931. By 1933, the agency sent a bill for another $7,821.30 in taxes.[422] The accountants had won a precious delay, and a settlement was reached in 1934. The ranch accounting system was tightened up considerably by that time.

Frank was harried on all sides. In one audacious incident, in New York Frank received a telegram from Bartlesville.

> Osage County authorities have raised your nineteen thirty three assessment on ranch fifty thousand dollars stop Washington County authorities raised your residence and personal property approximately seventeen thousand dollars stop we are endeavoring to reduce these amounts substantially and will attempt to hold final assessment open until your return.[423]

Frank flew home immediately and met with the county commissions. He did get an adjustment to a more reasonable rate. Personal property taxes remained a serious problem, and as late as 1939, the Frank Phillips Foundation was struggling with attempts by the state to levy taxes on intangible personal property belonging to the Foundation.[424]

In 1926 Phillips signed a contract with Frank for their obligation in operation of some parts of the ranch. They operated a pumping station, a small electric plant, and maintained telephone lines and the dams.[425] The 1934 tax agreement forced a general reassessment of the business delineation between the company and the ranch. The directors resolved to reimburse Frank Phillips $100,000 for entertainment expenses at the ranch from 1926 through 1933.[426] Their New York accountants advised that they formally split accounts into ranch operations and other expenditures.[427] The 1934 entertainment expense was $15,000.[428]

About the time he was starting the Frank Phillips Foundation, he ceased making private purchases of art and began to purchase through the vehicle of Phillips Investments. Also concurrent with formation of the Frank Phillips Foundation, the Phillips Petroleum Company signed a lease agreement with Frank Phillips for the operation of the ranch. Frank retained responsibility for operation of the farm, animals, and animal's buildings. For the aging country squire, this was a first step in passing the responsibility for Woolaroc on to the company and eventually to the foundation. As early as 1928, he told T. A. Latta, "After I am finished with it, after I have completed the thing, the State will get it. I would like to quit now—but I can't."[429] He was unable to let go of his creation during his lifetime. Right up to the end, he most enjoyed sitting on his front porch at the lodge, overlooking Clyde Lake. Fortunately for Woolaroc and the taxpayers, he provided for the future maintenance of the ranch with his own money.

V

YE OLDE CURIOSITY SHOP: THE COLLECTIONS

PHILOSOPHER GEORGE BERKELEY once questioned, if a tree falls in the forest is there a sound? One might ask if there was a roar from the rushing water that swept down the Pennsylvanian era river 300,000,000 million years ago. Those tropical summers brought annual monsoon rain, winds, and flooding to the river delta that is now Woolaroc. It was one of those flash floods that swept through the tropical cane breaks on the distant shores, tearing up some giant horsetail along the way, floating one of the logs with the waters far out into the delta, and depositing it along some muddy shoal as the flood tide slowly ebbed. Weeks, months, and years later other muddy inundations deposited more flood silt around the log, burying it in an anoxic mass that slowly petrified.

There lay the fossilized log, part of the rocky outcropping of the ageless Osage, the area that became the Woolaroc Lodge. By some quirk of fortune, Frank's construction crew noticed the unusual formation and set it out for display near the early lodge where T. C. Sherwood, one of Frank's geologists, happened to spy it. Inspired to imaginative raptures that only a geologist could appreciate, when back in the office, Sherwood typed up a report and sent it to Frank Phillips.

> This piece of petrified wood was unearthed while workmen were blasting on the F. P. Ranch in the vicinity of Woolaroc Lodge.
>
> It is a specimen of giant Horsetail, a species of tropical plant life that in prehistoric times grew to a height of from sixty to eighty feet with a diameter of two feet.
>
> This special piece of giant Horsetail grew millions of years ago in the swampy margin of a lake or shallow sea that once covered the area in and around the F. P. Ranch. It was possibly broken down by a high wind, covered with sand, then petrified when other beds of shale and sand were deposited on top of it. . . [430]

A record shot of the interior of the Museum after the 1939 addition. In the foreground was the speaker's desk from the House of Representatives of the General Council of the Choctaw Nation, given to Frank by Herbert Hoover's secretary of war, Tulsan Patrick Hurley. The inside walls of the room were *trompe l'oeil* painted rock. Courtesy Woolaroc.

Frank was delighted, "I do not know of anything that has interested me more than your report on the fossils which you examined on my ranch."[431] No doubt. For Frank had many friends who were interested in collecting fossils or ethnological specimens or art or stamps or all kinds of other pursuits and hobbies. Frank had never been one of them before, but he was already in the process of becoming one of the great collectors of his era.

Even as construction was still under way, on that chilly April day in 1926 when Frank entertained his directors, local dignitaries, and investors at the very first barbecue and Wild West show at the Frank Phillips Ranch, the lodge was nearing completion, and its inspiration was evident. We know that Grif Graham hung his collection of horns in the lodge first thing. Maybe the collection was already hanging for the directors or maybe the horns were sitting around in boxes, but it was enough to inspire Amon Carter. He sent a pair of steer horns, measuring 6 feet 9 inches, as a house-warming gift.[432] Frank's beginning collection consisted of about two hundred sets of horns, and he was already interested in finding rare specimens.[433] Like so many serendipitous events at Woolaroc, the petrified horsetail and these horns were some of the early inspirations that launched Frank's first collections.

Bert Gaddis, the local Ford automobile dealer and a close friend, had presented a "gun collection" to Frank at Christmas.[434] The collection consisted of about 43 weapons: some Civil War guns and swords, several swords from the Far East, and a Chinese hand cannon. By March of 1926, Frank was actively seeking artifacts and memorabilia to decorate his lodge. A Mr. Roddy, a curio man from Pawhuska, came out to see if he had anything Frank could use. Grif talked to a Mr. Finney in Bartlesville about his Indian collection and to a Mr. Kahler in Dewey, then went to Nowata to see if there was anything there that might work.[435]

Fortunately the Millers' friend, Emil Lenders, visited the lodge when it was nearly finished in time to offer Frank some expert advice about decorating the place. He made such suggestions as hanging Kentucky flintlocks over the mantel, placing mounted owls and squirrels in the rafters, making bed posts of rustic pine, putting Indian pottery on the mantels, and animal skins and Navajo rugs on the furniture and floors. Some of those ideas were already in the works; all can be seen in the lodge today. By fall, Frank was actively implementing Lenders' suggestions, "E. W. Lenders of the 101 Ranch is helping me decorate my Country Lodge and suggests that you could furnish a few things which I might need."[436]

More important, Lenders significantly influenced Frank's early acquisitions to more thoughtful ethnological themes. He wrote, "Of course, there are nowadays many Indian relics offered in stores, but as a rule they are more or less imitations and poor ones at that."[437] Lenders was a lifelong collector of Western memorabilia and Indian artifacts and a dealer of reputation. Among his clients were the American Museum of Natural History and J. P. Morgan.[438] Though Frank had repeated opportunities for many years to acquire parts of Lenders' own ethnographic collection, he did not do so, but he did take his advice. It was Lenders who painted the faux Indian rock paintings on the ranch in the summer of 1926.[439]

Frank did buy six of Lenders' paintings in 1926. In March of 1927, Lenders sold Frank a painting called *In the Teeth of the Blizzard* that seems to have been the cause of a cooling in their relationship. For some reason, Frank wrote Lenders, "Frankly, while I think the painting is wonderful, I don't like the coloring. Who ever saw pink or purple buffalo or colored snow? Please come over and fix it."[440] Lenders responded with a lengthy letter explaining the use of color and also citing other artists who approved of the painting. Frank answered, "I was raised to manhood in a blizzard country of the far north and you have not impressed me by your opinion."[441]

About the same time, Robert Lindneux, a Colorado-based Western artist of the same genre and a friend of Colonel Lillie, who had once painted for Buffalo Bill's Wild West Show, visited the lodge and offered Frank some detailed advice on arrangement of the decorations on his walls.[442] Lindneux hoped to sell Frank some of his own paintings. Frank already owned Lindneux paintings titled *The Homeseekers* and *Bawling For Help,* evocative paintings purchased April 1, 1926. He also bought *American Bison* the next year on January 1,1927.

Frank's first twoWestern paintings were by Henry Balink, titled *Indian On A White Horse* and *Chief Grey Fox.* He bought one on August 26, 1925, for $425, and Mrs. Phillips bought the second on December 31, for $300.[443] Frank had done business with Balink before.[444] He was a Santa Fe, New Mexico, artist from Amsterdam in the Netherlands and trained in the Royal Academy, one of the European artists that enjoyed the robust color of Southwestern ethnicity. Frank eventually purchased another twenty portraits of Indians by Balink.

Horns, Hides, and Heads

The April directors' meeting inspired other remarkable house-warming gifts for the Woolaroc Lodge. On the first of June, Frank's good friend and director, E. E. DuPont, gave him the Stanley Arthurs painting of *George Rogers Clark*.[445] From the beginning, the gifts of Frank Phillips' friends began to form a nucleus of the collections that are housed at Woolaroc. Felix DuPont sent a turkey gun that arrived the same day as Amon Carter's longhorns.[446] Arthur Ruble of Pawhuska sent an elk's head.[447] It seems the early lodge was already taking on the character to titillate a hunter, for one of L. E.'s Kansas City friends, sent a photograph of his last big game hunt in Africa.[448] Jess Leach, the owner of the *Bartlesville Enterprise,* sent the Hopi telegraph drum that still calls guests to meals in the lodge.[449] H. V. Foster's house-warming gift was a totem pole from Hoonah, a village near Juneau, Alaska, carved in yellow cedar by a man named Moses.[450] Frank placed it just southwest of the lodge. What could be more delightful than a two-headed calf that Frank sent off to Denver to be stuffed, a gift from neighboring rancher John Irwin?[451] Los Angeles oil man R. A. Broomfield sent as thanks a mounted marlin, "as a filler for the space reserved during the time I spent a wonderful evening at the 'Gimme' Club."[452] The animal skins, heads, and horns; the Indian blankets and ethnographic items; the paintings; the guns and swords were integral parts of the beginnings of the collections at Woolaroc and a sign of the early success of the Wild West ambience that Frank hoped to weave at his resort.

Frank began to build his collection of horns and animal heads even before the lodge was complete. When neighbor Cook's dog killed a Japanese Sika deer, Grif and Alec Gay skinned and dressed the deer and expressed the hide to Jonas Brothers.[453] Jonas Brothers were Denver furriers who had an expert reputation with hides and taxidermy. By far, they enjoyed the largest portion of Frank's extensive taxidermy business over many years. When so many animals died in 1927 and 1928, it was Jonas Brothers who tanned the hides and mounted the heads for Frank. Frank often gave his guests a beautiful hide as a memento of their visit at his ranch, and sometimes he sent his friends a prize animal head. Exotic hides graced the floor of his Bartlesville home, New York apartment, and office, and were gifts to Fern Butler. To Frank's horror, in 1934 moths attacked the trophy heads in the

Top: L. D. Bertillion holds the "world's record set of horns, 14 1/2 in. cir. 9 ft. 4 in. spread straight across, price $2500.00 for sale by L. D. Bertillion, Mineala, Texas." It was a set of horns that Frank literally coveted, but would not pay his exorbitant price. After Bertillion's death, Frank eventually bought them from his widow. Courtesy Woolaroc.

Bottom: Searles Grant is cleaning the horns collection arrayed on the floor during the 1960 renovation of the lodge. Grant was a craftsman in the shop from the early days. He was one of the few who knew the secret of the Woolaroc veneer process. Courtesy Woolaroc.

The interior of the southwest corner of the first room of the museum around 1936. Notice the anthracite block, the trophies, cases of Frank's gifts and Emil Lenders paintings. The chandelier in the upper right corner is one of four that came from the old Waldorf Astoria, and is now in the lodge. This old photograph is a record of the presentation of the collections before Frank began to give his museum some philosophical direction. Courtesy Woolaroc.

lodge. All the staff was called to a general quarters rediness and Jonas Brothers were brought in to treat the predators.[454] Arsenic was the remedy of the times. The museum still uses animal hides, draped over stands, as part of the decoration, and animal heads still loom on the walls.

Lenders recommended Ragghianti & Weber of Philadelphia, Pennsylvania, especially for mountings, and Frank did do some business with them.[455] But he clearly preferred Jonas Brothers. Frank also bought mounted trophies from Abercrombie & Fitch in New York, Edwin Dixon of Unionville, Ontario, and Rowland Ward Ltd. of London. The Rowland Ward purchases were very involved because of the import tariffs of the time, but Frank minutely followed every step because this was the dealer that supplied one of his most desired trophies. Frank used every means he could think of to ease the transfer. He even loaned A. P. Hill, a Department of Treasury employee living in Oklahoma City, $393 at 7 percent interest.[456] Not withstanding, the transport of Frank's exotic trophy heads from overseas generated huge shipping files for the few items actually imported. It was A. P. Hill who told Frank he should have his trophies listed as natural history specimens to avoid the tariffs, and he personally worked with the import broker to be sure all the papers were in order to facilitate the processing.[457]

Frank began to pursue his horn and trophy collection with great enthusiasm early in 1926. Dr. Weber loaned him a collection of seven mounts that eventually became part of the permanent collection. Frank was interested in purchasing the longhorns collection from the Buckhorn Saloon in San Antonio, Texas. That correspondence brought him into contact with Albert Friedrich. Friedrich sold him several sets of horns and a few heads over the next few years. C. E. Autry of Fort Worth was another longhorns source, W. G. Muter of Del Rio, Texas, sold Frank some locked deer horns, William Wolfe of Edmonton, Canada, sold him a moose head, and Claude "Smug" Byler ended up being Frank's scout for all sorts of curiosities. Byler chased down longhorns, minerals, fossils, Southwestern wildlife, and even cacti and a jar of rattlesnake rattles in 1927 and 1928.

Approximately parallel to his acquisitions of exotic animals, Frank began to collect exotic trophies. By early in 1927 Frank was bragging that his collection was nearly complete. A ranch memo enumerated "the only remaining horn bearing animals that are not represented in the Frank Phillips collection."[458] Eight species were listed, then a ninth, overlooked species was penciled in. That day Frank wrote his friend Major General Roy V. Hoffman, "one of them is the horn of that kind of animal killed by your friend, Roosevelt, in the heart of Asia; I've forgotten the name of the darn things now."[459] Hoffman responded that Frank did not own an *Ovus poli,* a species that Theodore Roosevelt, Jr. recently secured for Marshal Field's Chicago museum.[460] Frank took the letter to be an offer by Hoffman to try to help him secure some of the rare horns too. Hoffman promptly wrote Roosevelt who answered, "Write to Thaddeus Avery, c/o Cockburn Agency, Srinagar, via Kashmir, India, and ask him if he will buy the pair of poli horns that Harrison at the bank has."[461] Frank promptly contacted both Avery and Roosevelt. Roosevelt invited Frank to lunch, but Avery responded that the owner of the specimen was on vacation in England. The whole episode of high excitement was finally resolved by General Hoffman. He sat next to a big game hunter at a New York banquet and learned that Frank could purchase the needed horns from Roland Ward, Ltd. in London.[462]This was the all-important shipment that generated so much maticulous paperwork.

Frank was still avidly collecting in 1928 when he wrote L. D. Bertillion in Texas about some longhorns, "As you perhaps have heard, I have an immense collection. It is said my heads and horns are now equal to, if not excelling, any in America, and, of course, I get offers from everywhere which gives me an opportunity to make the best selections at low prices."[463] After his visit in 1929, Heinrich Hagenbeck sent Frank a shipment of 30 trophies for examination, and Frank kept 8.[464] By that time he had learned the ropes.

> In making shipments to me in the future they should be sent free of duty as all the heads and horns I have purchased from abroad have been allowed free entry, marked 'natural history' specimens.[465]

Frank had M. G. Terry take an inventory of the specimens at the ranch as of April 15, 1929, which listed 279 specimens and which suggested 34 specimens that were still needed.[466] Evidently the inventory of exotic trophies exposed a glitch in the records at the lodge, and Marjorie Loos wrote George B. Spencer of Archer-Daniels-Midland Company in Minneapolis, Minnesota, for a list of trophies that Frank had purchased from him in January of 1927.[467] Mr. Spencer located a list of 59 specimens of American fish and game trophies. Several of these very specimens are still evident in the dining room of the lodge today.

The Depression restrained Frank's trophy acquisitions, as it did most of his other pursuits in the early 1930s. Occasionally one of his friends gave him a trophy for his collections. In 1931 Frank's friend, L. L. Marcell of White Eagle Oil Company in Kansas City, visited in the home of C. F. Meyer of Standard Oil of New York. Meyer had a fine musk ox trophy hanging, which was presented to him by Captain Robert Bartlett of Admiral Richard Peary's artic explorations after a trip to Greenland. Marcell said he thought Frank would like to purchase it if Meyer was interested, so Meyer wrote Frank, offering it as a gift to the museum. He assured Frank it was moth proof.[468] Of course, Frank accepted with delight. In 1935, Frank acquired a collection of 206 prize trophies from L. P. Waldrip of St. Louis. In 1939, he purchased a sizeable collection of horns from J. C. Voorheis of Broken Arrow.

The *Bartlesville Morning Examiner* did a Woolaroc story in 1934 in which the breathless reporter described the wonders then housed in the museum. Among them were "horns of a buffalo killed by W. F. Cody" and "the horns of a milk cow that belonged to the mother of Frank and Jesse James" and, best of all, "horns of an animal purported to have been killed by Powhatan in 1591."[469] It looked like a clear case of Grif Graham "woofin'" another tenderfoot, but checking soon revealed that, in 1926, L. D. Bertillion offered Frank just those items.[470] It was Mrs. Bertillion who finally made a deal with Frank in 1945 for the longest pair of steer horns in the world, 9 feet 6 inches.[471] It seems that, in 1926, Bertillion had found a legendary site in south Texas, where a large herd of longhorns had been lost in a canyon during a blizzard in 1812. From the treasure trove of bones and horns that he had salvaged and polished, he sold numbers of prize specimens, including the pairs Frank purchased.[472]

Probably the most famous trophy given to Frank Phillips was a gift from his friend, Amon Carter. Carter sent a very fine example of a mounted longhorn steer's head. The specimen is so fine that it would have been gladly received in Frank's collection, but this one had been remarkably rigged so that, when a switch is flipped on the wall, the animal's eyes light up and flash, and smoke comes from it's nostrils. Lucille Zühlke wrote, "Amon Carter's man was here yesterday and installed the steer head. I had it put over the balcony so that people coming in the front door can be greeted by the fiery eyes and smoking nostrils—it is really quite an elaborate thing."[473] When Frank got home he immediately wrote thanks to Amon,

> The ranch is now complete. I am going to get a lot of fun out of the steer head which incidentally is one of the finest specimens of a real Texas steer that I have seen and a real piece of art. I think the whole set-up is a real engineering feat and I am honored that you would share the pleasure of this exclusive patent with me.[474]

The steer head still hangs from the balcony over the great room, facing the front door. It is good working order. Lucky guests at the lodge on rare special occasions still delight in the flashing eyes and smoking nostrils when it is turned on.

ROCKS AND FOSSILA

One of the showpieces of early Woolaroc was the largest block of anthracite ever mined. Frank's good friend J. M. Davis, President of the Delaware, Lackawanna and Western Railroad, helped him produce this wild idea. Frank expressed his interest to Davis who asked W. W. Inglis, President of Glen Alden Coal Company, if he would mine the desired block. On September 7, 1927, Davis wrote that Inglis said the 1,200 pound block of coal was ready to ship but would require very special handling.[475] Davis was so exuberant that he sent a thumbnail sketch about anthracite coal.

> The Glen Alden Coal Company mines more than eleven million tons of anthracite coal per year. Anthracite coal, after being mined, is taken to the top of very tall collieries, or what we commonly call breakers, where the coal is handled over a series of moveable screens, each screen having a different sized mesh, with result they market about one dozen different sizes of coal, known in the trade as lump, grate, nut, stove, pea, barley, rice, etc. The larger sizes wholesale are about eight dollars per ton.[476]

Frank claimed to be bemused. "I knew you were going to send me one but was under the impression I had asked you to attend to getting it for me and you were to let me know the cost so I could reimburse you."[477] Davis delightedly responded,

> About the only way you could repay us for this coal will be to use your influence with the people of Oklahoma to have them discontinue using oil in their power houses, etc., and substitute therefore the good Glen Alden anthracite.[478]

Frank returned that he accepted the Pennsylvania Black Diamond with Davis' compliments, "We will start right away on a campaign to have the people of Oklahoma to use this instead of fuel oil."[479]

So the largest block of anthracite was ensconced at Woolaroc where it became one of Frank's natural history wonders. Two years later the *U. S. Air Services* reporter wondered why anyone would even want such a thing.[480] Visitors to the museum can still see the 2 feet by 3 feet by 1 foot block of coal, cut and polished in a manner that is reminiscent of a tombstone, unobtrusively displayed beneath the case of H. V. Foster's minerals.

Meanwhile, Frank liked his giant horsetail fossil so much that he soon was asking his field men to keep a

For a long time Woolaroc's fragment of dinosaur egg that Dr. Roy Chapman Andrews of the American Museum of Natural History found in the Gobi Desert was the only such display that was privately owned. Frank had good reason to proudly show these Army officers his dinosaur egg exhibit. The guests were at a dinner honoring the War Manpower Commission and Petroleum Administration for War on 26 June 1943. Courtesy Woolaroc

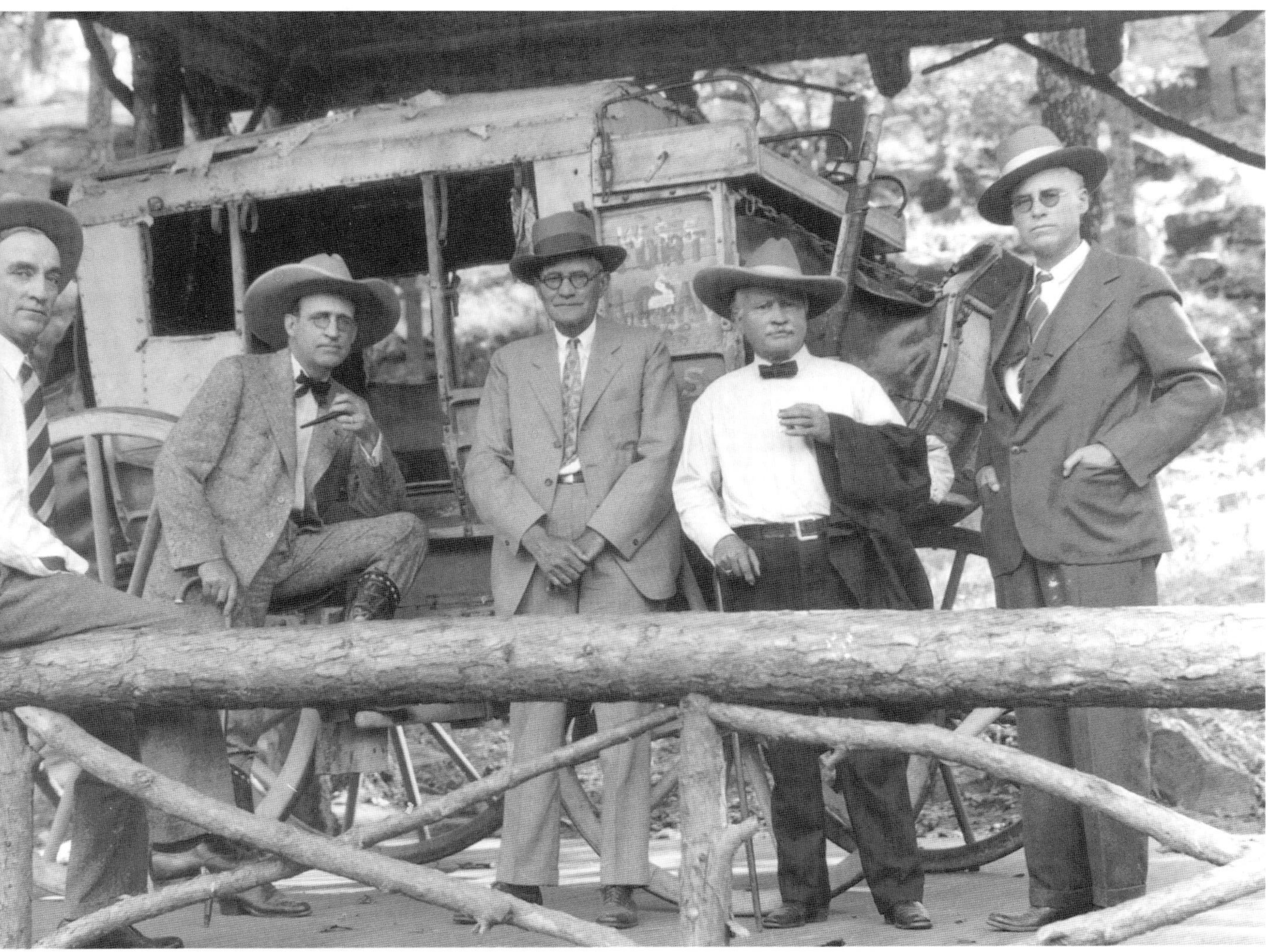

For the 1928 Cow Thieves and Outlaws Reunion Frank ordered L. E. Fitzjarreld to, "find a real stagecoach or don't come back." Just in time, Fitzjarreld's find, a stagecoach that had begun its career in Montana in 1869, arrived at the ranch. It made its Woolaroc premier at the party. Posing in the publicity photographs for the stagecoach are (left to right) George Miller, Frank Phillips, Chief Brown, Pawnee Bill, and Gid Graham. Courtesy Woolaroc.

lookout for some other interesting fossils.[481] How successful this technique was is not clear, but his San Angelo, Texas, district agent eventually put him in contact with Smug Byler of Valentine, Texas, a fellow that had a fossil business. Byler produced a good shipment of fossils in January of 1928. Then, in May, he was on the hunt for the really big one.

> Frank, I want you to know how things are here on this fossil business. I believe I can get you some real interesting fossils but I might fail, but as I say, I don't think so. But to get these a fellow will have to get way back in the sticks away from the beaten trains—places that are hard to reach in and near the river here in the big bend from 100 to 200 miles from railway where there are practically no roads at all, it is hard on rubber and takes gas; I am more than willing to go and try and get these things, but I wanted you to understand the lay.
>
> I will go over to Mexico at places where I here [sic] that some of the large mastadon [sic] bones are still there.[482]

Weeks later Frank asked Smug to find some rock crystals with water in them. Smug replied,

> I will take a trip after the water rocks you mention and will get the best that can be had. They are mined near Abeline [sic], Texas, two days car trip from here one way. There is an old fellow living here that knows where they are and I'll take him along with me.[483]

As promised, on June 1, Smug sent a set of mammoth teeth. He claimed each tooth weighed 17 pounds but warned they were brittle. Sure enough, they arrived badly broken. He had not located a water crystal, yet, but had sent a piece of mammoth tusk and was on the trail of some petrified fossils. At last, on June 18, he sent one of the water rock crystals. It was quite a feat. "The old man here valued this rock at $200.00 and I traded him a 40 acre lease for it which I could sell at $40.00. . . "[484] Finally, in August, Byler was discouraged about finding good mastodon fossils. Along the way, he shipped Frank a pair of Golden eagles, a jar of rattlesnake rattles, some coyote pups, and offered a jaguar. The coyotes were not happily received. Smug also shipped Frank lots of cacti—even some of the giant saguaros—but none survived in the Oklahoma climate. The crystals were probably imbedded in the fountain outside the lodge where, over the years, they seem to have been broken off as souvenirs.

The Lotos Club in New York was one of the important points where Frank's wide network of acquaintances made contact. The club feted writers, artists, politicians, generals, scientists, musicians, and explorers—just about all the names at the cutting edge of their era appeared at Lotos Club state dinners. Through the Club, Frank's growing interest in fossils had brought him into contact with Dr. Roy Chapman Andrews of the American Museum of Natural History in New York City. Andrews was a noted explorer of Central Asia and had spent the previous 12 years heading rewarding and expensive expeditions in the Gobi Desert of Mongolia. There he discovered the very productive areas where modern paleontologists are again finding some of astounding revelations from the Age of Dinosaurs. Among his discoveries on that trip were the very first dinosaur eggs.

Frank was interested in Andrews' work and was a supporter of the museum. It was to Andrews that Frank turned for help with a very personal problem. In 1932, John Phillips' marriage to Mildred broke up. Deeply concerned for his son, Frank made a hefty contribution to the Museum of Natural History, and Andrews arranged to send John along on an archaeological survey expedition to Bolivia with Dr. Wendell C. Bennett. The evening before the expedition sailed for South America, Frank and Jane gave a bon voyage dinner for 35 friends in New York. At the dinner, Dr. Andrews presented Frank with a dinosaur egg—or at least a stand with a fragment of the dinosaur eggs he had discovered in 1923, along with a plaster replica of an entire egg, belonging to the Colgate University Museum, nestled in some of the Gobi Desert sand. At the time, it was the only dinosaur egg that was privately owned.[485] Frank promptly placed the egg on display in his growing museum at Woolaroc, another of his remarkable collection of curiosities. Today the display is downstairs in the same room as the *Woolaroc.* It is still a well-known feature at the museum and now as much of historical interest as of scientific.

The piece of giant horsetail must have still been on display at Woolaroc in 1936, for C. O. Dobbins, of the First National Bank in Bartlesville, presented the museum a piece of petrified wood from Labette County, Kansas. It seems to have been another piece of horsetail, from the Marmaton Formation of the Lower Pennsylvanian age. Dobbins referred to the age of the giant tree-ferns which may mean he was thinking of the original horsetail when he made the gift.[486]

Frank's field men located one of his most spectacular fossil acquisitions in 1939. It seems the Phillips 66 filling station in Lamar, Colorado, was constructed from the local petrified wood. In June, Phil Phillips wrote Frank that Ted Lyon, the division manager in Wichita, had located a source of two carloads of petrified wood.[487] It was a difficult deal to make. Lyons was very careful that the parties did not realize who was buying the fossils. He learned that the land was mortgaged to the Federal Land Bank in Wichita and got their permission to acquire the petrified wood. Meanwhile they learned of other fields near Lamar and considered the possibility of simply buying the land. It was all over in days. W. E. Carlin wrote the assistant vice president of the Federal Land Bank, "Most of the petrified logs that were readily available have been carried away and I believe it is a good idea to get part of this petrified wood in the hands of some who will appreciate having it."[488] Frank's agent bought 48,000 pounds of petrified wood from Robert Colson, the lessor, in Township 27 of Prowers County, Colorado. The fossilized logs still lay where Frank had them placed in front of the museum.

Frank's mineral collections are most significant as

markers of events and friendships in his life. One of the most meaningful collections is the last, posthumous, gift of H. V. Foster. Vernon and Frank, two of the giants who built the Oklahoma oil industry, spent their entire adult lives living in the same town. They shared many a dinner party, many a poker game, and many a smoke-filled room. They were good friends. H. V. died in June of 1939, and Frank was an honorary pallbearer at his funeral. The next year, Marie Foster decided to make a gift to Woolaroc. Frank wrote,

> Referring to our conversation at Mr. Burlingame's the other night, I want you to know how grateful I am to you for advising that you are going to give me Vernon's mineral collection for the ranch. I have nothing of the kind and therefore it certainly will add greatly to my museum.[489]

The collection was on display before Christmas. "I have never received anything in connection with my museum project which has pleased me more."[490] The Foster mineral collection is a beautiful and thoughtfully assembled collection of mineral specimens. True to his word, Frank displayed the collection in a place of prominence, in a permanent case, a loving memorial to his old friend, one of the kings of the American petroleum industry.

One of the last curios in the mineral collections came three years after Frank's death, but is so in character with the spirit of his collections it can not be passed by. The Atomic Energy Division of Phillips Petroleum Company, in Idaho Falls, Idaho, managed to get "a sample of the desert sand, fused by the first atomic explosion created by man on July 16, 1945, near Alamagordo, New Mexico."[491] A generation of Bartlesville school children remember staring wide-eyed at that exhibit. Among the wonders of Woolaroc, the atomic sand takes its place, an odd reminder of the progressivism of Phillips' research and the amazing era in which Frank Phillips lived.

All Kinds of Stuff

In 1934, a newspaper reporter described the Woolaroc Museum as "a collection of curiosities," but already the character of the collection was beginning to coalesce.[492] It was a frontier collection, especially an early Oklahoma collection. Frank had the lodge decorated in Western style, with comfortable furniture, Western paintings and animal horns and heads on the walls, and Navajo blankets and rugs. His friends quickly pitched in with generous and enthusiastic gifts that were usually very appropriate to the place. An undated list, from 1927, gives an early peek at the beginning of the collections.

Dining Room

Large collection of swords, guns and relics—Bert Gaddis
Sword fish—Bert Gaddis
Old-time turkey gun—Felix Dupont
Frontier model ivory-handled six shooter—L. U. Gaston
Old-time percussion cap Kentucky
Squirrel rifle—H. V. Foster
Indian beaded scarf—Shoshone tribe—Arthur Lamb
Old Indian telegraph drum—Hopi tribe-Mr. & Mrs. J. S. Leach
Braided calf-skin riding bridle—Uncle Bill Childers
Indian drum—Mrs. H. V. Foster
Camel hide—I. S. Horne
Diamond back rattlesnake skin—Geo. B. Keeler

Patio

Suit of armor—J. Steinfeld
Mounted Hooded crane of India—I. S. Horne
Wooden figures—Chief Woolaroc and squaw—L. E. Phillips

Big Living Room

Pair of horns from Texas longhorn steer—Amon G. Carter
Small table clock—Mr. & Mrs. John Kane
Bronze statue of cowboy roping calf—New York friends
Mounted moose head—Bert Gaddis
Painting of Western cowboy (over east mantle)—Robt. Shipley
Mounted elk head—Bert Gaddis
Mounted elk head (over east mantle)—Mr. Ruble (Pawhuska)
Pieces of carved wood with Mexican emblems—John Phillips
Chinese pipe—E. W. Lenders
Walrus skull and tusks—V. Foster
Oil painting "Unwritten History"—Bert Gaddis
Indian waterjug and sling—Dorothy Wentz
Hunting horn—Texas Longhorn Society
Coyote hide—Waite Phillips
Bobcat hide—Waite Phillips
Gray fox hide—Waite Phillips
Small stand table with red marble top—Mrs. Frank Phillips
Table with onyx top—Mr. & Mrs. Burlingame
Stand table with painting of Mexican bull fight on top
—Mrs. Frank Phillips

Moro Rice pot—Philippine Islands—Mrs. Gibson
Western cartridge belts—L. U. Gaston

Balcony

Combination library, or otherwise, table—John Phillips
Oil painting "George Rogers Clark—1777"—Eugene duPont
Oil painting "The Arrow Maker"—M. C. Findlay

Gun Room

Old time Osage Indian pictures—Geo. B. Keeler

Outside

Totem pole used by Northern Alaska Indians (Southwest corner of Lodge)—H. V. Foster
Prairie Schooner used in Crossing Plains in Days of '49 —G. C. Clark493

This list of gifts does not fully describe the first months of Frank's collection. Early letters show that Frank also bought things that pleased him, such as some Indian ethnographic items from Arthur Lamb, a Pawhuska curio dealer, and a tomahawk from Mary Uffelman in Kansas City. Reverend O. M. Millsap, one of the ministers Frank had helped, brought him an old spinning wheel and loom from Tennessee.[494]

After the ox towed Frank's stalled car at Thanksgiving in 1926, Frank had another idea. In 1928, Frank managed to acquire a genuine old stagecoach in time for the Cow Thieves and Outlaws Reunion. Paul Endacott said that Frank told L. E. Fitzjarreld to not come back until he found one. The appointment logs show that Fitzjarreld was in the office February 8, 1928, and not again until September 29, just in the nick of time for the party.[495] How he located the Montana coach is unknown, but Frank bought it for $2,500. Eastern guests were carried from the gate in the vehicle at the Cow Thieves Party, and it saw regular use at various Woolaroc functions for several years before it was brought into the museum display. The vehicle was impressive even in those days.

> Not a single piece of the original materials has ever been replaced. The huge leather straps on which the body of the coach swing and which serve as springs, are still strong and well preserved, while the heavy oak and hickory woods in the wheels and body have weathered year by year until they approach the hardness of steel.[496]

John Gaddis ordered the vehicle from a firm in Concord, Massachusetts, and, beginning in 1869, the coach drove a route from Fort Logan to Helena, Montana. With the ebb and flow of Montana mining and the arrival of the railroad, the stagecoach route changed somewhat over the next forty years, and 625,000 miles later it was retired in 1912. The stagecoach is still one of the most vibrant displays in the museum. Many a visitor has leaned in to look in interest and wonder at the travel conditions of that past era that is illustrated all around them in paintings on the walls.

At the 1929 Cow Thieves and Outlaws Reunion, Frank's neighbor, Mert Keefer, presented a real old-time chuck wagon. It was reputed to have been a veteran of the old cattle drives, brought to the area by Jake Bartles himself.[497] At the picnic, it was hung with pots and kettles and was a feature in some of the photographs taken that day. The cowboys gathered around. Then more of a makeshift bar than a traveling pantry, the wagon was a hit. It, too, was a regular feature of Woolaroc events for years until it was finally retired to a shed with other old wagons, and eventually discarded by Manager Bill Blakemore in the 1970s.

While on vacation in Taos, New Mexico, in 1939, Frank spied an old ox cart and plow which appealed to him and asked Bert Phillips, one of his Taos artist friends, if he would buy them for him. Bert had the things shipped to Frank by June 25.[498] Frank asked for a statement of its origins from the Indian who owned it, and he responded,

> This cart was very useful in the old days, all crops were hauled in on the cart, the ox teams were used, but always a man led the team; four or five men worked together because the carts were scarce and they helped each other with their crops. The plow was used with an ox team with one man leading the ox and another guiding the plow. The cart and plow were made by Lorenzo Casador Martinez and Santiago Martinez.[499]

Evidently, there was a long delay in sending the letter from a Mr. Martinez for, on September 2, Frank had no specific information on the cart. Meanwhile it was put on display, credited as a veteran of the Santa Fe Trail, presented by John G. Phillips.

In 1929, local rancher Mert Keefer presented a real old-time chuck wagon to Frank for the Cow Thieves and Outlaws Reunion. It was claimed that this veteran of cattle drives had actually come to Oklahoma originally with Jake Bartles, the founder of Bartlesville. In the photograph some of Frank's cowboys were making an authentic show of the chuck wagon at the annual shindig. Courtesy Woolaroc.

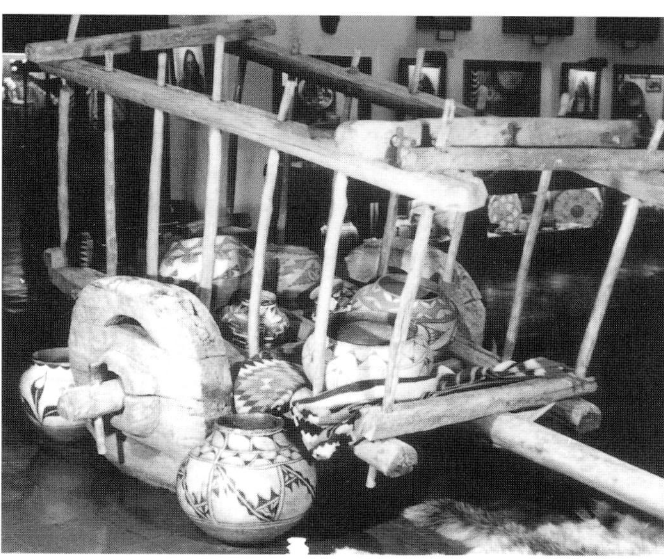

Frank bought this ox cart in Santa Fe on an impulse. Its owner stated that it was made and used locally in the 1890s, but Pat Patterson spun a yarn that it had traveled on the Santa Fe Trail. Here the wizened old cart is displayed in the Museum with an arrangement of Southwest Indian pots. Courtesy Woolaroc.

One of Woolaroc's impressive displays sits quietly beneath the painting *The Run,* amidst a grouping of horn chairs in the museum. It is an unobtrusive small antique desk that was built for the House of Representatives of the Choctaw Nation and served as the Speaker's Desk, Frank was told, of Principal Chief Edmund McCurtain in 1884 until the last meeting in 1911.[500] Pat Hurley presented the desk as a gift to Frank in 1931.[501]

Then, there was the bear trap. As the formal cataloging of the collection began to take place, Marjorie Karch wrote Grif Graham, asking about it. Grif responded in his own inimitable style:

> This old trap belonged to an old time trapper, who worked on the construction crew when the Ranch was first started. His name was Sam Parkhurst. Sam had a lot of traps and had a camp down by the old spring before the big fence was completed. I saw this old trap there in the camp and tried to buy it. He asked $50.00 for the old trap, which was a little unreasonable. Tried several times afterward to buy it, but he would never take less than $50.00. I seized a golden opportunity one time and hid his trap. When Old Sam was preparing to leave out there, he missed his trap and stayed over two or three days, trying to locate it and accused everybody in the place of stealing his trap, but me. I made sure he was plumb out of the country before digging it up, for the very good reason that Old Sam would have had me climbing the black jack trees on the place if he had known I had purloined his trap.[502]

The huge old trap hangs on the wall in the museum shop. Who would guess such an absurd tale is attached to it. And an even sillier curio is the hair ball taken from the stomach of a steer, painted with shellac, and given to Frank by M. L. McClure, Chairman of the Federal Reserve Bank in Kansas City.[503] Such curiosities of old times tend to strike us as random and disorganized, and there is a sense where that is correct, but there is also a unity in the agglomeration that was accumulating. It represents a contact with those things that were sometimes common or sometimes curious to the last generation of frontiersmen who were disappearing from the scene in those days. It was a way to call attention to that disappearing world and to treasure that heritage.

Frank and the Academe

Another early thread was the beginning of a library. As one of the earliest contributions Walter B. Wolf ordered a set of *A Natural History Of The Ducks* from Houghton Mifflin.[504] Frank was beginning to collect good and rare books about natural history and the West. The files contain numerous book orders from Brentanos in New York or orders to bind periodicals. Before 1930, Frank began to build a fine collection of books about the West and about Southwestern Indians. Sources included Dauber & Pine Bookshops in New York, Arthur H. Clark Publishers in Cleveland, Ohio, the University of Oklahoma Press, Oklahoma Geological Survey, *Folk-Say* in Norman, Oklahoma, and the United States Government Printing Office. A few people also gave him historical books and documents. George B. Keeler, a Bartlesville rancher and businessman who married a Cherokee, gave Frank a Cherokee New Testament and hospital bulletin.[505]

Frank was not an educated man but recognized a civic duty and responsibility to support education and academic pursuits. His good friend, E. W. Marland, funded Dr. Joseph B. Thoburn's archaeological expedition at Fort Ferdinandina in northern Kay County and established a local museum for the artifacts. Some of his other friends, such as Marshal Field, had been generously supporting research and exploration for many years. It was only natural that Frank's new-found interest in historical preservation and natural history would quickly lead him into contact with academic circles. By 1927, Frank was seeking resources to help him with his interest in Oklahoma history. Frank's good friend, Patrick Hurley of Tulsa, who became Herbert Hoover's Secretary of War, told him of Grant Foreman's new book, *Pioneer Days in the Early Southwest,* and sent him a copy.[506] Hurley was anxious for Frank to become acquainted with Foreman, so Frank wrote a friendly letter to Muskogee, Oklahoma, and invited Foreman to drop by the ranch.[507]

For such an auspicious beginning, the Grant Foreman correspondence is that of a potential relationship that never really gelled. Foreman was intently focused on his writing and his research. Frank was more interested in a resource person and not interested in the day to day work of a historian. Foreman sent an animated, handwritten letter from the Cosmos Club in Washington, D. C., where he was staying while researching his new book. On his return to Oklahoma, he wrote Frank of his excitement in discovering a treaty between the Osage and Cherokee on August 9, 1822 to end their bitter warfare, and of his discovery that one of the signers was an Osage man named Skitook.[508] Frank referred him to the Indian Agent, George Wright, for further information.

A few months later, Foreman was back in Muskogee, in the full bloom of a successful research trip; he wrote Frank a 14-page essay on the extensive resources of early Oklahoma history, and the deplorable condition of the archives. "I have the authority of a very eminent historian in the East that a number of years ago, perhaps fifteen or twenty, I have forgotten exactly, the head of the Interior Department directed those in charge to 'strip the files' in these old records." He suggested that Frank might be interested in funding a massive project of copying and publishing the old archives. He thought there were probably 10,000 useful pages in the Indian Office alone.[509] The letter arrived in New York while Frank was in France, so that the response was delayed until December. Probably the project was not showy enough to appeal to Frank. He pled absorption in too many other projects, "together with the present depression in the oil business" as his excuse for turning Foreman down.[510]

Grant Foreman kept Frank apprised of the publication of each of his books over the next several years, and they are in the Woolaroc Library. In 1938, Grant Foreman was a guest at the ranch. It was the only record of any visit by him. He sent Frank an autographed copy of *A Traveler in Indian Territory* inscribed, "As a token of appreciation for your gracious hospitality and a delightful evening at Woolaroc on May 3, 1938. . . " He tried one more time to interest Frank in his scholarship, "I used to have grand visions of some great achievements in the realm of research and the accumulation of a wealth of material for others to use. But I have given that up and my ambition now is to complete a few more books. . . "[511] Frank did agree to buy all the remaining copies of his *A Traveler in Indian Territory.*[512]

The University of Oklahoma was more successful in interesting Frank in supporting scholarly programs. In the winter of 1927, Dr. William Bizzell, the President of the University of Oklahoma, followed up on a suggestion made by Frank that some biology students might do summer field work at the ranch.[513] The arrangement did not work out, but it is the earliest indication that Frank was looking to the university for some credibility for his new interest in historical preservation. By spring E. E. Dale of the history department was in Frank's office. This was probably serious talk about Frank's $10,000 gift to the university for the purchase of historical documents for what would become the Frank Phillips Collection in the library, for John Kane was the next person in Frank's office.[514] Things must have been in the works for several months, and Frank was chummy enough with Dr. Dale, that in February, he asked Dale to help him get the springs on the ranch analyzed by some medical authorities.[515]

Such a large gift in 1928 was a tremendous boost to the university. Frank got what he wanted too. The University of Oklahoma Press sent him a copy of Dr. Dale's new book, *The Cattle Range Industry.* They commented, "Not only myself but all of the people of the state and particularly in University circles are interested in your estate and the things you have been doing for Oklahoma. . . "[516] Frank's gift provided that the University would spend $2,000 each year for five years on the purchase of historical documents. Over the next few years, Dr. Dale was an occasional guest at Woolaroc. A former graduate student of Frederick Jackson Turner, he was a person Frank enjoyed rubbing elbows with, and he may have given some advice and guidance as Frank began to accumulate a private collection and began a small museum.

Ellsworth Collings, of the University of Oklahoma education department, dropped by the ranch and left a copy of his new book, *The 101 Ranch,* and inspected the growing little museum. It was one book that Frank read right away.[517] In 1936, Frank gave another $20,000 to the university, and the Frank Phillips Collection was moved to expanded space in the main library. Grant Foreman's suggestion seems to have born some fruit in the long run. A Wichita paper commented, "The donations are responsible for 100 photostatic manuscripts and documents brought directly from Spain and Mexico."

Spiro

As with most of his other interests, Frank knew practically nothing about archaeology in the early days of the ranch, while he was buying an occasional arrowhead collection or tomahawk from a local collector or receiving as a gift from one of his friends. Indian artifacts added a lot to the Old West ambience at Woolaroc. Archaeology as a science was just moving beyond the age of treasure trove. When Tutankhamen's tomb was discovered in 1922, the gold of kings was all the rage, and humbler pursuits at Pre-Columbian sites in North America barely stirred the dust in academic museums. Still, generous businessmen, like E. W. Marland, funded interesting digs like the Ferdinandina site in Kay County where Taovaya people processed buffalo hides for trade with the French in the 18th century. Such digs added significantly to our developing knowledge of Oklahoma and forestalled looting at significant sites.

By 1935 occasional potholing at the Spiro Mound had escalated into wholesale looting and vandalism after the state legislature passed the first antiquities preservation act in the nation. As a spiteful *coup de grâce* the looters dynamited the ravaged mound. Frank Philips funded the lab that enabled the University of Oklahoma to conduct salvage archaeology at the site. This is a photograph of the mess left by the vandals, before archaeological excavation began. Courtesy Oklahoma Historical Society.

In that context, imagine Frank's visions of himself—virtually supporting another William Flinders Petrie—when, one day in 1936, a man appeared unannounced and showed him a fist full of ancient pearls.[518]

> A fellow showed up in the Phillips offices in Bartlesville. He just appeared there one day out of the blue. He was an old cowboy type, with grizzly sort of looks and he had a beat-up old ragged hat. I went ahead and saw him and he came walking in with a hat filled with pearls. There must have been two or three hundred pearls in that hat. He said he'd been down digging at Spiro and came across some things that might be good for Mr. Phillips' museum. The man wanted to sell the pearls. I immediately brought the old timer in to see Mr. Phillips. It was soon after that that he became involved with the digs at Spiro.[519]

In fact, this was not the first time Frank had been offered contraband from a Mound Builder site. Late in 1935, a J. W. Hale from Wyandotte, Oklahoma, left a box a flints for Frank to consider for purchase. He wrote,

"The flints I left in your care were taken from the burial mound on Elk River about 15 miles south of this place."[520] After a few letters, negotiating the price, Frank purchased 20 arrowheads for $75. This purchase was not especially different from many others small representative collections now displayed on the walls in the pre-history room of the museum. It did not especially presage Frank's important involvement in Spiro.

The Spiro Mound was known to locals for about 100 years before Joseph Thoburn of the Oklahoma State Historical Society discovered and photographed them in 1913. It was a story that is well known to Oklahomans and one of the most startling scandals in the annals of American archaeology. The locals in LaFlore County were mostly Choctaw people who knew the big mounds were burial sites and respected the ancient interments. But, in 1933, a new property owner leased the land to the Pocola Mining Company. This was a partnership of some local people and outsiders who wished to sell the treasure on the antiquities market. Minor pot-holing quickly accelerated to a fever pitch that became wholesale commercial mining. In 1934, Dr. Forrest E. Clements of the University of Oklahoma visited the site, and in 1935, the horror he had witnessed induced the state legislature to pass one of the first acts in the nation prohibiting the digging of archaeological sites. Believing the new antiquities law protected the site, Clements went out of the state during the summer. The looters took the opportunity to ravage the mound and, finally, spitefully dynamite the remnant. The results are an inestimable loss to the understanding of Mound Builders culture in North America.[521]

It was at that moment that Jack Reid pushed his way into Frank's office on May 10, "to see some pearls unearthed in Ark."[522] Frank picked up his ears, and shortly he received a letter from his agent in Muskogee, apprising him of a remarkable collection of Spiro artifacts being offered by John C. Pfalzgraf of Poteau, Oklahoma.[523] Marjorie Karch immediately wrote Pfalzgraf who wanted $2,800 for the lot. On September 3, Frank invited Pfalzgraf to come over to show him the collection for his consideration. Woolaroc archive has a bill of sale from Pfalzgraf and inventory of his collection, dated September 14, 1936.[524] Only weeks after, Lysee wrote Frank about Pfalzgraf's artifacts, Frank was again in contact with Jack Reid of Fayetteville, Arkansas, about his Spiro collection, including about 1,500 pearls.[525] By that time, Reid had made a couple of trips to Bartlesville, hoping to see Frank, only to find him out of town. Frank wrote that he had consulted a New York jeweler who counseled him that the pearls were probably of no value.[526] On September 5, about the time Frank purchased the collection from Pfalzgraf, Reid wrote, "I fully realize that these boys peddled many things from this mound at ridiculously low prices. I am also aware of the fact that I have charge of the only complete collection left, and I can assure you that it is not going to be peddled."[527] There is no record that Frank even answered that letter. Whatever the result, within days Frank's museum director, Lucille Zühlke, wrote Dr. Clements for advice about displaying some new Spiro acquisitions.[528] As a result, she met with Dr. Clements after a talk he was giving in Tulsa, and a few days later wrote him,

> I spoke with Mr. Phillips at length about the work you are engaged in. He was very much interested and I feel quite confident that he would be willing to assist the University, although of course I am not authorized to say so definitely. However, it has occurred to me for you to stop at the Ranch this week if possible as he will be here. . . [529]

Jane Phillips' diary shows that Dr. Clements was a guest at the Ranch that Halloween weekend.

More than a year went by before Clements wrote again. He was sending some Spiro specimens for display in the Woolaroc Museum which had just completed construction of its first addition.[530] Clements was an irregular correspondant, but Lucille Zühlke took a personal interest in keeping the dialog running. "I think Mr. Phillips would be pleased to have a word from you now and then, even though your plans are only an outline. He is taking quite an interest in Oklahoma's very early history."[531] By this time Frank's $6,000 grant had enabled the new archaeology lab at the University of Oklahoma to buy equipment and hire specialists.[532] Frank's involvement was just beginning.

Late in 1938, the university sent a film crew to Woolaroc. They were producing a film about the excavations at Spiro and wished to feature Frank, and Phillips Petroleum Company, as one of the major private benefactors of their research lab. For the filming, Clements brought along Sarah White who was the curator of the Museum of Anthropology at the University of Oklahoma and who was directing part of the film.[533] Sarah White was a beautiful and vivacious young woman with significant intellect and artistic gifts, and she charmed Frank Phillips. Sarah seemed to understand what would appeal most to Frank. "Dr. Clements has been very busy completing a detailed report on his work for Washington. As a direct result, the Works Progress Administration (WPA) office in Oklahoma City received a letter from Washington, D. C., saying our project was the best archaeological project in the United States. That means, among other things, a very wide circulation for the movie."[534] From the time Sarah came on the scene, Frank developed a much closer interest in the Spiro work and the development of the Amerindian story at the museum.

Sarah kept up a lively correspondence with Lucille Zühlke, who became a personal friend, reporting on the various aspects of Spiro and other archaeological interests in the department at the University of Oklahoma, and she encouraged Dr. Clements to provide a more detailed accounting of his expenditure of Frank's initial grant. By the end of the year, Clements produced some additional materials for display at Woolaroc, promised that more was eminent, and went on to praise Frank's museum at Woolaroc.

> It is nice you liked the historic specimens I recently brought to Woolaroc. In a few days the skeleton from this burial will be completed and I think the two together will make a most interesting display. Of course you understand that this is only a small part of the material you will eventually have for your museum. I was delighted with the many acquisitions you have received since I last visited Woolaroc. You are doing a very fine thing with this museum and one which the public institutions of the state seem either unwilling or unable to perform.[535]

Sarah White became actively involved in developing the museum's prehistory exhibits. Access to her expert consultation may have encouraged Frank to add more rooms to the museum. She worked closely with Lucille Zühlke in arranging the archaeological exhibits and moving into the new rooms, which were probably a big part of Lucille's lenghtened tenure and success in the job as museum director. It was Sarah White who designed and constructed the model of the Great Temple Mound Village for display at Woolaroc just in time for the annual directors meeting.[536]

It was Sarah White who convinced Frank to commission the murals on the east wall of the prehistory room.[537] Frank wrote that he always required a sketch for approval. Sarah responded,

> I have talked with the two artists I have in mind to paint the murals. They are graduates of the university so I am familiar with their work and know that it is good. Mr. Ward is head of the Art Department at Oklahoma City University and Mr. Meeks is director of the Art Center in Oklahoma City. By two artists, each one working on a mural under my supervision, I know their research will be authentic and we will obtain the finished murals in half the time. Needless to say, I would not touch a project without your full approval. . . [538]

Before the murals were completed, Sarah married Forrest Clements, and because married women did not pursue careers in those waning days of the Depression, Sarah was forced to do some freelancing.[539] Three months later, Frank was happy to acquire her services at $15 a day.[540]

Clements' work at Spiro was one of the most important archaeological excavations in the United States in those years. There was concern, as WPA funding dried up, that they would not be able to continue the dig. Frank became evasive about renewing his private support. There was relief when the WPA okayed the project for another $100,000 in 1940. Sarah redoubled her enthusiasm for the Woolaroc exhibit, which was an encouragement for Frank. Lucille Zühlke wrote that Frank was asking if there was a chance of securing Sarah as curator at Woolaroc.[541] He must have known that trouble was brewing. The Zühlkes gave notice they were resigning in July. Evidently, Sarah blamed Gordon Matzene for the rift, for when he offered to bring her a basket from New Mexico, she wrote Frank that she did not want Matzene to buy anything for her.[542] Despite their disappointment that Lucille was leaving, it fell to Sarah White and Dr. Clements to try to help Frank find a competent replacement. They recommended two or three people, and Frank finally settled on Miss Margaret Elliott, a University of Oklahoma anthropology graduate who was then working at the University of Texas museum.[543] She only lasted in the job a few months—Frank complained that she was too young and inexperienced and begged Sarah to come and bring Dr. Clements along. "May I say that if you could let me know whenever it is convenient for you to come up for a day or two, or longer, in practically every instance I could arrange to send a plane to the Oklahoma City airport and also return you there. I made the round-trip one day last week in ninety-two minutes. . . "[544] They devoted two weekends right away. Sarah White was a first-class unofficial development officer for the university.

After working most of December to get the new pre-history room exhibits set up, she wrote they would be needing more grant money after the first of the year.[545] Out of the blue Frank responded, "Arizona and New Mexico authorities seem anxious to make contributions to me rather than me give to them."[546] It did not take Dr. Clements too long to learn why Frank was feeling peevish. "I have heard that you have been told that a man in Tulsa has a much better collection of prehistoric material than you have, and that he obtained this material from the university."[547] He explained that Clark Field of Tulsa took an early interest in Spiro and had a small collection that he acquired before the University of Oklahoma became involved, but that he did have a very large collection of Indian baskets and perhaps that was the collection his informant was thinking of. "You have the only complete collection of Oklahoma archaeology on display anywhere."[548]

Frank was completely charmed by Sarah White who was the beautiful and immensely talented curator of the archaeology collection at the University of Oklahoma. When he became balky about funding the Spiro grant for another year, Sarah invited Frank to the dig, and saw to it that he made some finds. In this snapshot Frank and Sarah admire a burial and ceramic find on the spring 1941 day when Frank participated at the Spiro dig. Courtesy Woolaroc.

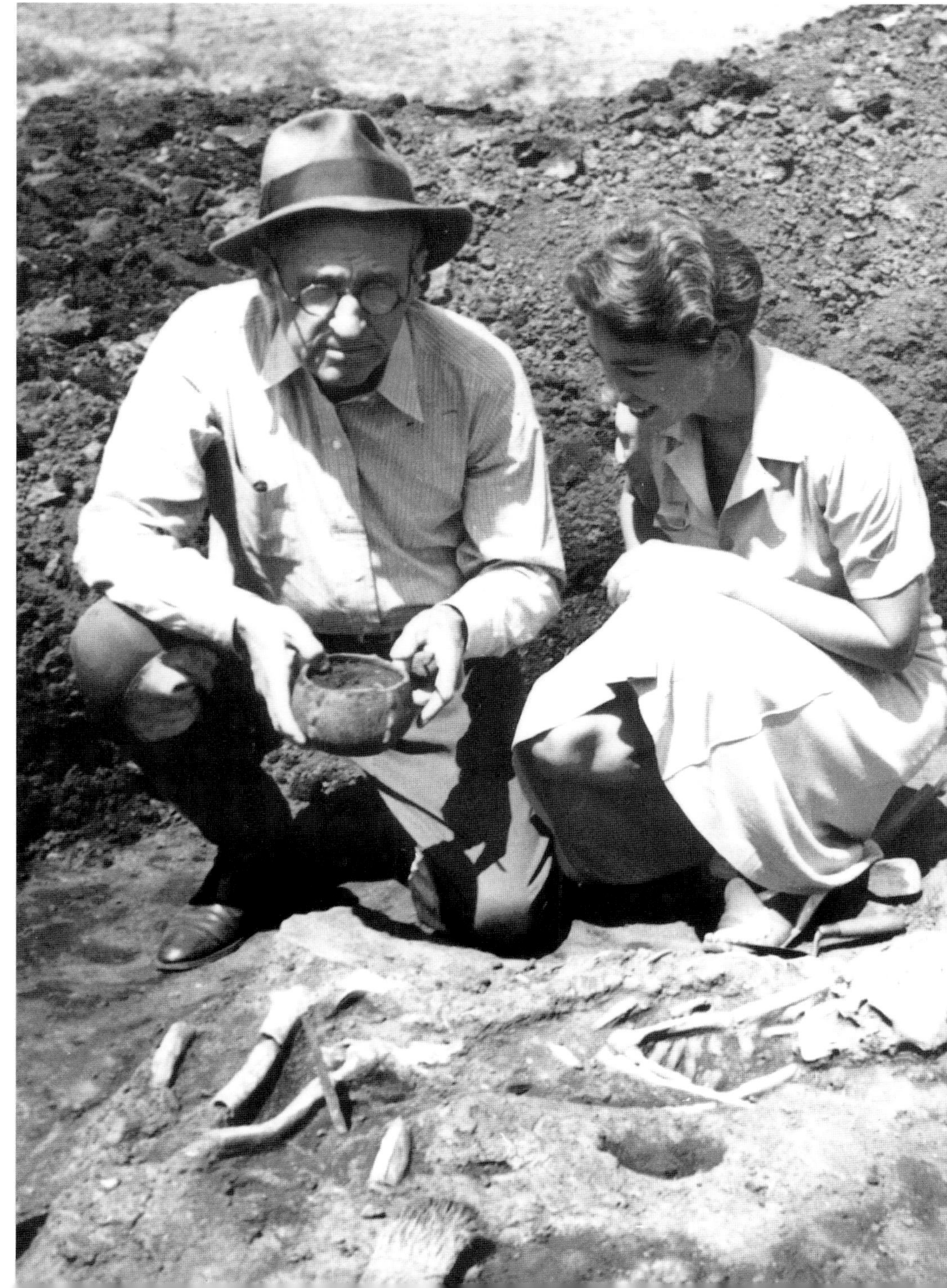

They hoped Frank was placated. To their relief, in March, they were able to report the WPA project funding was continued. After convincing Frank to do the murals, they proposed another grant, this time $6,300, but, disappointingly, this time the foundation only gave $3,000.[549] Undaunted, they thanked him enthusiastically and arranged for Frank to come along on a dig. On June 14, Frank left his office at 9:00 A.M., dressed in his riding jodhpurs, to fly over to Fort Smith, Arkansas, to participate in the excavation. When he returned 12 hours later, Frank had had a great time.[550] Why not? Grubbing around in the dirt, Frank miraculously managed, in one afternoon, to locate a burial and find a boatstone which sheltered a ceramic bowl and two projectile points.[551]

Frank was charmed by Sarah and Clements always had been fun for Frank. An irreverent academic, he was just bohemian enough to attract Frank's fancy. One episode belongs in the annals of Woolaroc's most audacious moments. Dr. Clements wrote Frank, asking a favor for an older anthropologist. Dr. John P. Harrington of the Bureau of American Ethnology was respected in his time as the foremost ethnologist in his field. Clements enclosed a copy of Dr. Harrington's letter.

> When I bad farewell to an old Navajo medicine man, Sam Tilden, at Fort Wingate, N.M. last fall, he charged me with obtaining certain "medicine" which he needs for his special line of singing to make no doubt a barren woman "birth" a baby. He told me that the way to make a hit with him was to get the c-u-n-t of a female buffalo, and the p-e-c-k-e-r of a male buffalo, to cut them out with a butcher knife and put them in a box full of salt, to "salt" them this way and send them to him through the mail, and he by his buffalo chant will be using the same — evidently to knock up the hard cases which he accepts in medical practice. In all sincerity the old fellow needs these parts, and if he receives them will no doubt be willing to come across with a lot of mystical information.[552]

Of course Frank came through, and the staff mailed the shipment to Tilden in August.[553] Doubtless the local grapevine clucked and Frank's cosmopolitan Eastern friends chortled for months—anything for the advancement of science.

World War II ended the active University of Oklahoma dig at Spiro. The WPA money ended, and the manpower went off to war. But, Frank's academic contacts with the university were well established. However fitfully, Frank had made a large contribution to higher education in Oklahoma. His grants in history and archaeology are still bearing fruit for another generation of scholarship. The academic community was grateful, and along the way he had made genuine friends. Dr. Dale was the president of Phi Beta Kappa at the time. Whatever the genesis of the suggestion, in 1942 Frank's friends at the university were in enthusiastic agreement that Frank, who had not even graduated from high school, ought to be inducted into that most honorific fraternity. Sarah Clements wrote, "Phi Beta Kappa is an international organization and neither Forrest nor I nor anyone else could politic to obtain membership for you—it had to be earned."[554] Clearly the sentiments were genuinely held that Frank's generosity toward academic research merited recognition, and the quality of the museum program at Woolaroc by that time was an immense contribution to higher learning in Oklahoma. Frank himself was a man of personal intellectual accomplishment. Frank's Phi Beta Kappa key was one of his most cherished awards, and he wore it the rest of his life.

Frank was able to augment the pre-history room with a small collection of South American artifacts brought from there by John G. Phillips. John had an arduous adventure in the backcountry of Bolivia with Dr. Wendell C. Bennett of the Museum of Natural History in New York in the summer of 1932. Not a scholar by inclination, he participated in an expedition that surveyed sites in Bolivia and seemed to take an interest in their archeological finds and the cultural continuity of the people in the area.[555] Dr. Bennett forwarded some relics from Nasca and Chimu, Pre-Inca burials that John presented to Frank.[556] These included a mummy, in poor condition and buried in a flexed position, textile burial shrouds, and burial goods from the American Museum of Natural History. John also presented several items from the historical period. A year later, John sent his father two Ecuadorian shrunken heads as a Christmas present, with a letter describing the shrinking process.[557] Until recently both displays were still to be seen in the pre-history room, the shrunken heads still stirring the same excitement in every class of grade school children that passed through the museum.

In addition, Frank purchased a collection of Peruvian artifacts from Rudolph Rhein of Tulsa in 1937.[558] In 1938, John H. Kane presented an authenticated Inca topos, or hair ornament, which once belonged to Atahualpa, and, in 1939, Pete French of St. Louis gave a small collection from the Bush Negroes of Dutch Guiana.[559] Together, they all make a very diverse and disjointed collection of assorted South American interests.

Sarah Clements had reason to take personal pride when she wrote, "Forrest was very pleased with the 'Dawn of History' room. He says it is the best archaeological display he has ever seen anyplace."[560] Ellsworth Collings wrote similar sentiments after a visit in 1945. "I recently had the pleasure of visiting again the museum on your ranch. I want to congratulate you on the improvements you have made since I visited it the last time. I consider it one of the most interesting and valuable museums this side of New York City."[561]

Cowboys and Indians

The collections of guns, spurs, Indian ethnology, saddles, and so forth, just naturally came with the growth of Woolaroc. Bert Gaddis' gun collection, the long guns given by DuPont and Foster, and occasional notable weapons, donated by L. U. Gaston of the Bartlesville Police Department, soon graced the walls or hung over the bar at the lodge. Guests gave him Indian moccasins or buckskin and beadwork clothing items that they knew were important but were only problems in their own homes. Spurs, bridles, saddles, even the skull of Henry Wells' horse began to accumulate in earnest as the museum took on the character of a Western collection.

The various weapons never did coalesce as a collection. Gaddis' guns and swords decorated the lodge early. Police Chief Gaston occasionally gave Frank a gun, probably those taken from criminals. The local American Legion Post presented Frank with some captured German trophies.[562] J. A. Richards presented a half dozen swords in 1930.[563] A friend, A. V. Muzzy of Tulsa, displayed his collection at Woolaroc for a time in the early 1930s, but the collection was returned to him a few years later.[564] Major General Hoffman even contributed his own presentation sword and some dueling pistols in 1939. The collections never assumed a unified character. Some were returned, some given away, some traded. Hoffman's sword is now in the 45th Infantry Museum in Oklahoma City.

From an early date L. E. Phillips had loaned Frank some family treasures and an assortment of items he picked up on his various travels. The L. E. Phillips Collection included numerous items such as a soap dish that had belonged to their mother, containing a piece of her homemade soap; Lewis Phillips' Civil War discharge papers; some McGuffey Readers; a stone from Nazareth and some water from the Jordan; an assortment of curios from Japan, China, and Mongolia; and some spent ordinance from World War I. In 1938, L. E. wrote Frank to remind him that several trophies in the museum were loans from him. "While I am not an 'Indian giver' and at this moment I have no intention of asking for the return of any of these articles, I am detecting in my own sons the desire to become collectors. . ."[565]

He was sure enough right about his boys' developing proclivities. Only a few years later his son, Phil Phillips, was seriously collecting guns, and he gave one to Frank as a gift. Unlike most of the other guns at the ranch, this one was a collector's item, and Frank realized it. "While I thanked you personally for the gun you gave me, realization of its importance in value and the fact that it came with your compliments makes me want to write this little note."[566] His appreciation was prophetic.

Phil Phillips became a true collector, especially of Colt Paterson firearms and a devoted patron of Woolaroc Museum. Before his death, he gave Woolaroc the nation's most extensive collection of Joe Beeler artwork, Thomas Moran's *Ruins of Old Church, Cuernavaca,* and his collection of Colt firearms. The Phil Phillips Collection of Colt Paterson firearms is one of the best in the nation, and the Paterson handgun portion is possibly the best in the nation. It was his pride and joy, and he took personal interest in the special room built downstairs to display his guns. Woolaroc finally has a gun collection of which to be proud.

Besides these, Phil also gave the peace medals and Indian, Oriental, and Steuben crystal, and contemporary Western artists' collections. Phil and Lee Phillips and the Lee Phillips family have given large collections of Western art, including works by Frederic Remington, Charles M. Russell, Frank Tenney Johnson, and others. Other collections of Doughty birds, books, graphic art, sculpture, and miscellaneous other items have come from the L. E. Phillips branch of the family as a memorial to L. E. and Node Phillips, occupying most of the lower level of the museum. These well-organized collections are the product of thoughtful and persistent collectors and the continued generosity of the Phillips family.

Shortly after the museum first opened, Frank received correspondence from E. W. Lenders in which he willed Frank several items presented to him by Buffalo Bill back in 1910 and it was witnessed by his wife Carrico Lenders.[567] Only a few days later, Lenders wrote Frank a desperate letter. It seems he owed Bert Gaddis for a long-overdue loan on a car, and Gaddis had finally located and attached Lenders' valuables in storage in Tulsa. From New York, Frank declined to intercede. The case was thrown out of court, and Lenders recovered the Buffalo Bill saddle.[568] The danger passed, Lenders seems to have forgotten his former urge to philanthropy and a couple of years later he suddenly died. To everyone's shock, it was learned that the gift to Frank of the Buffalo Bill saddle had been scratched from the will. Right away the Phillips legal department determined the change to the will probably would not hold up in court because it had not been witnessed and dated. While Frank was in New York, M. S. Kerr and R. B. Fummer of the company's Oklahoma City Office went to visit with Mrs. Lenders. To their relief, they learned she intended to eventually turn the saddle outfit over to Frank. Frank quickly wrote her, "I am not personally interested in taking part in a contest."[569] Over the next several years, she attempted to sell Lenders' collection of ethnographic specimens. She thought it was "worth about $37,000; you to advance her the sum of $15,000 on same and take her note with the collection as security," a tremendous sum in those days, and far beyond what Frank was willing to pay.[570] The Gilcrease Museum bought the collection in 1950 from Carrico's heirs for $17,500.[571] Sadly, Frank had missed a significant opportunity.

In 1937, some of Frank's friends surprised him with the Buffalo Bill saddle and other items as a gift, for which Frank thanked them profusely.[572] Years later, the *La Crosse Tribune* contacted Senator Robert S. "Bob" Kerr about how he managed to acquire the saddle for Frank. He responded that he had no recollection of how they were acquired.[573]

In 1926, Lenders was in possession of another historic saddle.[574] It was the saddle that Theodore Roosevelt used when visiting the Mulhall Ranch the summer of 1900, when he came to Oklahoma City to attend a Rough Riders' convention. When Lenders sold it is not known, but it was an undated early gift to Woolaroc from Mrs. Blanche Lucas of Ponca City. Gordon Hines of Ponca City offered Pancho Villa's saddle to Frank for $250, but Frank declined.[575] Another undated historic saddle was a gift from Pawnee Bill, the sidesaddle Mrs. Lillie used when she made her appearance before the crowned heads of Europe.[576]

Whatever saddles were displayed in the early days, before the historic saddle collection was assembled, C. E. Hochstetler of the comptroller's department thought the museum had a glaring omission. "While viewing the saddle collection, it was remarked that there was no ladies side saddle of the early time style included therein. . . "[577] Hochstetler's mother happily donated a saddle she had used around 1900. It had a fancy upholstered seat of red tapestry design mohair. Some time after that, Mrs. Leonard Copple of Sedan, Kansas, donated a plainer side saddle from about 1880.[578]

One saddle can be called the genuine article. It is displayed with a horse's skull and hoofs; it is Henry Wells' saddle.

> Henry Wells, Silas Meggs and Al Spencer, famous bank robbers of the early days were returning on horseback from Stroud, Okla., to their hideout in the Osage, after having gone to Stroud to look over a bank they planned to, and did, rob the next day. On a spot not more than 400 yards to the southeast of the museum they ran into a posse consisting of the following men: H. M. Freas, Osage County Sheriff, Deputy Sheriff Hedgepath, Big Carlo Marion, C. S. Cooksey, Dick Paris, Uncle Bill Childers, Ed Ellis, and Grif Graham, who shot Wells' horse from under him. Henry escaped however with two of his companions. Passing the same spot the next day, enroute to Stroud for the robbery, he found his horse still breathing, but beyond help, so he shot him through the forehead. Last year (1934) he recalled the incident which took place in 1915, to Grif Graham, the only surviving member of the posse. The animal's skull, shoes, and saddle were found and presented to Mr. Phillips by Mr. Wells, who in 1935 is now living within a few miles of F.P.R.[579]

The 101 Ranch Saddle is part of the collection of items from the 101 Ranch. There is also a dimutive saddle and chaps used by Zack Miller as a child. Much of the collection—photographs, spurs, bridles, lariats, and show stuff—came to Woolaroc as a gift from the Ellsworth Collings' estate. Collings had a small museum at the Bar

C Dude Ranch at Turner Falls, Oklahoma, that he called The Cowboy Museum where he had managed to assemble very respectable collections from the cowboy era. After his death, in 1974, his widow called Woolaroc to ask if the museum would like Collings' collections. Bob Lansdown, Curt Sydebotham, and Clyde Moore quickly drove to Davis, Oklahoma, to pick them up. When they got there, Mrs. Collings had already packed things up neatly to help them out.

Unfortunately, all the labels had become separated from the articles. It is a sad thing to shuffle through the Collings' file in the office. Scribbled in pencil, often on the back of The First National Bank of Davis checks, are the orphaned tags. One tag says, "37 Will James' spur—spur used by Will James great cowboy & artist." Another tag says, "This spur was worn by Henry Frass for 5 years. They were made by Gene Hays at Huntsville Prison. Gene Hays cowboy stole some of Frass' cattle and was caught, convicted, and sentenced to prison. He gave Frass the spurs to show the old spirit of the West. I got caught and am taking my medicine like a man. I'm not mad at you Henry."[580]

In the cases are beautiful pairs of gal-leg spurs that must have been the pride and joy of some cowboys, working spurs that must have seen some real cattle drives, an historic branding iron collection, a barbed wire collection, and bridles. Among these were 101 Ranch things and photographs. They are accoutrements that augment the display of the 101 Ranch show saddle.

As the 101 Ranch's financial troubles compounded in the late 1930s, Zack Miller sent three show saddles to Woolaroc as collateral for a $500 interest-free loan. Two were jeweled and inscribed "Joe C. Miller," and the other was silver mounted, inscribed "Zack T. Miller."[581]

Frank's Bartlesville jeweler examined them immediately and thought the jewels were mostly doublets.[582] Frank followed with correspondence to the New York jeweler who made the ornamentation. He responded that the saddle made in 1910 contained about $3,000 worth of ornaments at the prices of the day; the saddle made in 1914 contained about $1,500 worth of ornaments, but many of the jewels were imitation.[583]

Zack was becoming desperate for cash to pay his legal expenses. He hoped that Frank would loan him the money or buy the jeweled saddle. When Frank demurred, he began to try to find buyers. Finally, Frank purchased two of the three saddles, the Buffalo Saddle and the Myres Saddle for cancellation of Zack's debt to Frank.[584]

The Buffalo Saddle is made of buffalo hide and has copper trim; the Myres Saddle was the one with the imitation jewels, made by Sam Myres of Sweetwater, Texas. The third saddle, the Wyeth Saddle, or the 101 Ranch Saddle, from Wyeth Hardware in St. Joseph, Missouri, was returned to Zack Miller. It is now displayed in the Texas Ranger Hall of Fame Museum in Waco, Texas.

Not long after this, Frank contacted Mable Mix, the widow of actor Tom Mix, about buying her husband's saddle.[585] Mrs. Mix offered the entire Tom Mix collection of memorabilia, but Frank only wanted a saddle. A month later, the trust officer at the bank wrote that the estate had a buyer, and Frank missed another chance to acquire an interesting collection from the Hollywood Wild West. In November, Jane Phillips gave Frank the saddle he wanted. There is no record of how she acquired it.[586] It was the first saddle used by Tom Mix. It was possibly used by Mix on the 101 Ranch, and he also used it in his first movies.[587]

The Frank Phillips collections became a museum of ethnology and natural history, a Romantic vision of the Old West. By 1942, the following collections were at Woolaroc: the Frank Phillips collection of heads and horns; articles received from L. E. Phillips, June 6, 1941; pottery from New Mexico; the Phoenix collection; the Sharp Indian Rug Collection; Matzene's jewels; the lodge inventory; the Matzene collection of oriental and South Seas art; miscellaneous; the library; South American, Philippines, Australia, and South Seas collections; arms; mounted fish, birds, and reptiles; plaques and trophies; American Indian collection.[588]

As Frank hoped, the legacy has persisted. The most recent exhibit opened in the summer of 1999. It was the result of another fortuitous accident. For a long time, curator Ken Meek had been asking for a complete buffalo skeleton for exhibit. Late in 1998 an opportunity opened. Glen Miller said his ranch hands had just worked the buffalo in December of 1998, and the following day it had turned cold and there was ice on the pond when they found one of the biggest bulls by Stone Lake, gored and with a broken leg. He had been fighting—as bulls are wont to do. In the wild he would have died mercilessly in the elements after days of suffering. Glen quickly called the museum to ask Bob Lansdown what to do. It was

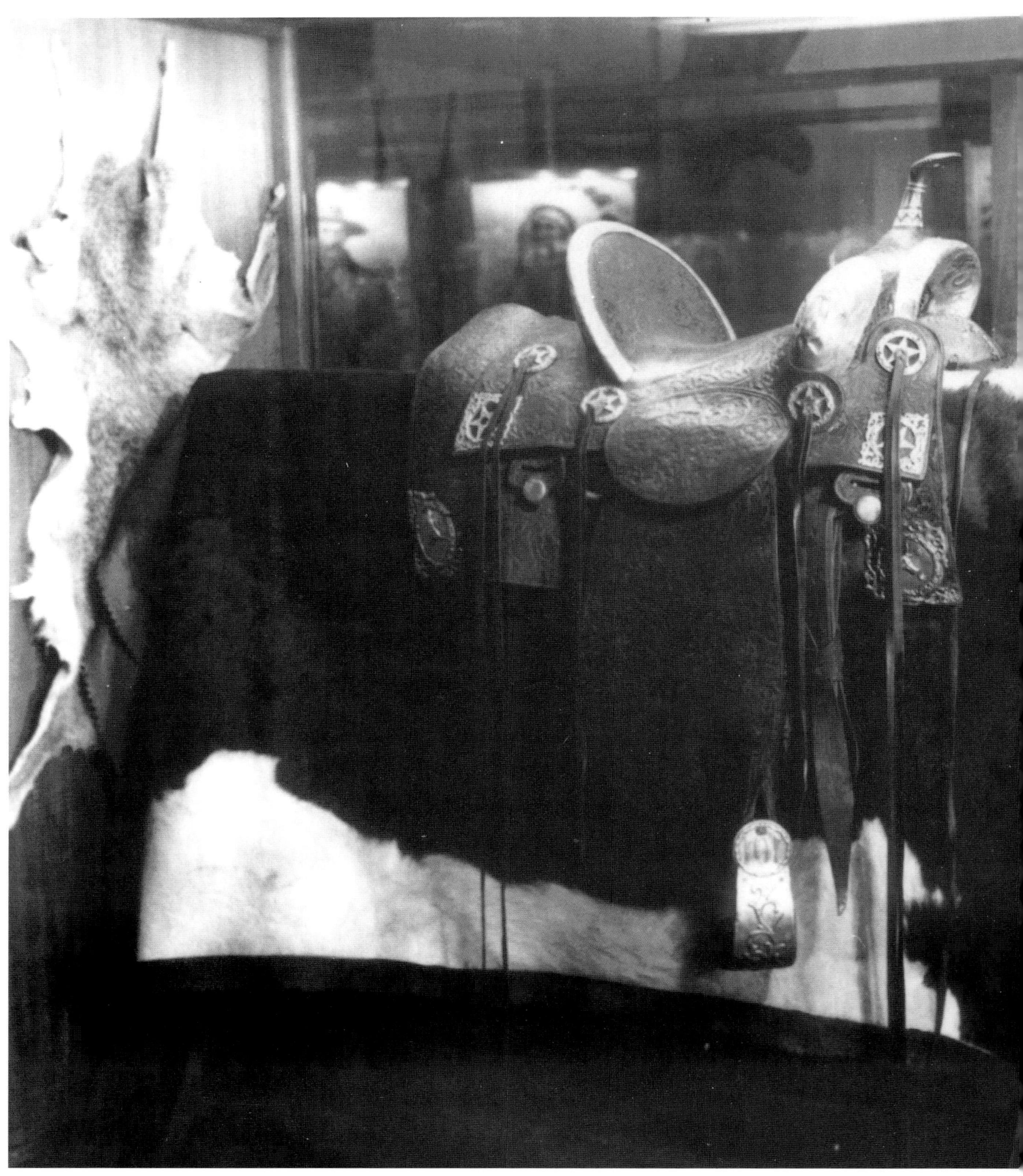

decided to try to get a full mount from the 1,600 pound bull. The men shot the old bull, and Ralph Thomason carefully field-dressed the carcass. It took an hour to flesh and salt the skin for Thomason to take to Lakeside Taxidermy in Copan, Oklahoma.

By January, everyone knew the full mount would work out, and there was an air of excitement about the new display they hoped to have by spring. Ken Meek began plans for an exhibit about the days of the buffalo. The men in the work shop, Curtis Sydebotham and Clyde Moore, began to build tall, triangular kiosks for hanging the displays. Every few days, General Manager Dick Miller talked to Ralph Thomason, and a buzz of anticipation would ripple through the office and out into the shop. The job was a big one; the buffalo was slow coming along.

The museum hosted a book signing for Michael Wallis' new book, *The Real Wild West,* in May. It included an exhibit of the Murphy 101 Ranch Collection, which was an opportunity to bring together two principal collections of 101 Ranch memorabilia. That event slowed down the preparations for the opening of the buffalo exhibit, but finally on July 17, the exhibit was opened at a preview for Friends of Woolaroc. On the day of the opening, the taxidermist spent the afternoon fluffing the hair on the buffalo, a perfection he had never enjoyed in life. People gathered at 6:30 in the evening for drinks and hors d'oeuvres and slowly walked among the new displays, and round and round the gargantuan trophy. After a while, they sat in chairs or stood around the perimeter while Dick Miller explained about the full mount buffalo as an inspiration for the new buffalo exhibit, then Ken Meek gave an engaging talk about the natural history of the buffalo. Around the room buffalo heads that Frank collected long ago glared down on the crowd. *In the Teeth of the Blizzard* hung on one of Curt and Clyde's triangular kiosks, a reminder of the Woolaroc herd that came the same year as the Lenders' painting, the very symbol of the Frank Phillips Ranch.[589]

Frank purchased the 1914 (Myres) 101 Ranch Show saddle from Zack Miller in 1940 in cancellation of his debts to Frank. Frank's inquiry to the jeweler who made the ornaments for the saddle found that the saddle contained $1500 worth of jewels (in 1914 dollars), but also that many of the jewels were imitations.
Courtesy Woolaroc.

THE RUN
Noble

VI

PIÉCE DE RESISTANCE: THE ART

> DID YOU HEAR about our tragedy? The day after you left I gathered up all the baskets to treat them with beeswax and gasoline. I put the gasoline in a pan of hot water, as you suggested, but thought the water wasn't hot enough, so I set an electric hotplate under it. After I had treated a few baskets one basket I had in my hands went up in flames. I called Joe and he got the men with fire extinguishers, so the damage was not great. I burned my arms and face, but not badly. However all the little California baskets were destroyed, and the "Old Indian Bag," is badly charred on one side. I have been cleaning it, but it crumbles if I'm not careful. What I'm most worried about is the Peruvian sewing basket excavated by John Phillips. It's badly charred, especially on the bottom and inside the top. It's the one I was working on when the fire started. I have some scraps of Peruvian tapestry which I think I can arrange to cover the burnt part, and there were balls of yarn, bodkins, etc., in the basket (they were not burnt) which will also fill up space. I wonder how I can treat the basket so it will stay together. How about a thin solution of ambroid and acetone? I haven't done anything to this basket yet.[590]

Margaret Elliott knew that this was probably the end for her. She hoped against hope that the new archaeology room would placate Frank, "I hope he will like it so well that he won't think too much about the baskets." The accident struck directly at some of Frank's suppressed anxieties—the evidence of one of the few activities from which John ever got satisfaction, and a fear of fire. Seemingly an unfortunate incident in the museum, the accident marks a milestone in the history of Woolaroc.

By the first part of January, Sarah Clements' letters began to refer to Pat Patterson doing things at the museum. Pat Patterson was a complicated and difficult character who grew larger with the passage of time. In January of 1941, he was hired to replace Margaret. He was the son of a circus painter and he claimed to have grown up in the circus. Along the way he was afflicted with crippling polio, so that a circus career was not open to him.

John Noble began painting The Run around 1920 from his recollections of the Oklahoma land run of 1893. He hoped that the state would purchase the painting, but the chronically strapped legislature never was willing to make the appropriation. In this 1935 publicity photo, Frank and Amelia Noble pose with her late husband's painting at the time it was purchased for Woolaroc. Courtesy Woolaroc.

Exceptionally bright, he went to the University of Oklahoma where he received a degree in drama and studied set painting. He was enrolled as a graduate student in anthropology and doing some work at Woolaroc in the fall before Margaret Elliott was dismissed.[591] Though there are no letters in the file, it is possible that the Clementses suggested he might be right for the job. He was just the man Frank needed. He had good relations with the anthropology department, a flare for the artistic and dramatic, and he was "4F"and therefore immune from the draft.

Before the Depression, most of Frank's paintings were purchased in 1926 and 1927. At that time, he acquired a number of paintings by Emil Lenders and by Robert Lindneux. Other notable works were by Henry Balink, E. I. Couse, and Bert Phillips, mostly purchased from the artists themselves. Partly, Frank came in contact with these people on his many trips to Santa Fe and Taos. Also, from an early date he was dealing with the Findlay Art Gallery in Kansas City. *The Magic Flute* by C. I. Couse and *The Buffalo Hunt* by Charles Russell were the first paintings he bought from Findlay for the lodge on 1 December 1926, but there was correspondence with Findlay from several months earlier. Possibly Findlay was advising Frank about some of his purchases. Probably the ultimate connection was J. C. Nichols. There is little doubt that J. C. Nichols was very influential on many aspects of the Frank Phillips Ranch.

Another early influence was J. Steinfeld of the Lotos Club. Early on, the enthusiastic Steinfeld sent Frank an antique Tibetan Buddha and a very old suit of Italian armor, along with a book of collected menus from Lotos Club State Dinners.[592] Most of the art at the Lotos Club was more traditional than Frank's Western art, but Steinfeld sold the Phillipses some paintings for the town house, and also *Feeding the Flock* by W. A. Knip in 1927, and *Landscape and Cattle* by William Hart for the ranch. It was the last painting purchased after the stock market crash of 1929.

By 1929, Frank had 33 paintings hanging on his walls, including the Russell and one Frederic Remington, *Indians Escaping After the Burning of Julesburg.* He did not acquire any more paintings until 1936. By that time, Frank had built his museum, added a room, and was already planning another addition. This time, things were serious. He was not just buying fine paintings to decorate his lodge. He was acquiring for a real museum.

Early in 1936 Frank purchased the John Noble painting called *The Run* from Noble's widow. Noble was a Wichita, Kansas, native who had a varied career, but studied painting in Paris, France, and Brussels, Beligum, and became a member of the National Academy of Design. The large canvass is the work of a man who was actually at the Cherokee Oultet land run of 1893. Noble began his sketches for the painting in 1920 and hoped the state legislature would commission it. Though disappointed in his hope, he continued to work on it periodically for about 10 years. After Noble's death, in 1935, William Allen White convinced Governor E. W. Marland that the painting ought to hang in the state capitol. Amelia Noble brought it to Oklahoma City and it hung in the Blue Room for five months. She valued it at $15,000. When the appropriation was not forthcoming from the state legislature, she removed it to the lobby of an Oklahoma City hotel. There some unnamed person altered the inscription to make it appear to be an older painting. Shortly afterward, Frank Phillips acquired the painting.[593] Frank paid a premium for the singular piece—$5,200—much more than he had even paid for Remington and Russell. This is probably the point where a philosophy for his collection began to coalesce.

An exchange of letters shows his thinking and some of the influences at this stage. Frank was keenly interested in a very expensive painting by John Young-Hunter, which he did not buy. It was at Young-Hunter's studio in New York, where an agent saw the painting and panned it to Frank.[594] An Oklahoma City art dealer, the artist's agent, subsequently lent it to the Nelson Gallery for an exhibition there and Frank asked J. C. Nichols for his opinion on the painting. By this time Nichols was chairman of the board of the William Rockhill Nelson Gallery of Art, so he asked the director of the gallery to give an opinion. It was the director's judgement that because Frank was only collecting Western pictures, this one was pleasing, but not comparable to more progressive American artists.[595] Two years later Frank told a New York dealer he was "only" interested in Western scenes depicting Indian or pioneer life.[596] Of course, Frank did buy the best art he could lay his hands on, but his chief interest was in telling a historical story.[597] Finally the museum was taking a coherent direction.

J. C. Nichols, as always, was influential and very helpful in providing contact points with the Taos group of artists in the early days, and finding good consultation along the way. In New York Fern Butler had an ear to the ground and a good eye for quality. As early as 1928, Fern wrote she had visited Williams' studio and he had nothing that would interest Frank.[598] It was Fern who purchased *Custer's Last Rally* and Aelbert Cuyp's *A Herdsman Tending Cattle* at an American Art Association auction.[599] Fern purchased seven bronzes at Grand Central Art Galleries.[600] "Miss Butler may be able to indicate whether or not Phillips would be interested," wrote Marjorie Karch.[601] Indeed, Fern Butler, as much as anybody, had a feel for what Frank wanted, and she had reliable good taste.

Galleries

In the early days Frank looked to the Miller brothers and Pawnee Bill for some of the sources of his Western art. Both Lenders and Lindneux were contacted through them. Zack Miller had a showman's eye. One time he gave Frank a painting that was more of a crowd thriller than an aesthetic piece. ". . . I didn't consider this picture much from the art standpoint, but the man who painted it and made the frame had a very bad reputation being 'Gypsy Bob' the killer of eight men and is now confined to a cell 8 ft. square for the rest of his life. . . "[602]

Frank had an interest in this kind of joking around but was well aware of his need for serious art. Henry Balink's paintings were an early demonstration of this awareness. As usual, he looked to his Kansas City connections for resources. The Findlay Galleries in Kansas City was the most prominent name among early dealers that Frank felt comfortable with using. An Oklahoma City dealer, The Colonial Art Company, tried very hard but only made one sale in 1936. In other major purchases, Frank also bought *The Bolter* by Russell from William McBeth, Inc. on December 1, 1926, the same day he bought another Russell and a Couse from Findlay.

He made art contacts through the several clubs that he belonged to in New York. The Lotos Club was notable because art exhibits were one of its *raison d'être* and Frank and Jane bought several works mostly for the house in town there. Frank bought *The Old Soak* at the Calumet Club dispersal sale in 1937, but then spent several months getting proper authentication.[603]

Early in 1941 Frank took a series of artists to see *Sailing of the Pilgrims from England* which hung on the fortieth floor of the Bankers Club. Finally Charles Shimmin, a friend of Gordon Matzene, got the job of copying this picture.[604] This was a common practice in old American museums, but by then was fading from use. Matzene worked with Frank about the composition in order to avoid an absolute copy.[605] Frank worried because Shimmin's hands shook.[606] Matzene knew that Shimmin needed the work badly so he went to Chicago to supervise the painting.[607] All went well, and Frank later purchased more of his paintings.

In the middle 1930s, Frank became very active in his search for appropriate works for his museum. After years of quiescence, suddenly in 1936, Frank started to buy again. Not until the end of 1935 did his appointments begin to show art activities, but 1936 and 1937 were busy:

In New York City:

8 May 1936, "went to John Young-Hunter studio to see *Santa Fe Trail*"

9 May 1936, "went to Ehrich Newhouse Galleries to see Russells"

In Bartlesville:

7 July 1936, "Rawsom Cut Gallery—OKC"

In New York City:

January 25, 1937, "up to some galleries to see Russell and Remington paintings"

January 26, 1937, "to Reinhardt Galleries to see Gilbert White exhibition; Mrs. Bowman's to see bronze of Frank Phillips"

26 March 1937, "Grand Central Art Galleries to find out about sculptors for Post/Rogers busts; to Bryant Bakers to see sculpture work"

27 March 1937, "Mr. Hirschl of Fred'k Frazier brought in a picture of Geronimo"

7 April 1937, "went to National Sculpture Society to see President, Gregory"

In Bartlesville:

8 and 13 May 1937, "Lindneux, artist of Denver"

The interior of the museum some time before the October 1937 expansion began. The Woolaroc was still upstairs. The collection was beginning to take the shape of a museum of Western history, though it still retained some of the old catch-as-catch-can aura. Courtesy Woolaroc.

> *In New York City:*
>
> 14 July 1937, "Findlay Art Gallery to see paintings"
>
> 30 November 1937, "Grand Central Art Galleries with SFB; met Frank Begrisch; lunch with Begrisch; to gallery to see Jane's painting."[608]

News got around that Frank Phillips was collecting seriously. He was making the right contacts, and knew the right people, and it was not long before he began to get solicitations from many galleries and information that certain privately held paintings were available. As the Depression ground on, the owners of fine collections began to sell. For example, Mrs. J. Warren Sanders of Tulsa offered seven paintings, including a Thomas Moran in 1936.[609] Often the prices were just too high, or Frank was unsure of the advisability of the purchase, and usually he simply could not use them. He wrote, "I am not out paying fancy prices; unless I can get what I consider real bargains [I] am not interested. So many good pictures are available now and, you know, the market is very thin."[610]

It is astounding to realize the sort of paintings that were on the market in those years. For an example, in 1940 Frank was offered Gilbert Stuart's portrait of *George Washington* for $70,000.[611] It did not fit Frank's collection, and besides, the price was out of Frank's range, but it is clear that the market was flooded with top paintings. Frank made some mistakes and missed some opportunities, but he had a remarkable opportunity in a very short span of time to purchase exactly the sort of art that would tell the story of the West.

Frank's reputation also won him entry into two very important sources in New York. In December of 1935 the Grand Central Art Galleries began to appear on Frank's appointment calendars. He went there on March 26 to find out about some sculptors for the Wiley Post and Will Rogers busts, then to Bryant Baker's to see some of his works. The Grand Central Art Galleries was a non-profit organization, founded in the interest of American artists. The artists became members by election, and lay members paid $350 for membership. Lay membership was limited by the number of artist members. Every year each artist member contributed a painting that was distributed to the lay members at an annual drawing. Of course the artists were able to exhibit their work at the gallery.[612] Frank made very important contacts at the Grand Central and bought some very important paintings. He bought *Thanksgiving Dinner for the Ranch* by Frederic Remington in 1938; *Open Season* by Carl Rungius; 12 paintings by

Frank Tenney Johnson in 1938 and 1939; an E. I. Couse in 1939; and 6 William Leighs in 1939 and 1944. Similar sources were the American Art Association where Fern bought *Custer's Last Rally* and the Park Bernett Galleries where he bought *Battle of Wolves* in 1940.

GETTING ORGANIZED

In the midst of all this activity, a New York dealer offered Frank a painting named *Bartering for a Bride,* ostensibly by Charles Russell. He claimed it belonged to an English friend and that the Prince of Wales had a companion piece.[613] Fern went to look it over, but, something bothered Frank. He wrote Betty Rogers, "I just wonder if Russell always used the same style of signature. The Russell I have in New York was painted in 1904 and the one I am considering purchasing was painted in 1905."[614] Nancy Russell answered quickly that if the dealer would send her the picture to examine, she could identify it immediately if it was authentic.[615] Sure enough, the dealer sent that Russell back to its owner post haste.[616] Frank became very nervous about Remington and Russell purchases.

> As you know pretty well my attitude about purchasing any further bronzes or Remingtons. I think definitely and positively, they are about the hardest thing there is to purchase and feel you are getting your money's worth, there is so much skullduggery about them. . .[617]

He had to find some way to get reliable advice.

Frank was at the very apex of his career. He was one of America's wealthy industrialists, one of the captains of industry. Presidents and senators, artists, movie stars, and princes of the Church were guests in his home; he was a friend of some of America's most respected families, Du Pont, Rockefeller, Roosevelt, Ford; he was beloved by his employees and the pride of his fellow Oklahomans. He had built well Number 8 into Phillips Petroleum Company, a major independent oil company that emerged from the depths of the Depression on solid financial footing, aggressive and progressive. Frank was a high-energy personality who thrived on work. But in July of 1936, Frank was among several petroleum industry leaders indicted on antitrust charges. For several months while on trial, Frank shared a Madison, Wisconsin, apartment with John Hughes' father, who was also under indictment. Of that time, A. M. Hughes gravely told his family that Frank really took the charges very, very hard.[618] Emotionally, he interpreted the charges as a questioning of his patriotism. It was a long time to be under that kind of pressure. Only a few months later, in March of 1938, when he checked into the hospital in New York for his annual physical, he had to admit he was just plain tired—and he had a grueling headache. He had had a headache for six weeks.

Frank spent several days in the hospital in New York in March, taking every test they knew.[619] When he was discharged he was warned to take it easy, and sent back to work with some vitamins. He still had the headache.[620] He took his records to Kansas City and checked in to the University of Kansas medical center there. The University of Kansas doctor's told him he had some myocardial damage and some atherosclerosis. They sent him home with some more vitamins.[621] There was very little else in those days. It is possible, that under the terrible pressures of the Madison Case, Frank had a "silent" myocardial infarction. His calendar appointments give the impression that he was staggered by the news, and probably frightened at what the continuing headache might mean.

A third visit to a medical center, this time in St. Louis, got no more satisfactory answer, but some headache relief following cocainization of his nasal ganglia.[622] In the meantime, in July, Frank decided to plea nolo contendere, pay his fine, and get out from under Madison. Only a month later, he bought a new pair of glasses that were unsatisfactory and wrote a curt letter to his ophthalmologist. The doctor responded that, after all, he did have glaucoma. Frank knew the meaning of that sobering diagnosis.[623] In rapid succession he was hit with news of heart disease and glaucoma, and he had an unremitting, frightening headache. About that time his close friend, H. V. Foster had a stroke and began to rapidly decline. Frank was his pallbearer in June of 1939. Not long after, Frank wrote, "Pictures are worth to me only what they bring at public auction in New York after my death."[624] It is the time when a man begins to seriously consider his legacy.

For a long time he had seen a legacy in his ranch. At first it was his game preserve, then his exotic animals, and lately it was his museum that gave him a stake in the future. Now he looked to his staff, as with each stone in the museum walls and new object in the collection, he built his memory. Sarah White was a museology professional, had an artistic eye, and was willing to give generous council. Lucille Zühlke in the museum and Marjorie Karch in the office were very competent, and Fern Butler was very valuable. Among them, they realized that Frank's collection needed to be properly cataloged. For the art, that included proper authentication. Early in the year the office generated a listing of the art at Woolaroc along with its cost, evidently for investment accounting.[625] In the process, and with the organization of the museum, and the problems with forgeries on the market, Frank ordered them to assemble the required documentation.[626]

Most of the records were in the New York office and they were gathered up and sent to Woolaroc. Many of the paintings were purchased from the artist and had no formal authentication, just a bill of sale. "We are sorely lacking in real authentication in many instances of course, but are getting everything together so that we can discuss the matter with Phillips and decide what can be done or attempted," wrote Marjorie Karch.[627] Marjorie and Fern wrote the artists, or their heirs in some cases, for proper letters of identification to authenticate the works, but a few proved elusive. Some of the galleries were just slow responding. Nelson of the Grand Central Art Galleries delayed as did the American Art Association. Anderson Galleries was frankly resistant.[628] Eventually most of the data was accumulated. To Frank's chagrin, a few did not stand up to the scrutiny, the most distressing was *The Buffalo Hunt,* thought to be by Charles Russell. When it was clear that a solid authentication was not forthcoming from Findlay Gallery, Frank resorted to inquiring with Nancy Russell who tactfully declined an endorsement. No wonder Frank became skittish.

Matzene

About this time, Frank's friend Lew Wentz suggested that Frank should talk with his art consultant, Gordon Matzene. Matzene was an Englishman who had a successful career as a society photographer in Chicago before moving to Ponca City where he became a consult for Lew Wentz. He was an artist and very knowledgeable about art and the aesthetics of decoration. Matzene was a world traveler with a special interest in oriental art. He had an international network of art contacts.

Matzene contacted Frank at Lew Wentz' urging. "Mr. Wentz gave me your letter to him, wherein you say that you, perhaps, are interested in some Western paintings."[629] Matzene had a listing of 18 paintings from a Ponca City collector. They were very top quality paintings: Albert Bierstadt, Nicolai Fechin, Joseph Henry Sharpe, William R. Leigh, E. I. Couse, and Thomas Moran. Matzene said, "Besides those listed there are quite a number by Henry Balink but personally I do not think his Indians compare with the ones by Fechin or Sharpe." Fechin was a personal friend of Matzene, but it is said that Frank specifically detested Fechin. This was probably a political distaste; the old capitalist war horse smelled Bolsheviks, and Woolaroc never owned a Fechin in Frank's lifetime. Frank could be cranky. So instead, this time Matzene sold Frank a Henry Balink and a Fletcher Ransom.[630]

But Matzene's trip to Woolaroc that first weekend in February was significantly more productive than simply selling some paintings. When Frank returned to Oklahoma in April, Matzene visited the ranch again and proposed to give Frank his oriental collection and that Frank should add an oriental room to his latest museum expansion. A few days later Matzene wrote, "I left a rough sketch for my idea of the building."[631] By spring he was involved in inside discussion for the plans of the new big expansion of the museum.

> Suppose you know I have a crew of men out now mining the rock for building the new museum and plans for the addition are being drawn. New material is gradually coming in from friends so it appears I will have no trouble filling it. Had word yesterday from Henry Ford that he was going to make a personal selection from his museum for my place here.[632]

Matzene's oriental room was not a settled issue for three years. He eventually gave the museum a sizable assembly of oriental collectibles such as snuff bottles and netsuke though both he and Frank knew they really did not fit in the museum.[633] Matzene pled that Jane really liked the oriental things; and Frank could not pass up the free collection—even if he did have to build a room to house it.

Meanwhile, Matzene was busily acting as Frank's agent in a deal for some paintings owned by a rancher near Kaw City. He tried to awe her. "Mr. Frank Phillips is a member of the Grand Central Art Galleries in New York and is

Gordon Matzene, right, advised Frank on art purchases and designed the interior of the museum after 1939. Matzene can be credited with bringing the museum art and collections into a coherent unity. He was a flamboyant and adventurous man with artistic contacts all over the world. His first love was Chinese art. This group was photographed with Matzene while on a trip to China during the 1920s. He remained something of a mystery to those who knew him. Notwithstanding, he became a valued friend of Frank and Jane. Courtesy Ponca City Public Library.

rather well posted on the values of paintings today."[634] Unfortunately, she had already had dealings with Frank, "I tried to lease to Phillips but they sent a curt reply, 'Not interested.' So I am making other arrangements."[635] By the end of the year Matzene was a fixture at the ranch. He commented on the new acquisitions that were beginning to arrive at the museum and took photographs at the ranch.

> I think everything is going to be fine as far as the building is concerned. I saw the two large pictures of Leigh's and I like the Indian pueblo immensely. The other one had good action but I think the color is too cold. [He was referring to *Custer's Last Fight.*] Amongst other things I saw a lot of Sharps. He must have cleaned up his attic. They are terrible. Don't you think that you have so many pictures now and that it would be a good idea to stop buying for a time to see what is needed for your spaces if any more.[636]

He brought over three paintings by E. L. Waldo that he thought were "as good as the Denver man's [Lindneux]."[637] Frank responded, "I appreciate your advice about things at the ranch because I think it is always good."[638]

Matzene prepared an inventory of his collection, interesting items from all over the Far East and the South Seas, and also a collection of "jewels" which he may have thought might compliment H. V. Foster's minerals. The oriental room was a growing problem. The planned space was 40 feet square and Matzene's collection was not sufficient to fill the space. Matzene's answer was to take a trip to China, on Frank's nickle, of course. Frank thought that was impractical, "I feel that conditions over there are such that it is too much of a risk for you to take."[639] Matzene kept pressing with plans for the voyage, asking to have letterheads and envelopes printed up:

Woolaroc Museum
Bartlesville, Okla.
Frank Phillips, Director
R. Gordon Matzene, Curator[640]

Frank finally put his foot down. "I would not care to fully or partly finance the undertaking just at this time."[641]

Oddly, what seems to have precipitated that declination was that Frank learned that Matzene had enticed one of Frank's Filipino houseboys into his employ.[642] Matzene skillfully repaired the damage, and blamed the whole misunderstanding on the Zühlkes. "After receiving this letter from you I can never visit the Ranch again."[643] Frank knew how to handle him, "If you decide to sever the most delightful friendship that Mrs. Phillips and I have had in years, then I will have to give serious consideration to returning everything to you..."[644]

For several months Matzene had been trying to elbow out the archaeologists. The Zühlkes were the first fatalities in the power struggle. He attempted to insert an alternative candidate to Sarah White's suggestion for the murals in the pre-history room, a frieze done by a friend who was an adjunct art instructor at the University of Oklahoma.[645] He encouraged an alternative interest in archaeological excavation being done by Odd Halseth who was director of Pueblo Grande ruins and museum in Phoenix, Arizona.[646] It was probably gossip from Matzene about the Field collection in Tulsa that miffed Frank so much that Dr. Clements, himself, had to do damage control to save their grant relationship.

The power struggle continued to focus on the murals. When the finished works were hung, Matzene was enraged. "This so-called mural is a terrible thing."[647] He wrote an irate letter to Professor Oscar Jacobson at the University of Oklahoma.

> A couple of days ago I was at the Phillips Ranch. I saw a mural that was recently done and I asked the young fellow, Patterson, who had done it. I was told that it was done at the University by students under your supervision. That's the most awful thing I have ever seen. Whoever did it can not draw nor do they know anything of anatomy, especially Indians. The central figure with the awful face has big bulging muscles—his arms are like a prize fighter's. It is quite well known that Indians have flat muscles and same are not visible in repose. I can hardly believe that you have ever seen it...[648]

The murals are hanging in the pre-history room at Woolaroc today. They are reminiscent of the Mayan frescos at, for instance, Palenque in coloring and composition, and also of the etchings on gorgets found at Spiro. They have a flavor of the muscular, populist Regionalist style that was current in the 1930s and 1940s era, and are really quite well done, but probably very offensive to a man of Matzene's sensibilities, not to mention the infighting tussle. Jacobson answered, "You are barking up the wrong tree. I have nothing to do with the mural whatsoever."[649] Victory was sweet when Marjorie Karch wrote Sarah White, "You might be slightly interested in the comments of a certain well-known artist about the front room."[650] What followed were three direct quotations from the same letters cited above.

During the summer Matzene wrote Frank, "I have in mind a proper arrangement of your museum, but as same did not agree with Mrs. Zühlke's idea I decided to drop the same. However the condition of your museum is disorderly and confused. It is quite alright for people who do not know anything about it as the crowd that mostly comes to the ranch, but occasionally people do come who know."[651] The very next day he mailed Frank a lengthy letter outlining his vision.

Side view of Woolaroc museum erected by Frank Phillips to house his extensive collections, including Indian relics and regalia. It embraces many items in memory of the old west.

Top: The front entrance of the museum as it appeared in the late 1930s. There had been many changes since the hanger showroom of 1930. The big plate glass windows were closed up with rock, and rooms had been added at the rear. A canopy and some lions were at the entrance and the drive curved up close by the petrified wood bench that is still in place today. Courtesy Woolaroc.

Bottom: A record shot of the south side of the museum after completion of the 1939 addition, the glass windows in the last section at the rear had been filled with rock. A section of recessed panels, an arched entry, and two more sections of recessed panels had been added on the east end of the building. Courtesy Woolaroc.

Top: Visitors to the museum are absorbed before *Custer's Last Fight* by William Leigh. Leigh's paintings were characteristically monumental in size and sentimental in nature. His version of Custer's battle is a compelling Woolaroc favorite. Courtesy Woolaroc.

Bottom: Jo Mora cast his four heroic-sized Western bronzes for E. W. Marland in 1925. They were displayed outside, on his estate in Ponca City for many years until Gordon Matzene bought them for Frank in 1940. In this unbelievable picture, Woolaroc trucks are at the Marland estate, loaded with the bronzes for transport to the ranch. Courtesy Woolaroc.

> I should make the very ancient Indians the beginning of your museum and follow same with the Indian objects from tribes that came later...After completing the Oklahoma part you can go to the other Indian tribes...take up the invasion of the white men...after that comes the cowboys...it will be necessary to remove the airplane...The South Sea things on the left as you enter should be moved to the basement...[652]

Frank was intrigued by Matzene's logical proposal and asked for more detail. Matzene responded with specifics about arrangement of the displays and the sorts of objects and paintings for each room. Frank was receptive to the plan, "This together with what you have previously sent gives me a very clear idea of your views on the museum and gallery arrangements. I am in full accord with all you say and we will work gradually to that end."[653]

Frank already had a few nice pieces of Southwestern Indian handicrafts, probably in the lodge. For example, in the early days, Dorothy Wentz, Lew's sister, sent him a basket, and the Frank Burfords sent a piece of Santa Clara blackware.[654] Once Matzene had the go-ahead, he took off on a buying trip in the Southwest. He reported to Frank, "My trip was successful as far as obtaining various samples of pottery from all pueblos known as pottery makers."[655] The invoice of his purchases lists 126 pots, which is today an irreplaceable complete collection. He noted that the pots approximately corresponded with the periods of Frank's blanket collection.[656]

In the same time frame, Odd Halseth presented the promised Phoenix Collection of Southwestern artifacts. This is a collection of 100 Colonial, Classic, and Sedentary period pottery items, and assorted flint, shell, and stone artifacts. Halseth was probably a contact of Matzene's. Frank brought him out to inspect Woolaroc and give an opinion. He also offered Halseth the director's job in May of 1940, and again in December of 1941. Halseth wrote perceptively, "...I have been trying to think of the museum as such and not a part of Frank Phillips. This is not easy to do, I can assure you, for your personality—not less than your money—is a vital part of the museum as I see it."[657] The war interceded. Had Halseth come to Woolaroc, the museum would certainly have taken a very different direction.

Early in 1940, Frank bought the J. H. Sharp blanket collection through a Phoenix dealer. Sharp, of Taos, collected the blankets over many years and it was considered a very representative collection. Sharp wrote, "I feel now that I am really separated from the rugs & sorry for quite a number of them are really works of art & skilled craftsmanship—old masters now."[658] In 1946 Woolaroc acquired the Walter Bimson collection of 51 blankets from a Phoenix banker friend of Frank's. The collections of Southwestern artifacts and handicrafts at Woolaroc became quite impressive at a rapid rate.

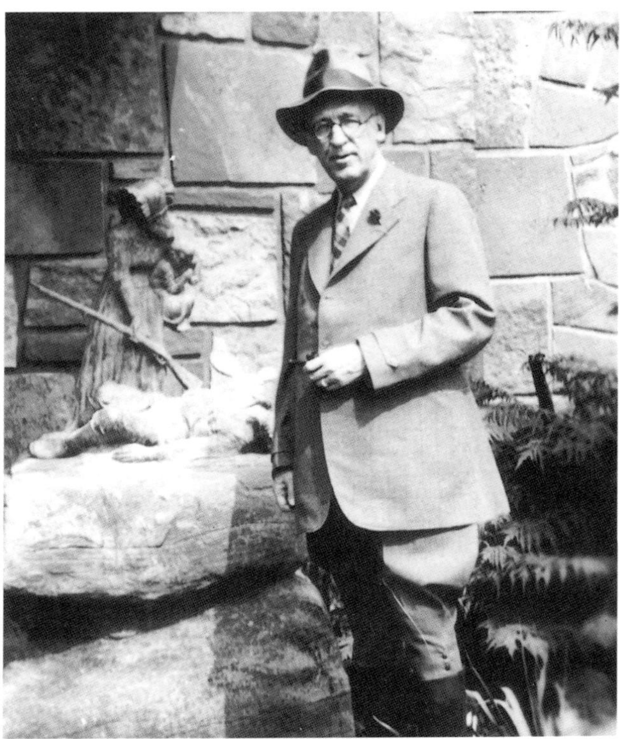

Frank in his casual clothes—riding jodhpurs, boots and his favorite hat—stands near the museum entrance next to John Gregory's *Pioneer Woman* bronze on 25 May 1941. This is the same outfit he wore a month later to the Spiro dig. When Sarah White invited him to dig, she offered to find him some work clothes, but he declined the offer. This outfit was what he evidently thought was appropriate digging clothes for an oil man. Courtesy Woolaroc.

Matzene's vision for the Southwestern Indian room, the second room of the museum, was inspired. In late September he toured the Rockefeller Museum of Indian Art and the museum in Colorado Springs, Colorado, to assess the competition.[659] He kept pressing Frank for a free hand with the arrangement of the museum. "I can, if you will let me, arrange your museum in continuity so the greater part of it will not only be a museum but also an educational institution."[660] The concept was novel for the time, and Matzene knew it. "It will take time, but when same is completed it will possibly be the only educational museum of its kind in the U.S."[661]

At last a philosophical direction for the museum was formulated. From an early date Frank planned a theme of American natural history and American art.[662] He had struggled with his own hodge-podge of collections for a long time, but his art acquisitions had taken that direction from the beginning. The fortunate association with the Clementses brought Frank access to professional consultation in the highest standard of museology of the times, and the only exhibit of all the archaeological cultures of Oklahoma that were known at the time. Matzene was able to bring all of these elements together logically, in a philosophical unit. His vision for an educational museum was ahead of his time. Organizing the upstairs with the first room for archaeology, then the Southwest Indian room, the Plains Indians and frontier, and the cowboy era, then moving the other assorted exhibits to the downstairs brought order to the chaos. When it was finished Matzene was pleased, "I have arranged the Southwest Indian room the way I think it should be and think to-day it is the most beautiful room in the museum."[663]

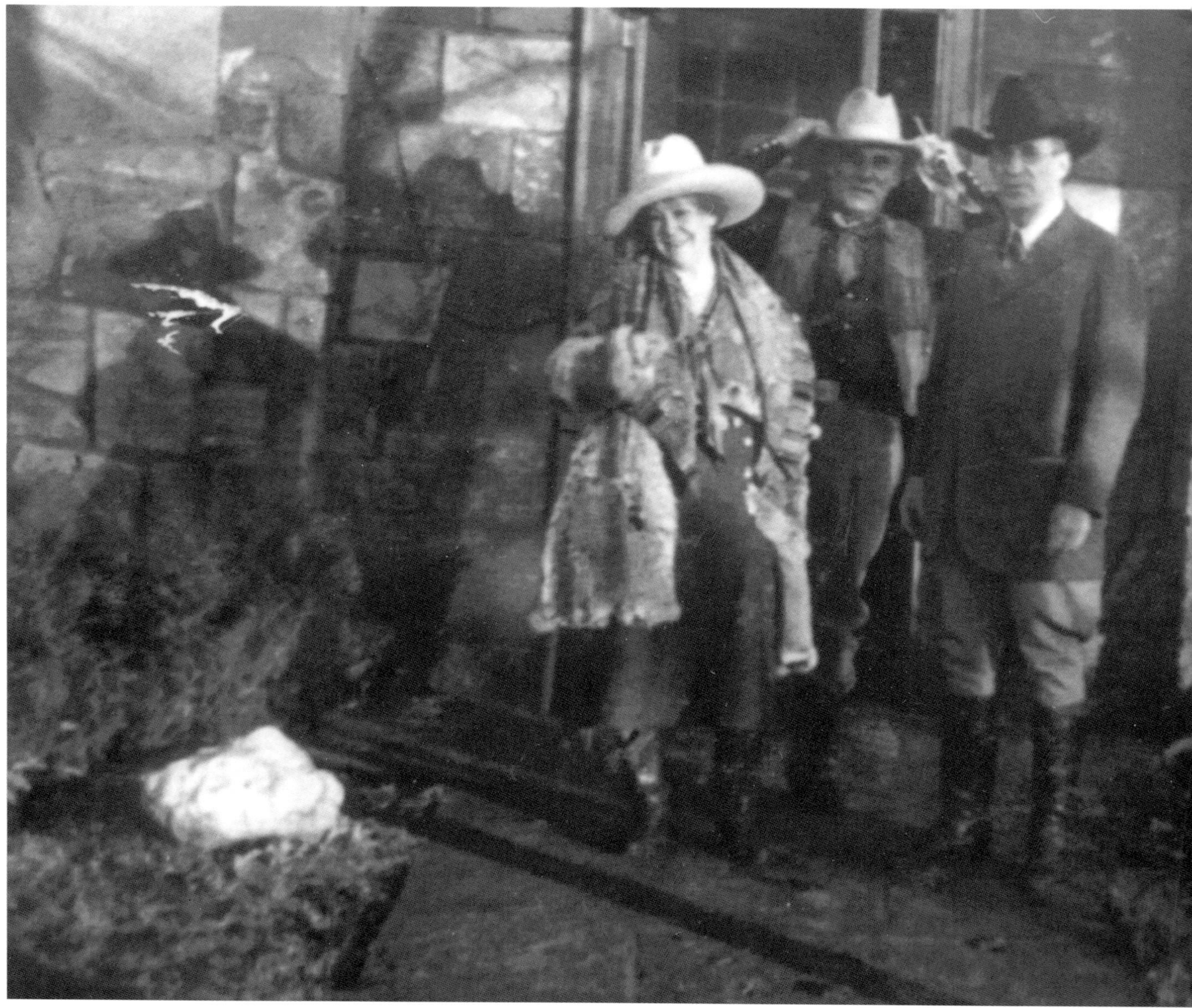

This is a snapshot of Powder River Jack and Kitty Lee with Frank at the side entrance to the museum. This couple were old Wild West and movie stars from Buffalo Bill days and Tom Mix movies. On hard times in the 30s, Frank helped them pay for Kitty's eye surgery. They tried to help Frank acquire some Charles Russell paintings in Montana. Courtesy Woolaroc.

Matzene enlisted the help of Dr. O. B. Jacobson in preparing the copy for the labels. Matzene said that Jacobson knew more about Southwestern pottery and baskets of the era than anyone in the country.[664] Matzene himself did the new labels. By fall they had the whole place torn up and a new coat of plaster was going on. "The museum of course is being correlated from one end to the other."[665] It must have been music to Matzene's ears. A few months later, Pat Patterson and his assistants were rearranging things, ". . . it is going to be time very soon for you to come over again to pass judgement."[666]

All the while Matzene was shepherding the development of the art collection. Sometimes it was quite a job! Frank had a tendency to buy everything Lindneux brought in, and besides Lindneux was more or less commissioned to do a series of portraits of frontier figures and Indian chiefs, so he was there often. In 1939, Matzene had once criticized the color in William Leigh's painting, and Frank must have taken it to heart. Pat Patterson reported to Matzene that "Lindneux came to the museum, bringing his paints, ready to paint the large picture of Leigh over."[667] Matzene had to plead with Frank that touching the painting would destroy its value. It must have really eaten on Frank because he wrote a Boston art dealer, "I would not be interested in any of Leigh's pictures. Think he is a good artist but he does not display the proper color in portraying animals. I have two of his major paintings and am not satisfied with them."[668] The whole thing must have sorted out, for in 1944, Frank bought four of the museum's most popular Leigh paintings at Grand Central Art Gallery: *Navajo Fire Dance; Pocahontas; Westward Ho!;* and *Visions of Yesterday.*

By 1940 Matzene was exceedingly chummy with Frank and Jane. He even regularly referred to Jane as "Her Highness" in his correspondence with Frank. He was in poor health—or possibly was hypochondriac—and there are many solicitous letters about his various doctor's reports. He often traveled with the Phillipses or met them at their resorts, and he wrote them friendly letters from all of his own exotic vacation sites. Matzene was involved in Frank's acquisition of some of the major art works from the Marland estate, the *Westward The Course Of Empire Takes Its Way* tapestry, the *Pioneer Woman* bronzes, and the Jo Mora bronzes. In one of the saddest letters at Woolaroc, Frank's friend, Ernie Marland wrote,

> My financial condition compells [sic] me to sell objects of art, tapestries, bronzes, rugs and paintings acquired by me in more prosperous years. . . I will sell at a price approximately 25 per cent of their original cost to me. And will consider it a kindness if you will come yourself or send some one to look them over with the object of buying anything you fancy.[669]

Frank was out of town, but he sent Matzene over.[670] He bought the tapestry right away, and negotiations began for the bronzes. Matzene thought the tapestry was Flemish and he went right to work on authentication. It turned out it was by Paul J. Baumgarten after the Leutze mural which decorates the ceiling of the United States House of Representatives, woven in this country for the 1915 San Francisco Panama-Pacific Exposition, a singular piece. Frank was exceedingly nervous about the purchase of the bronzes. Matzene had to assure him that there were no copies and Marland had the only rights to them. The four Jo Mora bronzes were cast in 1925. At that time, Joe Miller posed for *The Cowboy;* Mr. and Mrs. John Bull, both Ponca, for the *Indian Chief* and the *Indian Maiden;* William H. McFadden posed for the *Pioneer Man,* and the last was *Belle Starr.* When Frank purchased them, they were on the estate grounds. "As they are cemented to the stone he asked if he should pry same loose. I believe you have better men to do that in Bartlesville and should send someone with a truck to do that. They can, you know, easily be injured if care is not taken."[671]

In 1927, E. W. Marland sponsered a national contest for a bronze that most represented the American pioneer woman. The bronze models were exhibited and the contest was judged by a vote of the public. There were 75,000 votes cast and the sculpture by Bryant Baker was the winner. The full size statue is, today, a prominent exhibit for visitors to Ponca City. In 1940, Frank Phillips bought the 12 original entry models from Marland for only $6,000. Matzene declared the purchase was a wonderful bargain. He asked Marland to leave the stone bases on the bronzes and he personally designed the pedestals for the statues. Frank over-ruled him and ordered the dark wood pedestals that they stand on today.[672] The Pioneer Woman bronzes compose a moving exhibit at Woolaroc. It is a collection of illustrations of the respect accorded to the role of the women who settled the Plains, by the generation who were their children.

Frank and Jane's long-time friends from Oklahoma City, the Bullocks and Hoffmans, were frequent casual guests at the ranch. Here they pose around *Sundial* by Frederick Allan Williams with Frank and Jane. This bronze was purchased in 1929 for use as an outdoor sundial. Courtesy Woolaroc.

HOW FRANK MISSED THE RUSSELL COLLECTION

Even in his own lifetime, it was generally acknowledged that Charles Russell was among the most respected American artists. Russell's prolific work recorded the sights and memories of a real-life cowboy and was widely known and especially beloved through his illustrations for popular journals of the times. By Frank's time forgeries of Russell's work were a problem for collectors, and Frank managed to buy some fakes during his naive early collecting, and even in his more wary later years. He learned caution, but as a result, sometimes missed some great opportunities.

As Frank began collecting again, his network of friends sometimes told him of works that were for sale. "Powder River" Jack Lee and his wife Kitty were some of those friends, colorful Wild West showmen then living in California. Jack had performed in Buffalo Bill's show and worked with Tom Mix and Will Rogers. They were guests at the ranch many times, good enough friends that Frank once paid the medical bills for Kitty's eye surgery.[673] It was Jack who tipped Frank off on some Russell paintings that were for sale in Montana. He sent Frank the catalog of paintings hanging at The Mint, a saloon in Great Falls, Montana, owned by United States Marshal Sid Willis, who was a friend of Charlie Russell's, and of Jack's.[674] The letter came while Frank was in Los Angeles, calling on Nancy Russell, and viewing her pictures.

> It is really a fine collection and we enjoyed seeing them; however she did not indicate to me that the pictures were for sale. I spoke to her about the pictures in The Mint—she did not speak any too well of them and mentioned that there were only about five or six originals in the lot.[675]

Jack immediately answered the letter, defending the marshal's collection, but Frank was leery and he did not buy the paintings.

Nevertheless, this signaled that Frank was again in the market in a big way. Almost four years later, G. T. Nelson of the Grand Central Art Galleries wrote Frank that Harry Carr of Pasadena, California, was acting as Nancy Russell's agent in an effort to sell her collection.[676] Frank was planning a trip to California in the next few weeks and he certainly acted on the new information quickly. He made another call on Nancy Russell, and contacted Carr in January. Of course he wanted the collection so badly he could taste it. So began the game of negotiation.

Nancy Russell gave Frank some autographed books she had written; Frank sent her a buffalo head. Meanwhile, he invited Nancy, and also Harry Carr, to visit Woolaroc. Nancy's asking price for the paintings was high, and she had a miscellaneous collection of historical sketches, wash drawings, and assorted personal belongings of Charlie Russell's which she wished to sell along with

Who knows what impulse induced Frank to buy this set of ivory miniatures of United States presidents, Washington through Teddy Roosevelt, which were painted by A. J. Rowell for a commission from "Diamond" Jim Brady. The collection has been kept updated all these years. Courtesy Woolaroc.

the paintings, envisioning a whole exhibit devoted to the life of Charles Russell. Frank offered $80,000 and wrote Carr that Nancy Russell was asking about $20,000 too much.[677] He also negotiated for a collection of bronzes, including some that were in the hands of dealers.[678]

This was a business negotiation and Frank did not hold back. He offered to send a airplane to bring Harry Carr for a Woolaroc weekend. Harry enthusiastically accepted, "... you say when! You see, there would be no fun for me unless Uncle Frank was there (excuse the relationship, but I like that)."[679] Frank was making headway. "I like the relationship stuff. Which shows that I am getting pretty old and sentimental." But, he would not want to give the idea he was getting soft, "There never was a time when people with money felt so uneasy as now, and they are holding on to their cash. Art is among the things that are not moving."[680] The next weekend he sent the airplane to get Harry who spent a week at the ranch.

Carr's week at the ranch gave Frank some pause. He told Frank that he was determined to sell the Russell collection and that Nancy Russell had given him power of attorney. But, he overstepped decorum for a good negotiator.

This photographer was shooting a picture of the D. C. French 1916 bronze *Seated Lincoln*, the model of the Lincoln Memorial, for a museum publication. Frank bought this bronze, cast from the original plaster model at Grand Central Art Galleries in New York. It was an era when patriotism was a compelling theme and deeply held value in America. Courtesy Woolaroc.

> While in Bartlesville he was out at the Ranch, and one night when I was out of town I had Marjorie invite a number of young people out there for dinner. I understand it turned out to be a wild party. Carr claims to have lost $1,000 in drafts and $600 in currency. It worried me a great deal, but I have since about come to the conclusion that he didn't lose it.[681]

Frank was suspicious.

> He claims to have telegraphed for money on the 2nd and told me he received $100 on Monday, the 4th. He said that he wired a man named Bebee in Chicago for money. On the way out here in the plane he flashed at least $600, and in view of his conversation, my suspicion was again aroused. He likes his liquor and talks too much; has got me in a bad frame of mind with reference to him and I have lost my confidence.[682]

Frank wrote Boots Adams more particulars that he had learned about Carr, then asked Adams to investigate Carr both financially and morally.

A week later, Adams had a complete retail credit report. Carr had been an intelligence officer during the World War I, and had owned a Pierce Arrow automobile agency in Pasadena, California, which failed in 1937. He had been in a contracting financial position for several years, but did not have a bad record, and was well regarded. Still, Chief Gaston reported to Adams that on March 2, Carr wired Bebee, "I am still working on the deal. Have hopes of putting it over."[683] An unsigned memo shows that L. U. Gaston had found the telegraph and telephone records of Carr's stay in Bartlesville, and at Amarillo. "None of the telegrams sent by Carr requested the remittance of any funds and no money was received by wire by Carr at Bartlesville, nor at Amarillo, Texas."[684]

It could have been worse, but Frank decided to work around Carr. He kept up his groundwork on Nancy Russell. "In talking to your best friends I notice they all call you 'Nancy' so that is why I am addressing you in this manner. . . "[685] Then, he put Gordon Matzene on the case. Matzene was aboard the company airplane that returned Carr to California. He wrote Nancy Russell, "He knows so much about art and is such a good friend that I have asked Mr. Carr to take him to see your collection. . . "[686] A note at the bottom of the letter says, "(Matzene has rest of file)."

Students touring the museum admire *Navajo Fire Dance.* This huge William R. Leigh painting is so dramatic that these students must have thought they could hear the war drums. When Leigh sold the painting to Frank, he wrote him, "you are doing something for America. . . . " Courtesy Woolaroc.

They did not know that time was getting short. Matzene did schedule a luncheon and time to view the collection with Carr, but he telegraphed Frank in Phoenix, "Mrs. Russell ill. . . "[687] Had they realized the portent, they would not have delayed. Frank wrote Betty Rogers of Matzene's visit.

> I consider that he is one of the best judges of art in this country and knows so much more than I do about it that I trust him implicitly...He returned today and reports that he thinks it would add greatly to my museum if I built a shrine for Charlie. However, he thinks that $250,000 is entirely out of the question and that my original offer of $80,000, which was withdrawn, comes nearer to its value. . . In view of my present plans, I do not feel that I could afford or would want to pay more, free of commissions.[688]

The same day he wrote Lucille Zühlke that Matzene "likes the Russell collection, we haven't bought it yet. It looks as if you and Miss White may get a trip to California."[689]

Matzene went to work on Nancy Russell as soon as he got back to Oklahoma. He sent her a string of lapis lazuli beads. Then he planted doubt in her mind about Carr, added that the price she was asking was simply out of the question, and played on a fear of fire that he perceived she had, "Have you ever considered that a fire may destroy everything."[690] He sent Frank a copy of the letter and added, "I learned that Mrs. Russell was afraid of fire that may destroy her pictures. That is why I mentioned fire in the letter."[691] And, he encouraged Harry Carr a little bit in some friendly letters. Nancy Russell responded that she was firm on the price and they niggled about whether the collection contained copies. Finally, in April, Nancy wrote Frank that she was negotiating with the Rockefeller and Whitney Museums of Art. Frank did not panic, but continued negotiations by asking her to authenticate *Battle of the Wolves* that he had recently bought at Parke Bernet.

Things changed quickly. One of Frank's employees, D. C. Hempsell of the Land Department, received information from an old high school friend who was then an officer of the firm that handled Nancy Russell's securities account, "If he wants to deal with us direct he had better hurry as Mrs. Russell is pretty sick."[692] Frank did move rapidly, but on May 24 Nancy Russell died. The collection was caught up in the administration of her estate.

Frank immediately began negotiating with the executor, George R. Miller, who was CEO of the securities firm that Stivers worked for. Somehow in the ensuing months Frank gave the impression that he thought the price for the collection was too high—and worse—that he would no longer be interested in purchasing the collection, or so protested the executor. As late as October of 1940 Frank thought he would get an opportunity to bid for the collection. By that time the asking price seemed to be $70,000.[693] Now serious, Frank had Hemsell query Stivers about what was going on. The executors were firm in their response that the collection was worth $75,000.

Suddenly things turned bad. Hemsell's brother-in-law who lived in Los Angeles did some discrete inquiries and found a friend of Nancy Russell's with some information.

There had been three individuals trying to purchase the collection, among which was some man from Oklahoma. She also indicated that a sale had tentatively been made and that both the collection and the money were already in escrow. [694]

It must have been devastating disappointment, but the worst was yet to come. The collection was sold by the court for only $40,000 on May 14, 1941, with no one ever contacting Frank about the new developments.

Frank did not give up. Hempsell's brother-in-law who worked for the Department of Pensions checked on the court records and found the sale was made to C. R. Smith who was then the president of American Airlines in New York. He also learned that Smith had subsequently sold half of the collection to H. E. Britzman.[695] He managed to locate Britzman, a Russell collector, who by that time had also bought Trail's End, the former Russell home. Britzman was willing to sell several bronzes, paintings, and water colors from his collection for a premium price. Frank demurred, and so ends the story of how Frank missed buying the entire Russell collection.

Rounding It Out

Frank's missed opportunities are disappointing to contemplate, and probably more so for him. But in the longer view of the collection, he avoided the pitfalls of building a shrine for Charlie Russell or Matzene's oriental collection. It would have been very nice to have gotten the Lenders collection, or to have had the vision to pull together more of the 101 Ranch things. Overall, Frank stayed on task, and collected works that would illustrate a time-line of the historical story of the West that he wished to tell.

He does not seem to have had an early interest in sculpture, and pictures from the museum at that stage show there were only a few. In 1938, he bought seven bronzes at Grand Central Art Galleries: *Massasoit* by Cyrus E. Dallin; *The Sun Vow* by Hermon A. McNeil; *Magic Lilies* by Brenda Putnam; *Frog Baby* by Janet Scudder; and *Duck Baby*, and two of *Baby With Frog* by Edith B. Parsons. All of these are still to be seen at the rock garden pool. They joined a handful of sculptures that Frank was purchasing for his collection: *Man on Horse* by Russell; *Pay Day* by Sally Farnham; *Bull* by Rosa Bonheur; *Bull and Bear* by Isadore Bonheur all from F. Schnittjer & Son. *The Trapper* by Remington was purchased from Grand Central Art Galleries, and *Indian Warrior* by A. Phimister Procter was from Tiffany & Co. Prior to these there was *Cowboy Roping a Calf* by Clinton Shephard that was presented by the Directors in 1926, and *Sundial* by Frederick Allen Williams that was purchased in 1929. Jane presented a bust of Frank Phillips by Electra Waggoner in 1937. There was also *Horse and Boy*, purchased in 1938, and another Electra Waggoner, *The Golden Spear*, and five small incidental pieces.[696] It is easy to see the monumental addition made by the acquisition of the Marland estate bronzes.

Frank did gratify a few impulsive urges. He bought a collection of miniatures of the Presidents of the United States, hand painted on ivory by A. J. Rowell for "Diamond" Jim Brady. Woolaroc has always kept the miniature collection updated with each new president. At Grand Central Art Galleries he bought the bronze cast from the original plaster model of *Seated Lincoln* by Daniel Chester French. When Will Rogers died, Frank commissioned a portrait by Charles Shimmin and a bust by Bryant Baker which are exhibited in a corner of the pioneer room in the museum. He hung a pair of beautful pastel portraits of his friends Fred and Julia Lookout by Canadian artist Nicholas de Grandmaison.

A few more singular opportunities happened. Frank commissioned *The Trail of Tears* from Robert Lindneux in 1942. It and *The Run* are the two most requested pictures in the Woolaroc collection for reproduction in history texts. *The Trail of Tears* is a moving picture that evokes indignity at the injustice and pathos of the Cherokee Removal. The next year Bill Leigh wrote Frank wishing to sell him some paintings, *Navajo Fire Dance* and *Westward Ho!* among them.

> I want you to see them first because you are doing something for America in which I thoroughly believe; you have built a fine gallery and are collecting real art—the art that will live and be a prime factor in building a true, great civilization and tradition—you are collecting America. . . You will be known in time to come as one of the chief builders of America's art heritage.[697]

Frank's vision was influential even in his lifetime. Thomas Gilcrease dropped by unannounced, and missed Frank in 1944, but wrote a nice thanks, "You are doing a mighty fine thing in collecting and maintaining so many things of interest to the people of Oklahoma, and I'm sure they will appreciate it more and more as time goes by."[698]

FRANKLIN D.

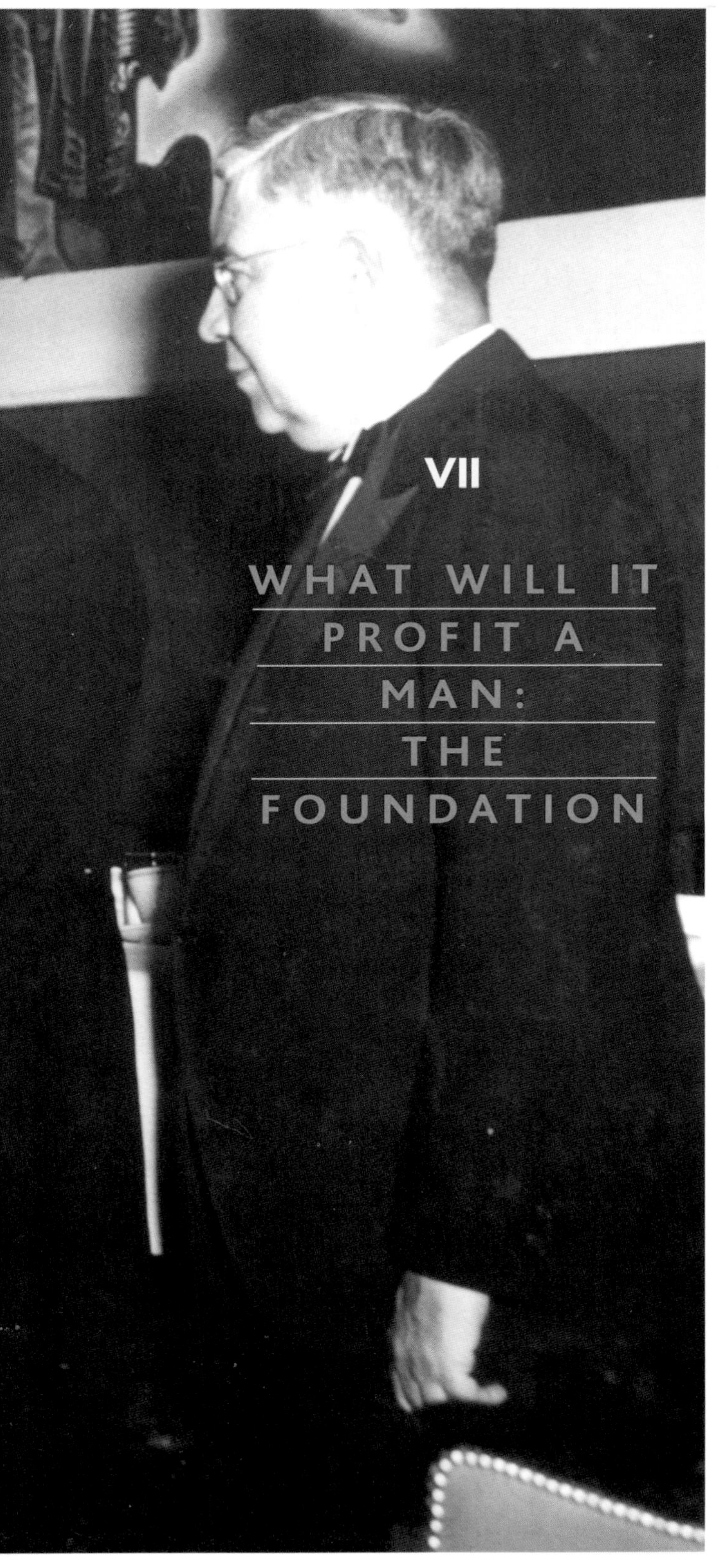

VII

WHAT WILL IT PROFIT A MAN: THE FOUNDATION

WHEN NATIONALLY SYNDICATED newspaper columnist, Ernie Pyle, visited Woolaroc for half a day in 1939, he was amazed that Frank and Jane were waiting for him on the front porch. "You wouldn't figure the richest man in Oklahoma would be easy to see, anyhow."[699] Frank and Jane fed him a couple of hefty Woolaroc meals, showed him the lodge, took him through the museum, and toured the ranch. Like Latta 11 years earlier, that afternoon Pyle enjoyed the full measure of Frank's open-handed Woolaroc hospitality. Writing with a populist-style cynicism that simply suspected a rich man to be mean and selfish, Pyle produced a couple of columns about Woolaroc that put a spin on his afternoon that had a faint tinge of resentment. Pyle observed, "I believe that Frank Phillips is a man who genuinely enjoys his money. . . You can sense that he is proud of the power and honor and recognition his money has brought him."[700] He was shocked to learn that Frank routinely rode the subway to work in New York, and he could not help busy-bodying about Frank's philanthropic habits. "He says he's pretty tight about money. But I guess he's like many other rich people—he'll pinch on a subway ride and then give $100,000 away without a thought."[701] If he only knew!

Frank Phillips' parents were early homesteaders in the North Loup River valley of what became Greeley County, Nebraska. Lew Phillips helped organize the county in 1872, and that year was elected the first county judge. He cut a farmstead out of the prairie and built a cabin of cottonwood and cedar logs for his family. Court sessions were held in that living room, the room Frank copied when he built the cabin at Woolaroc. Frank was born there in November of 1873, but only months later a grasshopper plague of Biblical proportions stripped their farm to the bare ground. They were ruined and returned to Iowa. In Iowa, Frank grew up as a child of an emerging

Frank Phillips received the Boy Scouts of America Silver Buffalo award at St. Paul, Minnesota in May 1942. The award is the highest honor that the Scouts give to a non-scout. It was in recognition of the work and tremendous financial support Frank invested in the Boy Scouts of America, without a doubt his favorite charity. (left to right) Ragnuald Anderson Nestos (former governor of North Dakota), Judge Campbell, John S. Hoyt, Frank Phillips, Chief Scout Executive James E. West, Most Reverend Bernard J. Sheil, and W. C. Smoot. Courtesy Woolaroc.

middle class. Though by modern standards the overwhelming majority of Americans lived in poverty in those days, Frank was one who always envisioned opportunities. By the time he married Jane in 1897, Frank was already a prospering entrepreneur.

All indications are that from the beginning, Frank was interested in rewarding the values of high character and hard work, and he was always generous. By 1920, the diaries and letters begin to give clear evidence of his generosity to the local churches, civic projects, political candidates, local efforts to relieve the needy, and youth programs. But, with real wealth came real responsibility, and a need to formulate a philanthropic goal. This became evident following the deluge of letters that were generated by the *Kansas City Star* article in 1926. His tax problems in the early 1930s complicated efforts at simple charity. Each pathetically desperate plea left him unable to respond at all, his alms only a pointless droplet in a sea.

During the Depression years, Frank, and other community leaders such as H. V. Foster, consciously tried to continue to provide jobs. For a while local wealthy men were able, consciously, to provide work for some men by building some of the big homes in the area around the new country club. Foster also built a ranch house, and Frank continued construction at Woolaroc. As the bad times deepened, Frank's employees took pay cuts, Frank doing all he could to keep family heads on the payroll. After the terrible labor dispute in East St. Louis in 1932, Frank worked quickly to shore-up the company image, and saw first-hand the circumstances of those desperate people.

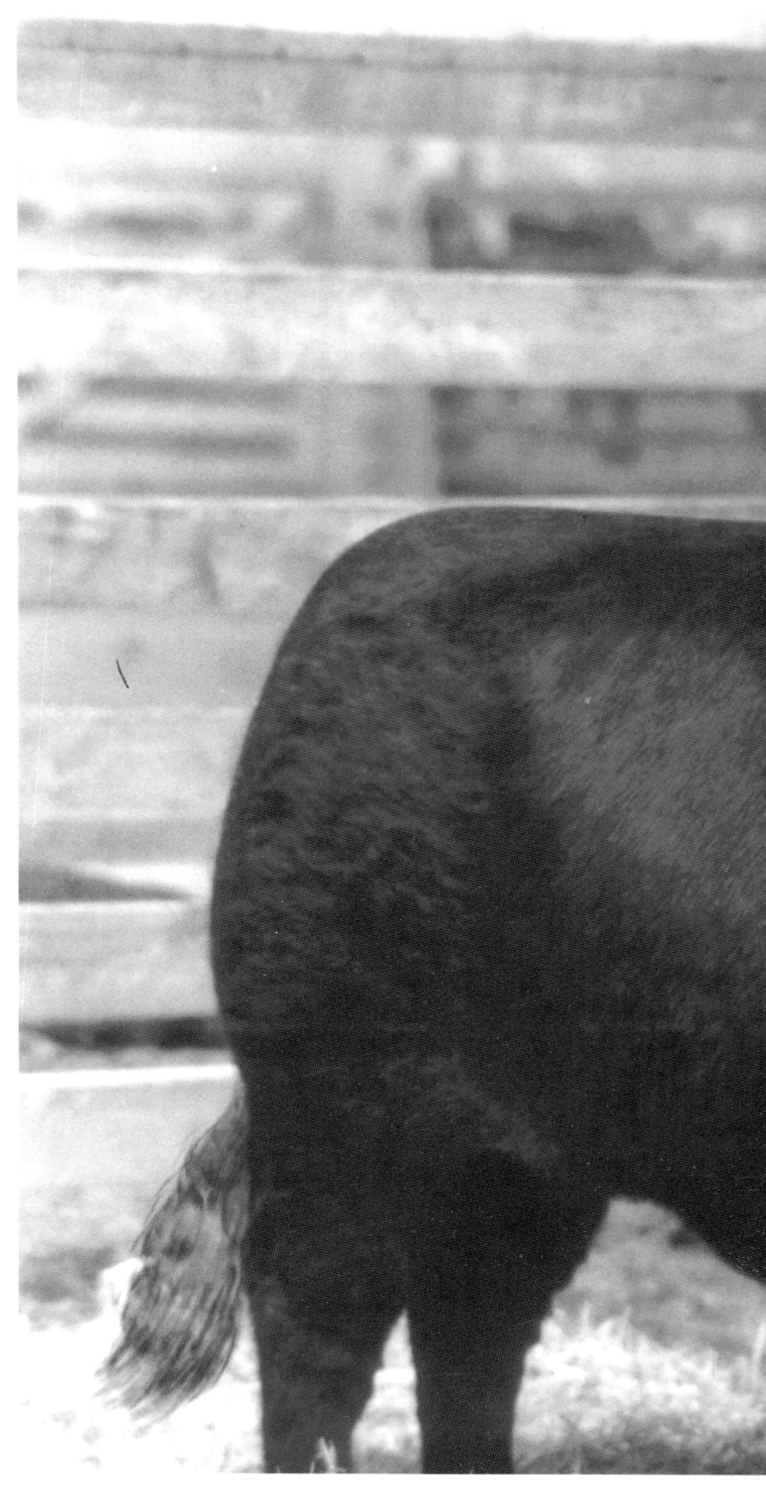

Frank had an interest in good programs that encouraged development of a solid work ethic. For several years in the 1930s and 40s the Frank Phillips Foundation purchased prize winning 4-H and FFA steers at the livestock show auctions. The beef was given to charity and the hide was tanned for the young agriculturist. Courtesy Woolaroc.

Frank's buffalo were worthless, and his prize Brahmans were not much better. Still, Frank had to cull his herds, and the drought made that routine imperative. Frank began donating large quantities of meat to the Salvation Army and the Bartlesville Welfare Association. This became regular at Christmas season, and sporadic during the year. In the summer of 1934, his beef fed 318 families, nearly 2,000 people in Washington County. Recipients were told by the Welfare Association ". . . to go home at once and cook the meat and take no chance of permitting it to spoil."[702] The Salvation Army distributed Christmas beef for Frank in East St. Louis. That season he distributed meat from 40 head of beef, also buffalo and elk.

Bartlesville had a civic organization called The Christmas Cheer Committee that distributed Christmas baskets to the needy each year. The local merchants donated to the fund, and each year Frank would anonymously finish off the drive to complete the goal, usually about half. Frank took a personal interest in these efforts and knew the needy recipients. For example, in 1940, he was out of town until just before Christmas. Upon returning, he perused the Christmas Cheer list and noticed three names had been left off. Shortly, arrangements were made for a delivery to be made to them too.[703] Frank was a canny contributor to programs for the needy. An internal memo of the Frank Phillips Foundation evaluated the five welfare agencies that were operating in Washington County in 1940, though they thought half of them were politicized.[704]

Long before the crisis of the Depression, Frank and his brothers took an enthusiastic interest in the new organization, Boy Scouts of America. The first troop in the United States had been organized at Pawhuska in 1908. It was the sort of organization that would have appealed to Frank on many levels. Frank put it in his own words:

> The hope of the future, in an ever-changing world, rests in the rising generation. The restless, adventure-loving, perhaps mischievous, boy of today is the raw material of tomorrow's unselfish citizen. Dedicated to the task of preparing young America for citizenship, in the best sense of the word, the Boy Scouts movement has become a great educational influence in the lives of a million boys.
>
> Emerging from a world-wide depression with the influence of communism, fascism and many other radical "isms" threatening to undermine our government and with war clouds hovering over the entire world, we of the present generation will leave to the next generation a heritage of debt, class prejudice, strife and unrest. We pass on to them the responsibility of untangling and solving the knotty problems of society, business, and government.
>
> Our only hope to preserve and maintain the traditional freedom and independence of our American Democracy is to raise men with moral and mental stamina who will have the courage to defend and uphold these ideals and principles on which our nations is founded. The least we can do is prepare our boys for their future responsibilities. This can be done by supporting those institutions which have for their purpose the training of the youth of our nation. There is, in my opinion, no better such organization than the Boy Scouts organization. Non-political, non-sectarian, this great organization supplies a need for physical and moral training during the formative period of a boy's life. Not only is an outlet supplied for all of his restless energies, but held constantly before him are the high ideals of honorable, useful citizenship. He is taught the virtue of self-reliance, self-control, community service and respect for the rights of others.
>
> My contributions to the Boy Scouts are made as investments in the future manhood of our nation. . .[705]

This remarkable polemic is a rare window to Frank's soul that gives the clear vision that stirred him.

Frank's early interest in Boy Scouts is evident in his early contacts with national leaders in the organization—men such as Pat Hurley, Marshal Field, J. M. Davis, Herbert Hoover, Theodore Roosevelt, and Bishop Kelley. In the 1920s, local scout troops were early visitors that took the opportunity to work on merit badges and ranks at the Frank Phillips Ranch.[706] The area council meeting was held at the ranch for the first time in 1929, as it was several times over the ensuing years.

He also had an interest in education. It was Frank that built the Phillipsburg school, and that good relationship was long-standing. Inadvertently, the Phillipsburg school children were the first beneficiaries of a Woolaroc tour, thanks to Grif Graham. The Phillipsburg School made an annual visit to Woolaroc into the 1940s, for which they always wrote a thank you note to Frank.[707] Curt Sydebotham remembers, with great loyalty, that "Uncle" Frank came to the school every Christmas to pass out silver dollars and candy to the children. School groups from all over the area coveted Woolaroc field trips for their students. One of the annual groups that was most grateful was Douglass High School, the Black school in Bartlesville. An imaginative principal established an annual trip in 1935. His articulate and gracious thank-you letter persuaded Frank to host a larger group the next year. The school's principal wrote, "Let me take this opportunity to convey the expression of appreciation, enthusiasm, and boundless joy of 100 Negro graduates from over the State of Oklahoma. . . "[708]

Frank's support of higher education has already been visited. He took a strong interest in vocational education as another means of providing genuinely marketable work skills and character development. Frank continued to contribute to his favorite charities during the Depression years when his own resources were constrained. Bishop Kelley could usually count on him to help with an emergency, as could the Scouts. The 1931 tax case about his ranch deductions nudged him toward providing a better means of making the charitable contributions that were clearly a pleasure to him. That opportunity emerged in 1932 when he was elected to fill the vacancy on the board of the Markle Foundation, created by the death of Alonzo Hebbard. The Markle Foundation was chartered "to promote the advancement and diffusion of knowledge among the people of the United States and to promote the general good of mankind."[709]

Formation of the Foundation

This was just the sort of vehicle Frank needed. His friend John Markle had the pleasure of charitable bequests through his foundation in his own lifetime, and his fortune was continuing to support his heartfelt interests even after his death. As soon as Frank was flush again he began making plans for his own foundation.

In October of 1937, a charter was granted, the bylaws adopted, and a board of trustees was elected for The Frank Phillips Foundation, Incorporated. The purpose clause reads as follows:

> To aid public religious organizations, charitable organizations, preparatory, vocational, and technical schools, institutions of higher learning, and scientific research; to establish, maintain, construct, assist, and endow public charitable, religious, literary, educational, and scientific activities, agencies and institutions engaged in the discovery, treatment and care of diseases and its endowments and funds shall be administered exclusively for such purposes.[710]

Though as yet there were no funds in the foundation, Walter Cooper of Barrow, Wade, Guthrie & Co. in New York, Frank's personal accountant, suggested it would be a good idea to make several small contributions to recognized public charitable causes that very year in order to establish the foundation for tax evaluation.[711] Accordingly, Frank's staff drew up a likely list and Frank checked it by November 1. It was a list of 23 charities that Frank usually contributed to, for a total expenditure of $2,300.[712] These included such organizations as Bartlesville Day Nursery, a pro-rated day care for children of working Black mothers, YWCA of Okmulgee, St. Anthony's School of Okmulgee, the Methodist Church of Ochelata, Catholic Sisters of Bartlesville, and the Salvation Army of Bartlesville.[713]

Predictably, the Internal Revenue Service sent out letters to many of these organizations, asking for information that would establish them as bona fide public charities. The above six did not return the form letter, which put Frank's foundation in jeopardy of losing tax exempt status.[714] Boy, was there ever a general quarters! W. C. Smoot called on the Day Nursury where the director confessed she could not read the letter. The minister in Ochelata denied ever receiving the letter and besides he could not find it; the nuns in Bartlesville and Okmulgee were overwhelmed by the task; the "Y" had not received a letter; and the army had lost it in their Oklahoma City bureaucracy. Smoot had copies made of the Treasury Department letter and saw that the parties had the necessary help in getting the forms filled out. It was all turned in by the end of March and Frank asked Hy Byrd to follow through to get the foundation approved.[715] Frank had no hard feelings and contributed to those same organizations in 1938. A bill before Congress at that time posed a second daunting obstacle to Frank's foundation plans. He hoped to make large stock transfers to the foundation, probably to avoid confiscatory income and capital gains taxes, but even if the bill passed, "it will not change his decision to give to charity a considerable part of his estate through the foundation."[716]

The new strictures imposed by the tax-exempt status required Frank to backtrack for documentation on some of his large commitments. He was particularly fussy with Dr. Clements' rendition of the expenditure of the Spiro grant; fussy enough to draw the intercession of Dr. Bizzell, the President of the University of Oklahoma, who praised Frank for his support of important research and promised unfailing and continuous cooperation.[717]

In 1937 Frank paid off the first mortgage of all the churches in Bartlesville. First Baptist had no indebtedness, so Frank paid for the magnificent doors outside the old sanctuary of that church. Somehow he missed the Lutherans, but made it up with a $2,000 contribution in 1939.[718] It was a stunning gift that is still remembered by the older Bartlesville churches. At the time it garnered some national attention.[719] He said his object was "not to relieve the churches of their obligations, but to stabilize them and enable them to broaden their service."[720]

The year of the Madison antitrust trial that was so hard on Frank was 1937. The following spring began Frank's serious health problems, and the year he began to really think about his museum development. It was also a year when he made some spectacular, milestone foundation gifts. Through the foundation he gave $100,000 to the Boy Scout councils in Oklahoma and the Texas Panhandle.[721] In the same year he continued substantial gifts to other Boy Scout councils around the country.[722] Despite a great deal of publicity for the Scout gift, Frank remained testy toward nosey reporters. "It is not my intention to give publicity to any of my philanthropic work," he wrote a Tulsa newspaperwoman.[723]

It is no wonder, for he was evidently considering paying the church mortgages in Oklahoma City at that time. When the news leaked out in December, the Oklahoma City papers were all ablaze. The president of the Ministerial Alliance said that Frank wished "to build up a psychology to make us proof against Communism and Fascism and preserve our American Democracy."[724] *The Daily Oklahoman* declared the total local debt was about $2,000,000. In fact, Frank had already helped a few churches in the city, but when the news broke he wrote Smoot, "Recent publicity given to rumors that the Frank Phillips Foundation might make substantial contributions to Oklahoma City churches is indeed unfortunate and had embarrassed me considerably."[725] He simply did not have that kind of money and had to back away from helping out in Oklahoma City.

Late in 1938, Frank reached an agreement with the company to rent the ranch to furnish a place for meetings and entertainment of employees, friends, and customers of the company.[726] In exchange, the company took over financial responsibility for large parts of the ranch's functions—all with the consent of Frank Phillips, of course. This is a relationship that continued for many years. Meanwhile, Frank continued to build and expand his museum. It was a work in progress that he enjoyed for the remainder of his life.

The foundation quickly became the vehicle for Frank's charitable, as well as philanthropic giving. He made a small donation in 1938 to The Blue and the Gray Women's League to help fund the transportation for Oklahoma Civil War veterans to the last encampment at Gettysburg, Pennsylvania.[727] The foundation was an insulation from the pitiful, and frequently deranged, letters he often received. One woman from Larned, Kansas, sent him a 55-page, handwritten letter, reciting every misfortune of her life since 1908.[728] It was a relief to be able to respond that the foundation was not permitted to make loans or gifts to individuals. Still, Frank was never deterred from helping when he thought it was worthy. When the Bartlesville Department of Public Welfare asked the foundation to fund a new prosthesis for a 71-year-old janitor so he could continue to work, Frank was happy to help.[729] The foundation also provided a scholarship to osteopathy school for the son of a Methodist minister in Iowa. The foundation purchased prize winning 4-H and FFA steers at the livestock show auctions, then gave the beef to charity and had the hide tanned and sent to the young agriculturist. The foundation made frequent contributions to Memorial Hospital in Bartlesville to be used to support charity care. Doubtless, because of his experience with the unrelenting headache in 1938, Frank gave substantial support to headache research at Barnes Hospital in St. Louis, associated with Washington University, for several years.

At the solicitation of the governor of Nebraska, the foundation gave $50,000 toward youth programs in Nebraska.[730] This philanthropy backfired. Working overtime to ferret out a meaty scandal that would make good newscopy, the *Hastings Morning Spotlight* charged that Frank had given the gifts because the State of Nebraska vehicles used Phillips Petroleum Company credit cards. Frank's division manager wrote that the state credit cards were not a major business, but that Phillips had a contract with most of the federal agencies in Hastings, and even more important, Phillips had 90 percent of the state tank car business.[731] Because of the publicity, Frank had to back away from foundation gifts for Nebraska youth.

The Nebraska experience was unsettling enough that Frank polled his executive committee for their reading of the Phillips' employees opinion of his gifts to Boy Scouts. He wanted to make sure of his employee's approval, and loyalty. Partly because of this, and partly because of Frank's interest in education, another major foundation program was scholarships for children of Phillips Petroleum Company employees. The foundation fussed with a fair means of awarding scholarships. Hy Byrd conferred with Dr. Harry Woodburn Chase of New York University, and Dr. Nicholas Murray Butler of Columbia who recommended that he talk with the College Entrance Exam Board. Significantly, Frank funded the scholarship program for the first year of 1940 with $66,000.[732]

Catholic Charities

Frank continued to make very substantial gifts to Boy Scouts during his lifetime. He also made a practice of supporting other youth organizations such as Girl Scouts and Y.W.C.A. Through the Scouts connection, Frank's personal friendship with Bishop Kelley developed into another facet of Frank's philanthropic interest.

Over the years Frank was a reliable friend when the Bishop was hosting a retreat. The truth was that the Oklahoma church really did not have facilities for its growing duties. In 1939, the Oklahoma Diocese was dealing seriously for the William T. Hales estate in Oklahoma City. Bishop Kelley wrote he had picked out a suite for Frank, but the estate's trustees were asking $75,000 for the property.[733] He was ambivalent about the purchase. The opulence bothered him, but he knew the diocese needed a residence, offices, and a place for meetings and retreats; at the same time, he wanted to use the money for some of the needs around the diocese, and he really needed Frank's help with these. The foundation sent $10,000 toward purchase of the estate early in May.

While this exchange was going on, Frank was also helping the Catholic church in Pawhuska buy a new car and helping George Labadie purchase some property in Pawhuska for the local church. The church also was soliciting regular small contributions to maintain an indigent food and clothing fund. The foundation also made a nice contribution to the Catholic Youth Fund in New York. The Archbishop of Santa Fe solicited $5,000 to build a chapel for their vocational school for boys.[734] Frank had a continuing interest in the New Mexico school with a special fund to combat communism in the state.[735]

Frank's help to Oklahoma Catholic organizations in those years was truly remarkable. In the previous summer, just as the foundation was becoming established, and at the time Frank was hoping to help out the Oklahoma City churches, Bishop Kelley wrote with a knotty problem. "A bishop ought to have been given the shell of a turtle and a heart like an oak," he mused.[736] The Benedictine Sisters of Oklahoma were responsible for three large ministries: Monte Cassino Junior College in Tulsa, a small college in Guthrie, and an Oklahoma City orphanage and seven parish schools there. They had managed to accrue a collective debt of $250,000. In order to make interest payments the sisters were practically without food to eat, living on what their gardens could produce. Bishop Kelley had loaned them enough money to pay current bills, but wrote to Frank, "If you have done all you can for this year, just forget this letter."[737]

Frank had done all he could for the year. He put the Bishop off while he traveled to the West Coast. Meanwhile, by fall W. C. Smoot asked for, and received the financial statements from St. Joseph's Convent, St. John Vianney Training School, and St. Joseph Academy. Bishop Kelley was begging, as it were, for funds to rescue his Benedictine nuns' work. He confided to Smoot that he had a greater interest in Vianney, but dutifully pled the case for the entire work.[738] Frank made a stop-gap donation to the Vianney school. Finally, in December, from the newspapers Frank's bewildered friend realized the dilemma. A man with a great heart, the Bishop wrote, "If all the news about paying the debts on Oklahoma City churches is true it will be consolation to me."[739]

The foundation did come through with substantial help for the Bishop after the first of the year. By 1941 Frank's initial $10,000 gift to Vianney, along with $30,000 in donations their board pulled together, had reduced their debt to $30,000.[740] St. John Vianney School was a boarding school for wayward girls that taught vocational skills to the young women. They had a good track record of really helping troubled girls, which is why the Bishop was partial to the work. The trustees authorized a challenge grant to retire the debt of the school, and advance $5,000 at their fall meeting. By January, the money had been raised and the school was free of debt.[741] In time Frank also provided challenge grants for St. Joseph Orphanage, Cascia Hall and Monte Cassino schools in Tulsa. By this time Bishop Kelley was in failing health. He did not live much longer.

The news of Frank's big challenge grant to St. Joseph Orphanage set Oklahoma City astir. It was not long before the Baptists approached Frank for a similar grant for Baptist Children's Home. In Oklahoma, Baptist resources are substantial. One of their resources was Robert S. Kerr who was then governor and who was happy to use his influence to persuade Frank that the Baptist home was a very worthy work.[742] Frank agreed to give $100,000 to match $150,000 to be raised by the Baptists.[743]

THE FINAL DIRECTION

Starting in 1944, Frank began to change the focus of his philanthropy, transferring the deeds for the ranch properties into the foundation. The foundation did continue, in Frank's lifetime, to support his favorite philanthropies generously, and continued to make grants for many years after Frank's death. The National Y-Indian Guide Center, built in the 1970s just across from the museum is one of the last of these programs.

Frank's foundation has had its influence beyond Frank's own philanthropic interests. In 1948 C. H. Wright of Sunray approached J. A. Thompson of Phillips Petroleum Company about information on the foundation. Shortly Frank asked Smoot to give the information. "While I was in Florida with Mr. Phillips, Mr. K. S. Adams advised that you were interested in securing an outline of the Frank Phillips Foundation, Incorporated for Mr. John Mabee of Tulsa, who is planning to set up a similar organization."[744]

Just as Ernie Pyle postulated, Frank had had a lot of fun with his money. The great generosity of his foundation gifts had been a large part of that, and now he began to transfer the funds and property to endow his ranch and museum as a permanent legacy.

A lucky coincidence occurred as Frank was nearing this juncture—a coincidence named Pat Patterson. Patterson was a long-lived and difficult person in the history of Woolaroc, who serves a key spot as the bridge to the future. He is well remembered by many still on the staff at Woolaroc, yet he remains a mysterious and enigmatic person. He had crippling polio as a child. He managed to put himself through school during the depths of the Depression, a drama major who studied lighting and stagecraft. Shortly before he came to work at Woolaroc he was enrolled in a graduate program in the anthropology department at the University of Oklahoma. He also claimed he became director at Woolaroc in 1938.[745] It is possible, but not likely, that he worked occasionally, as a graduate student with Sarah White, at Woolaroc that in those early years, but certainly not as director. The earliest reference to him was by Matzene in November of 1940. This was shortly before Margaret Elliott was fired. For the next several months John Seward was in charge, probably quite capably, and Patterson worked under him as a helper.

After Seward's resignation in 1942, Patterson was the curator on site. At that stage the new building expansion had been completed, they were moved in, and Patterson was moving systematically through the upstairs rooms, executing the plans dictated by Gordon Matzene and Frank. The first report from Pat Patterson was February 1, 1942, and he called himself curator. He made some criticisms, "Our museum is not a collection of curios... It is a visual history lesson," but he was unable to articulate a vision beyond the mechanics of organization.[746] His training in the arts gave him good decorative sensibilities and he did a good job of arranging the museum along

Pat Patterson (left) poses, supervising the lifting of a caribou head into the old fumagator. The contraption was used for a while to keep moths out of the mounted animal heads. Courtesy Woolaroc.

Matzene's plan. He knew the jargon of archaeology and worked well for Sarah Clements. Both Clements and Matzene wrote to Frank that Pat was doing a good job.[747]

In September, Frank sent Patterson on a museum fact-finding tour of the East. Armed with a Woolaroc letter of introduction, Pat visited the Nelson Gallery in Kansas City; the Field Museum and Museum of Science and Industry in Chicago; the Peabody Museum and Boston Arts Gallery; the Museum of Modern Art, Reineart, the Metropolitan, Cloisters, Frick, Heye, Museum of Natural History, Marine Museum, Museum of Modern Science, and the Hayden Planetarium in New York; the Smithsonian, White House, Lincoln Memorial, and National Museum in Washington; and galleries in Philadelphia. It was probably money well spent, but there is no report in the file, only an expense account.[748] In fact, there are very few reports from Patterson in the archive, but it can be assessed that by the end of World War II he was showing some autonomy in his management. One of his suggestions, that Frank should build a gasoline station across from the Woolaroc entrance, fell on deaf ears.[749]

In some ways Patterson was probably a man way over his head, managing the museum by bluster and intimidation. In other ways he was an immensely talented man who understood the collection and who was responsible for much growth and refinement in the museum. He had the common sense not to change the basic plan, and during Patterson's tenure there were no philosophic changes in the exhibit at Woolaroc. The exhibit was shepherded through the destructive 1950s and 1960s when it was trendy for everything old fashioned to be disposed of with alacrity. Patterson resigned in 1971.

By the 1940s, both Frank and Jane were visibly aging. Jane kept her heart problems to herself. She looked exhausted in the photographs taken for their fiftieth anniversary in 1947. Mary Phillips Low happened to be at home for a visit with her mother the afternoon of July 29, 1948, when Jane had a heart attack. She only lived another month, dying on August 31. For several days she had seemed to be doing better. Frank was at the ranch when the news came. It was a crushing blow.

Some time before Jane died, they had already decided what their final wishes were. Paul Endacott told Michael Wallis,

> One evening I was out at the ranch for dinner with the Phillipses, and as we were driving back to town, Mr. Phillips had Clayton Fisher stop the car and he pointed to the side of the hill and said, "Betsie, that's where we are going to be buried."[750]

Things had crept up on them and now death interceded. So, Jane was temporarily enterred in the mausoleum at White Rose Cemetery in Bartlesville. And, as is so often comforting for the grieving, Frank threw himself into a new project. The trustees of the foundation executed a warranty deed for 23 acres at the site that Frank had shown Endacott on that day. Meanwhile, using the Will Rogers Memorial at Claremore as an inspiration, Frank had plans drawn for the mausoleum. The thing was built for the pharoahs. To begin construction, they blasted through 18 feet of sandstone. In a Frank Phillips quirk, the tomb was air-conditioned and a telephone was installed. It all took about a year, then Jane's casket was transferred from White Rose Cemetery to the mausoleum and a short memorial service was observed.

Frank tried to carry on. He was in failing health himself. On March 16, 1949 he resigned as chairman of Phillips Petroleum Company. But, he was as ever, the charming host to people the company brought to Woolaroc, and he kept up some of his old New York contacts. Cardinal Spellman was still a frequent visitor at Frank's Ambassador Hotel apartment.

Following his life-long pattern, Frank summered away from the Oklahoma heat. In 1950, he went to Atlantic City, staying at the grand old Traymore Hotel on the Boardwalk. There, in mid-August, Frank had a gall bladder attack. He never recovered from the surgery. Complications set in for the old man and he died August 23, 1950. He was taken home aboard a company DC-3.

Frank Phillips' passing at age 76 drew national attention. In Bartlesville, fitting memorials marked his funeral in the community that had been his home for half a century. He was layed to rest in his mausoleum with Jane, almost exactly 25 years after the beginning of his ranch. So much of his attention and satisfaction had been centered there. It was the place he most loved in the world.

FRANK PHILLIPS RANCH
BUFFALO AND WILD GAME

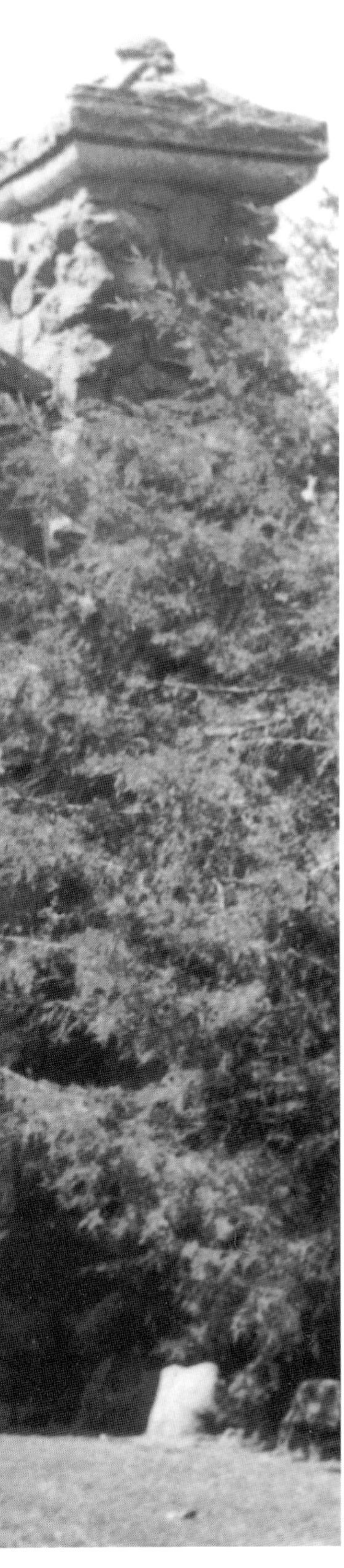

VII

THE LEGACY

FROM THE TIME THAT FRANK began buying the land for his ranch, the history of Woolaroc was inseparable from the person and fortunes of Frank Phillips. The earliest beginnings of the ranch were part of a grand plan of community development that aimed at making Bartlesville a progressive center, and the ranch an attractive resort where Frank could promote Phillips Petroleum Company.

Ranch estates with palatial country homes were a common hobby of wealthy friends, such as his brother Waite or friend H. V. Foster, or of famous acquaintances, such as William Randolph Hearst. In his vision of a rustic lodge and game preserve, employing the Oklahoma history of Indians and cattleman, and a showman's interpretation of the Wild West, Frank created an ambience of casual, homespun Americana in a private world of privilege and luxury during the heyday of Oklahoma oil.

Beyond this vision, for a long time there was no philosophy underlying what developed there. Frank's own gifts of humor and friendly hospitality and an incisive attention to detail generated instant enthusiasm among his friends, neighbors, and guests. Initially, Pawnee Bill and the 101 Ranch were his models and sources of much council. The early décor suggested by Emil Lenders was a direct result of Frank's contacts with Lillie and the Millers. Frank was not limited by the Wild West Show concept, and sought sophisticated council through his friend, Kansas City developer J. C. Nichols. Through Nichols, and through Waite's proximity to Taos, Frank had early interest in Southwestern art and especially the Taos School artists.

Frank's game preserve rapidly burgeoned into an exotic animal preserve. It was not in the original plan—it just happened. He was influenced and helped by George Miller who put him in contact with zoo men and exotic animal dealers such as John Ringling, Heinrick Hagenbeck, and George Vierheller. The Crystal Springs Farm was intended to be modeled on the idea of diversi-

Grif Graham was holding open the old entry gate to Woolaroc in 1936 for Messrs. Hutchinson and Tomison of the New York Transfer Department as they were leaving. Courtesy Woolaroc.

fied farming that was all the rage in those days, though it was always more of a bragging point than an actual profitable operation. The exotic animals, fine domestic stock, and fresh farm produce in that halcyon time at the Frank Phillips Ranch have been an untold story that adds richness and even humor to the saga of Woolaroc.

Entertaining was the main purpose for Woolaroc's inception. Frank was "champing at the bit" to open it up even before the lodge was completed. Before the year 1926 ended, a Woolaroc invitation was a social prize. Woolaroc hospitality was met, in the convention of the day, with great enthusiasm and often extravagant gifts. Many of those gifts and curiosities eventually ended up in the museum. It is easy to dismiss them as just a polyglot accumulation, which inspired historian Danney Goble to remark that Woolaroc was only the collection of a spoiled rich man. But, they might also be viewed as gifts that Frank's guests sent because they thought they would be appropriate, and they are that generation's interpretation of the significance of Woolaroc as a vehicle for preservation of the Western heritage.

The museum, itself, was an accidental development. It grew steadily, without a purpose other than to house the historic aircraft *Woolaroc.* Frank stashed his treasures there, and for a long time it was just a fun accouterment to a Woolaroc weekend. As Frank's financial fortunes emerged from the depths of the Depression, he also emerged with a nascent vision for the credibility of his museum that became inseparable from his quest for legacy.

A conscious decision to order his museum exhibit as a visual narrative of Western history contributed new order to the museum and Frank's acquisitions. His fortunate association with Sarah White Clements of the University of Oklahoma Museum of Anthropology was a milestone in Woolaroc development. The interest and devoted consultation of art authority, Gordon Matzene, at last, provided a definite, clear philosophy for the museum, and much needed help with the quality and aesthetics of the exhibition.

Portents of mortality and confiscatory taxes influenced Frank's move toward creation of the Frank Phillips Foundation. By transferring stock into the foundation, he could avoid capital gains taxes, and take a large charitable deduction that would only cost him 10 or 20 percent in those days of punitive marginal tax rates. At the same time he could follow his conscience, promote the company, and have a lot of fun. It had always been his plan to eventually give the ranch to the public. At first he thought he would give it to the state, but somewhere along the line he resolved to endow it through the foundation. Woolaroc was his beloved creation, and is his final resting place.

The museum collection, the lodge, and indeed, the Frank Phillips Ranch itself has fortunately arrived at an era when historical preservation is a national value. Woolaroc is a place of deep history. On the land Indian forebears often camped and hunted, leaving the occasional refuse of millennia to testify to their passage. In historical times, near Chouteau Spring the Osage traded with Frenchmen. Cattle drives passed by for water, leaving faint trails and wagon ruts. Outlaws and moonshiners once hid out in the gullies. When Frank closed in the acreage with his fence, a few small farmers tilled the good land along the creek that became Crystal Springs Farm. At the edge of the ranch pumped one of the most historic oil fields of the Osage.

Woolaroc entertained the rich and famous people of that age of the golden age of Oklahoma oil. Hoe-down music and swing combos played for flappers and Indian dignitaries. Bootleg whiskey, big black cigars, back-slapping humor, high-pressure business and political wheeling and dealing, and gun-toting gangsters were at the same place where grade school field trips, ladies teas, bishop's retreats, Boy Scout banquets, and church picnics often came. It was, at the same time, a family place, redolent in rich and warm memories for a family that is still closely associated with Woolaroc, and for many friends. The entire ranch is a living snapshot of that amazing lifestyle.

It is a place of continuity. The flash flood that swept over the low water bridge in 1999 is reminiscent of the flood that deposited a giant horsetail log there millions of years ago. In August of 1999, while this paper was being written, a daddy in cowboy clothes showed his rowdy little boys their great granddaddy's saddle in the Henry Wells case in the museum. Curt Sydebothem's son recently started working in the carpenter shop with his dad, a third generation of craftsmen to work at Woolaroc, a living memory of the days of Uncle Frank. At the Cow Thieves and Outlaws Reunion in October, Charles Chibitty's family performed the Indian dancing, and Charles himself told the party about his experience as a Comanche code-talker at Omaha Beach.

Frank's dream was to leave a legacy. Characteristically,

he has shared that legacy with many, many others. A skit at a docent's banquet in September of 1999 reviewed many of them: Will Rogers, Harry Blackstone the Magician, Harry Truman, Zack Miller, Elliott Roosevelt, the Baconrinds, and Osa Johnson. Memory has dimmed of some of the most influential people at the ranch. Grif Graham is one of these. Certainly, he was responsible for the beginning of Frank's collection of horns, which in turn, was the beginning of the Woolaroc collections. He was also the man behind the scenes who made those social events hum, and who added so much character to early Woolaroc visits. Sarah White Clements and Gordon Matzene who were the consultants who literally pulled the museum together are also faded from memory. Oddly, Pat Patterson, who was so self-destructive, was the person who carried the museum intact through the historically destructive 1950s and 1960s when, for example, in Bartlesville, the elegant old Delk Hillcrest Country Club clubhouse was razed to make way for a flashier California-modern edifice.

Today Woolaroc might be interpreted as a sort of virtual reality exhibit. Like postmodern literature of a novel within a novel, Woolaroc is a museum within a museum. It is, prima facie, a museum of Western art and artifacts. Just as in Frank's day, from the entry vestibule a visitor turns right into the "Dawn of Time" room where the exhibits that were arranged by Sarah White still stand. Her village model and the murals are still features of the room. The next room, in sequence of time, is the Southwest Indian room, changed little from when Gordon Matzene declared it the prettiest room in the museum. Then follow the Plains Indians, the Cowboys, and the Pioneers.

The sequence and order of the old arrangement reflect the Frederick Jackson Turner orthodoxy of the period, probably partly through the influence of E. E. Dale who had been a graduate student under Turner. A multiethnic character tempers the exhibits, probably because of the anthropological influence of Sarah Clements. The first class design of Gordon Matzene and excellent execution of the plan by Pat Patterson have kept the antique museology from seeming stodgy. Not only does the visitor see an excellent exhibit of the Old West, but he sees an exhibit of the exhibit. It is an experience in visiting a museum on the very cutting edge circa 1940, all the time among one of the finest Western art collections in the country today.

Downstairs the collection is augmented by excellent art acquired since Frank's time, mostly through the generosity of the L. E. Phillips family, and Phil Phillips' outstanding Colt firearms collection.

The Woolaroc aircraft, the Frank Phillips memorabilia collection, and outside, on the North Road, the Oil Patch collection, as well as the lodge, are part of the larger museum of the heyday of Oklahoma oil. This larger museum includes a preservation of Frank Phillips' vision, and so becomes a sort of living museum. It lives and breathes each year in the mountain man encampments, school tours, OK Mozart Woolaroc Concert, and Cow Thieves and Outlaws Reunion. The cooks still turn out real home cooking for the employees and docents, and a few lucky guests, in the kitchen each day, just as they did for Frank and Jane a long time ago. It is a place that captures the heart.

In my car, I leave the parking lot and drive past the office. One of the Indian statues signs good-bye just where I begin to drive over the low water bridge. There have been fall rains and the pasture is in better shape than one might hope, but that was a few weeks ago, and no water is trickling over the spillway now. The oak leaves are just beginning to change color. Rich green is mixed with burnt orange against a brilliant and cloudless cerulean sky. Among the blackjack trees fallow deer are calmly browsing on newly fallen acorns. It is deer hunting season outside the park, and out there the deer are frantic, but in this preserve, where there are no predators, the deer graze in idyllic calm. A pair of rheas pick their way along the road, wishing to cross the fence to join some other birds in the Scotch Pasture. Minivans loaded with children, and big Park Avenue Buicks with silver-haired couples creep along the winding blacktop, stopping to watch a buffalo with her calf or doe and fawn. The animals have good grass and are scattered throughout the ranch.

From the highway back to Bartlesville, I turn right at the microwave towers to return over the dusty County Road-2075. Soon I can look from this high spot, east across the Caney River Valley. From here, beyond John Hughes' fence, for a while I can see no houses or roads. Through this gap in the hills is a passage to higher ground, used in the Territorial days as a route into the Osage. In slavery days this way was sometimes used by runaways who could slip into the good hideouts of the Osage, on their way to Kansas. The gravel road winds down off of the hills and strikes straight east, crosses a railroad track, then dead ends at the Old Tulsa Road, just north of Ochelata. Across the road is H. V. Foster's beautiful ranch and just to its north is the old Tyler land where Louis Chouteau once had his cabin. At the bend of the road, a little way on, is L. E. Phillip's, Philson Farm. Turning north, toward Bartlesville I pass the site where Chouteau had his trading post, and the Osage encamped, and I pass Silver Lake where the Delaware first settled in Washington County. This country is rich in its history of oil, cattlemen, and Indians, and Frank Phillips' fingerprints are still everywhere.

BIBLIOGRAPHY

ARCHIVES AND COLLECTIONS

Bartlesville Public Library, Local and Family History Room. Bartlesville, Oklahoma.

Newspaper clippings, biographical information.

Osage Agency Minerals Office. Pawhuska, Oklahoma.

Drilling logs.

Osage County Clerks Office. Pawhuska, Oklahoma.

Deeds.

Phillips Petroleum Company Archives. Bartlesville, Oklahoma.

Audio tapes and video tapes of interviews with company employees for company history. Paul Endacott manuscripts and transcriptions of his interviews.

Washington County Clerks Office. Bartlesville, Oklahoma.

Deeds.

Woolaroc Archive. Woolaroc, Oklahoma.

The Woolaroc Archive is the major research resource. The Frank Phillips' appointment calendars were kept by his secretary from 1920 to 1942; 1940 is missing. They are a listing of daily appointments and travels. They contain only occasional elucidation. Two annual diaries kept by Jane Phillips in 1935 and 1936, and a European travel diary from 1937 have been found. They contain almost no personal information. The travel diary from John G. Phillips' trip to South America in 1932 is fairly lively, but contains little personal information. There are eight boxes of correspondence, containing as many as 20,000 pages. The correspondence is entirely business and some social, but contains no personal correspondence. It also contains foundation correspondence. Also maps, photographs, scrapbooks, some published material, blueprints, and a computer database, video transcriptions of old movies.

BOOKS AND PUBLICATIONS

"American Brahman Breeders Association History & Background." <brahman.org/history.html>. 1998.

Amick, Hugh. "Meet the Master of Woolaroc Lodge: He Thinks of Posterity While Enriching the Passing Hour." *U.S. Air Services* (August, 1929).

"A Remarkable Preserve in Oklahoma." *Outdoor Oklahoma* (May, 1927).

Barr, Thomas P. "An Archaeological Survey of the Birch Creek Reservoir." General Survey Report No. 6: Oklahoma River Basin Survey Project. Norman: University of Oklahoma Research Institute, 1964.

Bell, Robert E. *Prehistory of Oklahoma.* Orlando: Academic Press, 1984.

Collings, Ellsworth. *The 101 Ranch.* Norman: University of Oklahoma Press, 1971.

Dary, David A. *The Buffalo Book: The Full Saga of the American Animal.* Chicago: Sage Books, 1974.

Ellis, William Donohue. *Out of the Osage: The Foster Story.* Oklahoma City: Oklahoma Heritage Association, 1993.

Ewing, Sherm. *The Ranch: A Modern History of the North American Cattle Industry.* Missoula: Mountain Free Press, 1995.

Foreman, Grant. *Advancing the Frontier.* Norman: University of Oklahoma Press, 1933.

________. *Indians & Pioneners.* Norman: University of Oklahoma Press, 1936.

"Frank Phillips Adopted By the Osage Indians: First White Man To Be So Honored." *The Phillips Gas Tank,* (September-October 1930).

Franks, Kenny A., Paul F. Lambert, and Margaret Withers Teague. *Washington County: A Centennial History.* Oklahoma City: Oklahoma Heritage Association, 1999.

Friedman, S. Morgan. "Inflation Calculator.." http://www.westegg.com/inflation/. 19 September 1999.

Harper, Elizabeth Ann. "Trade and Diplomacy of the Taovayas Indians on the Northern Frontier of New Spain, 1719-1835." Masters thesis, University of Oklahoma, 1951.

Hoffman, Jacks, ed. "Archaeology and Paleoecology of the Central Great Plains," Arkansas Archaeological Survey research series, No. 48. Fayetteville, 1996.

Irving, Washington. *A Tour of the Prairies.* Francis McDermott, ed. Norman, University of Oklahoma Press, 1956.

Johnson, Paul. *Modern Times: The World from the Twenties to the Nineties,* revised edition. New York: HarperCollins, 1991.

Jones, Billy M. *L.E. Phillips: Banker, Oil Man, Civic Leader.* Oklahoma City: Oklahoma Heritage Association, 1981.

The Lotos Club. *The Lotos Experience: the Tradition Continues.* New York: The Lotos Club, 1996.

"The Markle Foundation." The Markle Foundation, 1999. Available at http://www.crossover.com/reus/mip.html; Internet.

Page, Barbara. "Artifacts Reveal 12th Century Culture." *The Gilcrease Magazine of American History* (July 1981).

Pearson, Robert and Brad Pearson. *The J.C. Nichols Chronicle.* Kansas City: Country Club Plaza Press, 1994.

Phillips: The First 66 Years. Bartlesville, Oklahoma: Phillips Petroleum Company, 1983.

Queen, Edward L., Stephen R. Prothero and Gardiner H. Shattuck. *The Encyclopedia of American Religious History.* New York: Facts On File, 1996.

Shelley, Richard C. *Applied Sedimentology.* London: Academic Press, 1988.

Troccoli, Joan Carpenter. "The Sketchbooks of Emil Lenders: Down to the Soles of the Moccasins." *Gilcrease Journal* (Spring 1993).

Wallis, Michael. *Beyond the Hills: The Journey of Waite Phillips,* Oklahoma City: Oklahoma Heritage Association, 1995.

________. *Oil Man: The story of Frank Phillips and the Birth of Phillips Petroleum.* New York: Doubleday, 1988.

________. *The Real Wild West: The 101 Ranch and the Creation of the American West.* New York: St. Martin's Press, 1999.

Williams, J. Howard. "The Rising Tide." The Baptist Messenger (December 9, 1943).

Wilson, R.L. with Gregg Martin. Buffalo Bill's Wild West Show: An American Legend. New York: Random House, 1998.

MANUSCRIPTS

Endacott, Paul. "Background To the Information in the Attached Maps of Early Phillips Oil Operations in the Vicinity of Woolaroc Ranch." Phillips Petroleum Company Archive.

________. "Prelude to Woolaroc." Phillips Petroleum Company Archive.

________.Transcription of an interview with R. B. Finney, 15 March 1979. Phillips Petroleum Company Archive.

________. "Woolaroc's Early Years." Transcription of tape recording of speech, 5 August 1989. Phillips Petroleum Company Archive.

"Highlights of Taped Interviews with H. A. Trower as Recorded on The Files in the Public Relations Department of Phillips Petroleum Company," September 9, 1960. Phillips Petroleum Company Archive.

NEWSPAPERS

Bartlesville Daily Enterprise. Bartlesville, Oklahoma.
Bartlesville Morning Examiner. Bartlesville, Oklahoma.
Christian Science Monitor. Boston, Massachusetts.
The Daily Oklahoman. Oklahoma City, Oklahoma.
Examiner-Enterprise. Bartlesville, Oklahoma.
The Greeley Citizen. Greeley, Colorado.
Kansas City Star. Kansas City, Missouri.
Kansas City Star Magazine. Kansas City, Missouri.
National Magazine. Boston, Massachusetts.
New York Times. New York, New York.
Oklahoma News. Oklahoma City, Oklahoma.
The Tulsa Daily World. Tulsa, Oklahoma.
Tulsa Tribune. Tulsa, Oklahoma.
Washington Daily News. Washington, D. C.
Woolaroc Bulletin. Woolaroc, Oklahoma.

PERSONAL INTERVIEWS

Brown, Jean Campbell
Gorman, Arthur P.
Hughes, John F.
Kane, Richard
Levold, Erwin
Phillips, Lee
Phillips, Bob
Roberts, Bob
Steele-Petrovich, Miriam

NOTES

1 Michael Wallis, *Oil Man,* (New York: Doubleday, 1988), p. 207. Wallis says a niece of Fern Butler was his source.

2 Richard C. Shelley, *Applied Sedimantology,* (London: Academic Press, 1988). Thanks to Dr. Miriam Steele-Petrovich for helping me craft a few intelligible paragraphs about the geohistory of the area.

3 Jacks Hoffman, ed., Archaeology and Paleoecology of the Central Great Plains, Arkansas Archaeological Survey Research Series, No. 48. (Fayetteville, Arkansas. 1996); Robert E. Bell, Prehistory of Oklahoma, (Orlando: Academic Press, 1984).

4 Bell, *Prehistory of Oklahoma,* p. 126.

5 Thomas P. Barr, General Survey Report No. 6: Oklahoma River Basin Survey Project, "An Archaeological Survey of the Birch Creek Reservoir," (Norman: University of Oklahoma Research Institute, 1964).

6 Harper, Elizabeth Ann, "Trade and Diplomacy of the Taovayas Indians on the Northern Frontier of New Spain, 1719-1835," Masters thesis, University of Oklahoma, 1951.

7 Grant Foreman, *Indians & Pioneers,* (Norman: University of Oklahoma Press, 1936); Grant Foreman, Advancing the Frontier, (Norman: University of Oklahoma Press, 1933).

8 Francis Revard, "History You Can Find It Close To Home," *Bartlesville Morning Examiner* (Bartlesville, Oklahoma), July 21, 1935. George B. Keeler was a clerk for Louis Chouteau when he was a young man. He was the one that told this story. Others claim the site was closer to Barnsdall.

9 Paul Johnson, *Modern Times: The World from the Twenties to the Nineties,* revised ed., (New York: Harper Collins, 1991) p. 2.

10 Henry Vernon Foster (1875-1939), a native of Rhode Island, signed a blanket lease with the Osage Tribe for the entire Osage reservation in 1896. The death of his father and uncles left inexperienced young H. V. Foster in charge of Indian Territory Illuminating Oil Company, ITIO. The tribe gave H. V. a second lease on the eastern part of the county in 1906. H. V. developed his interests into Foster Petroleum Company and a part of Cities Service, among other things, so that by the time of his death one newspaper called him the richest man west of the Mississippi. See Ellis, William Donohue, *Out of the Osage: The Foster Story,* Oklahoma City: Oklahoma Heritage Association, 1993.

11 "Highlights of Taped Interview with H. A. Trower as Recorded on Tape Filed in the Public Relations Department of Phillips Petroleum Company," September 9, 1960, Phillips Petroleum Company Archive, Bartlesville, Oklahoma.

12 Wallis, *Oil Man,* pp. 129-130; Ellis,p 129; Paul Endacott, "Background To the Information in the Attached Maps of Early Phillips Oil Operations in the Vicinity of Woolaroc Ranch," 2-27-87, Phillips Petroleum Company Archives. Osage Agency, Minerals Office: Drillers Logs SE 11-25-11, No.1, April 16, 1914, dry; No. 2, May 20, 1914, dry; SE 10-25-11, No. 3, June 26, 1914, dry. This shows that part of the lease had been tested in 1914, but Phillips did not resume drilling again until the 1916-1917 time period when they were selling Washington County leases, and concerned about testing the rest of Lot 185 or risk forfeiture. No.4, SE 12-25-11, 1 September 1916, came in at 15 barrels and quickly went dry; No. 5, SE 12-25-11, November 14, 1916, came in at 2 million feet.3 of gas, but the lease gave all gas to Foster, so it was of no profit to Phillips; No. 6, SW 10-25-11, January 5, 1917 was dry; No. 7, SW 12-25-11, February 23, 1917 was 100 barrels after it was fractured. This is the one that encouraged one more drill. No. 8, SW 12-25-11, March 22, 1917, was 1000 barrels.

13 Endacott, "Background to the Information..."

14 Endacott, "Background to the Information..."; Wallis, *Oil Man.*

15 Osage County Clerk. WD 22. p.522, p.6.

16 Thanks to Bob Roberts, retired Phillips vice president and chemical engineer, for a simple explanation of this old process.

17 Osage County Clerk. WD 23, p. 429, p.542.

18 Osage County Clerk. WD 23, p. 430, p.543.

19 The oldest royalties were 10 percent--later 2/16. These days it is usually 3/16.

20 Conversation with Arthur P. Gorman, May 8, 1999. The Gorman family were Frank Phillip's architects on many

projects since Frank built his 1909 mansion in Bartlesville. They do not have any of the old architectural records, but Art is a repository of his uncle and father's stories, and has many memories of his own.

21 Paul W. Endacott (1902-1996) came to work for Phillips Petroleum Company as a young graduate engineer and basket-ball player, He was President of the com-pany (1951-1962), and retired as Vice Chairman in 1967. Frank Phillips chose him as his successor to Chairman of Trustees of tht Frank Phillips Foundation. He had an active interest in the history of the oil industry and of Woolaroc and was an invaluable resource in his lifetime.

22 Frank Phillips Appointment Calendar, 1920.

23 Neal became a director of Phillips Petroleum Company, and J. C. Nichols was a director of Neal's bank.

24 Ibid.

25 Endacott, Transcription of interview with R. B. Finney, March 15, 1979, Phillips Petroleum Company Archives.

26 *Ibid.*

27 *Ibid.*; Prentice October 6, 1920; Prentice and Earnst October 7; Baruch October 8; Markle October 9.

28 Frank Phillips Appointment Calendar, 1921; Eastern Directors Meeting March 4, 1921; Annual Stockholder's Meeting April 5, 1921; Company Picnic Sunday, June 5, 1921.

29 *Ibid.*

30 *Ibid.*; Perry August 28 and September 9, 1921; Crawley September 11.

31 Frank Phillips Appointment Calendar, 1923.

32 The Lotos Club, *The Lotos Experience: the Tradition Continues,* (New York: The Lotos Club, 1996).

33 Telephone conversation with the club pro, May, 6, 1999. Apawamis Country Club, Rye, New York, is one of the oldest clubs in the country, organized in 1890, the golf course designed in 1896 by Willy Dunn.

34 *Ibid.*

35 Thanks to Richard Kane for a descrip-tion of the old club where his family were members when he was a child.

36 *Ibid.*

37 Phillips Petroleum Company, Annual Report, December 31, 1924 and December 31, 1925.

38 Billy M. Jones, *L.E. Phillips: Banker, Oil Man, Civic Leader,* (Oklahoma City: Oklahoma Heritage Association, 1981), p. 88.

39 Frank Phillips Appointment Calendar, 1922.

40 *Ibid.*

41 *Ibid.* Picnic, June 10, 1922.

42 *Ibid.*

43 Frank Phillips Appointment Calendar, 1925; Dr. Howard Weber was a Pennsylvanian and local physician with several oil interests. He developed the Weber Pool oil field northeast of town. He was very active in Bartlesville society. W. W. Jones was a local realtor and Sunday School Superintendent at First Methodist Church. He was the kind of trustworthy man who knew what was going on in town and who you would call in to put together a quiet deal.

44 *Ibid.*

45 Washington County Clerk, Index 30-26-13.

46 Calendar, 1925.

47 *Ibid.*

48 *Bartlesville Morning Examiner,* November 18,1925.

49 Perry Maxwell was an Ardmore, Oklahoma banker who also designed spectacular golf courses. Other notable courses are Dornick Hills in Ardmore, Oklahoma; Colonial in Ft. Worth; Southern Hills in Tulsa; Oklahoma City Golf and Country Club. Prairie Dunes in Hutchinson, Kansas, is presently rated number 13 in the world. Maxwell also remodeled hole number 14 at Augusta National.

50 *Bartlesville Morning Examiner,* November 9, 1926; November 20, 1926.

51 *Bartlesville Morning Examiner,* June 2, 1925.

52 Calendar, 1923; Information from Richard Kane.

53 *Ibid.*

54 Jones, L. E. Phillips, p. 99.

55 Calendar, 1922; Osage County Clerk, Index Township 25, Range 11.

56 Endacott, "Prelude to Woolaroc," Phillips Petroleum Company Archives.

57 Calendar, 1923.

58 Frank Phillips Home Movies, Tape 1, (Bartlesville: Frank Phillips Mansion), videorecording of 16mm movies.

59 Calendar, 1923.

60 Joe Williams, *Bartlesville,* (Bartlesville: TRW Reda Pump Division, 1978), p. 99.

61 *Ibid.*

62 *Ibid.*

63 Osage Agency, Minerals Office, Drillers Logs SW 12-25-11.

64 *Ibid.*

65 Calendar, 1923.

66 Osage County Clerk, WD46 p.168.

67 Osage County Clerk, Index Township 25, Range 11.

68 *Ibid.*

69 Michael Wallis, *Beyond the Hills: the Journey of Waite Phillips,* (Oklahoma City: Oklahoma Heritage Association, 1995) p. 196.

70 Ibid; Calendar, 1925.

71 Calendar, 1925.

72 "Charles 'Pop' Shirley dies; services Monday," *Examiner Enterprise* (Bartlesville, Oklahoma), February 23, 1979.

73 Jean Campbell Brown to Dick Miller, letter, September 16, 1996, Woolaroc Archives. Photograph accompanied the letter.

74 Telephone interviews with Jean Cambell Brown and Gladys Campbell Atkins, 3/22/01, These women are the daughters of Charles J. and Melia Campbell who lived at "Campbell Field" when Frank purchased the ranch. Their uncle Jim Campbell lived just across the field from them at the time. Their father built a new house and they moved just north of the ranch shortly after construction of the dam was completed. Gladys also described some memories of early Phillipsburg.

75 Walkup, Construction Drawing, "Detail of Ellwood Woven Wire Fence Rock Creek Game Preserve," June 9, 1925, Woolaroc Archive.

76 Joe Williams, *Woolaroc,* (Bartlesville: Frank Phillips Foundation, 1991), p. 14.

77 Boatman, Construction Drawing, "Flood Gate Across Rock Creek Sec 2-25N-11E Phillips Osage Park," September 26, 1925, Woolaroc Archive.

78 May 10, 1999 interview with Jean Campbell Brown, 2233 Venus Court., Bartlesville, Oklahoma.

79 Calendar, 1926, entry for October 3; Grif Graham to Frank Phillips, letter October 21, 1926, Woolaroc Archives.

80 Grif Graham to Frank Phillips, letter, May 20, 1927, Woolaroc Archive.

81 Jean Campbell Brown interview.

82 Frank Phillips to T. A. Latta, letter, June 9, 1927, Woolaroc Archive.

83 Frank Phillips to Clyde Alexander, letter, February 22, 1928, Woolaroc Archive.

84 Geo. Harris, Construction drawings, "Dam and Spillway Clyde Lake F. P. Ranch," March 19, 1928, Woolaroc Archives.

85 E. W. Evans to Frank Phillips, letter, April 30, 1930, Woolaroc Archive.

86 A. H. Riney to Frank Phillips, letter, August 29, 1933, Woolaroc Archive.

87 Wallis, *Beyond the Hills,* p. 145.

88 Ibid, 156.

89 *National Magazine* (Boston, Massachusetts), April 20,1925.

90 Ibid,; Calendar 1925.

91 "Frank Phillips Made Millions," *The Greeley Citizen* (Greeley, Colorado), December 16, 1926.

92 "My Apology," undated and unsigned, but internal evidence places it in late 1926, written by Frank Phillips, Woolaroc Archive.

93 Arthur Gorman, Architect, Construction drawings, "Mr. Frank Phillips' Private Club House," January 12, 1926, Woolaroc Archive. The front view is all that remains of this blueprint, no sides or floor plan.

94 Calendar, 1925.

95 Paul Endacott, "Woolaroc's Early Years," Transcription of tape recording of a August 5, 1989, speech, Phillips Petroleum Company Archives, p. 5.

96 Grif Graham to Frank Phillips, letter, December 16, 1925, Woolaroc Archive.

97 Grif Graham to Frank Phillips, letter, January 9, 1926, Woolaroc Archive.

98 Grif Graham to Frank Phillips, letter, February 8, 1926, Woolaroc Archive.

99 *Ibid.*

100 Grif Graham to Frank Phillips, letter, February 15, 1926, Woolaroc Archive.

101 *Ibid.*

102 Calendar, 1926.

103 E. W. Lenders to Frank Phillips, letter, March 28, 1926, Woolaroc Archive.

104 E. W. Lenders to Frank Phillips, letter, April 15, 1926, Woolaroc Archive.

105 Joan Carpenter Troccoli, "The Sketchbooks of Emil Lenders: Down to the Soles of the Moccasins," *Gilcrease Journal* (Spring 1993), p. 36.

106 Endacott, speech, August 5, 1989.

107 Calendar, 1926.

108 Frank Phillips to J. W. Jenkins, letter, August 10, 1926, Woolaroc Archive.

109 Grif Graham to Frank Phillips, letter, October 21, 1926, Woolaroc Archive.

110 Calendar, 1926. Buck Boren was the father of Kathleen who married E. C. Mullendore. The Mullendores are still a big ranching family in the area E. C. II was murdered in a famous, unsolved, case in 1970.

111 Gid Graham, "Private Preserve of 3,700 Acres in Osage Nation Abounds with Wild Birds and Game," *Tulsa Daily*

World (Tulsa, Oklahoma), May 16, 1926.

112 Calendar, 1926.

113 Frank Phillips to Amon G. Carter, letter, May 20, 1926, Woolaroc Archive.

114 William T. Duggan to Frank Phillips, letter, June 5, 1926, Woolaroc Archive.

115 Frank Phillips to A. L. Schell, letter, July 20, 1926, Woolaroc Archive.

116 Frank Phillips to W. R. Schell, letter, January 5, 1927, Woolaroc Archive.

117 Frank Phillips to Philip W. Thomas, letter, January 20, 1927, Woolaroc Archive.

118 Frank Phillips to Philip W. Thomas, letter, February 27, 1928, Woolaroc Archive.

119 E. W. Evans to Frank Phillips, letter, May 2, 1930, Woolaroc Archive.

120 Frank Phillips to Don Zühlke, letter, March 4, 1939, Woolaroc Archive.

121 Calendar, 1926.

122 Frank Phillips to J. C. Nichols, letter, April 20, 1943, Woolaroc Archive.

123 "Uses Riches to Preserve the Spirit of the West," *Kansas City Star* (Kansas City, Missouri), November 21, 1926.

124 Calendar, 1926. Promotional literature from Wilshire Lawn Improvement Company, Chicago, with note, "Dr. Miller called 10-25-26," Woolaroc Archive..

125 "At the Phillips Family's 'Reunion of Oil Millions' in Bartlesville, Ok.,"*Kansas City Star* (Kansas City, Missouri), December 19, 1926.

126 Arthur Gorman to Frank Phillips, letter, December 14, 1926, Woolaroc Archive.

127 *Kansas City Star,* November 21, 1926.

128 Bell, *Prehistory of Oklahoma,* p. 11.

129 Washington Irving, *A Tour of the Prairies,* (Norman: University of Oklahoma Press, 1956), p. 42.

130 Mac Hasler to Frank Phillips, letter, November 20, 1924, Woolaroc Archive.

131 A. R. Reeves to Frank Phillips, letter, October 29, 1925, Woolaroc Archive.

132 Grif Graham to Frank Phillips, letter, February 15,1926, Woolaroc Archive.

133 Freight bill, Oscar Smith, Eden, Tx. to Grif Graham, July 25, 1925, Woolaroc Archive.

134 Grif Graham to Tamblyn Commission, letter, October 31, 1925; Ed Kleisker to Frank Phillips, letter, November 9, 1925; Grif Graham to Tamblyn Commission, letter, December 2, 1925; "Statement Covering Items 9, 14 and 15 on W. G. Moyle Memorandum," Woolaroc Archive.

135 Grif Graham to Frank Phillips, letter, July 16, 1926, Woolaroc Archive.

136 "Statement Covering Item 9, 14 and 15 on W. G. Moyle Memorandum," Woolaroc Archive.

137 Waite Phillips to Frank Phillips, letter, December 11, 1932, Woolaroc Archive.

138 J. L. Lillard to Frank Phillips, letter, February 26, 1934, Woolaroc Archive.

139 Frank Phillips Appointment Calendar, 1934.

140 Frank Phillips to Tol Pendleton, letter, July 26, 1934, Woolaroc Archive.

141 Frank Phillips to Grif Graham, letter, December 24, 1925; W. T. Leahy to L. E. Phillips, letter, January 5, 1926; Frank Phillips to W. T. Leahy, letter, January 8, 1926, Woolaroc Archive.

142 Grif Graham to Frank Phillips, letter, December 16, 1925 and February 8, 1926, Woolaroc Archive.

143 Frank Phillips to Grover Hornstein, letter, December 28, 1925, Woolaroc Archive.

144 David A. Dary, *The Buffalo Book: The Full Saga of the American Animal,* (Chicago: Sage Books, 1974), p. 232.

145 Buffalo file, Woolaroc Archive.

146 *Ibid.*

147 E. M. Botsford to Frank Phillips, letter, February 12, 1926, Woolaroc Archive.

148 A. H. Leonard to Frank Phillips, letter, March 17, 1926, Woolaroc Archive.

149 Grif Graham to Frank Phillips, letter, July 28, 1927, Woolaroc Archive.

150 Inventories for 1927 and 1928, "Death Losses," Woolaroc Archive.

151 John T. Benson to Frank Phillips, letter, February 17, 1932, Woolaroc Archive.

152 P. P. Balentine to Frank Phillips, letter, June 17, 1935; Frank Phillips to P. P. Balentine, letter, June 30, 1935, Woolaroc Archive.

153 Frank Phillips to Roan Horse, letter, November 16, 1936, Woolaroc Archive.

154 Frank Phillips to Amon Carter, letter, April 8, 1936, Woolaroc Archive.

155 Frank Phillips to A. R. Reeves, letter, December 28, 1925, Woolaroc Archive.

156 Snake King file, Woolaroc Archive.

157 *Ibid.*

158 Grif Graham to Frank Phillips, letter, October 21, 1926, Woolaroc Archive.

159 Antelope file, Woolaroc Archive.

160 W. H. Fuqua to Frank Phillips, letter, January 30, 1926, Woolaroc Archive.

161 Antelope file, Woolaroc Archive.

162 *Bartlesville Morning Examiner,* September 24, 1927.

163 Frank Phillips to Grif Graham, letter, January 11, 1926, Woolaroc Archive.

164 Grif Graham to Frank Phillips, letter, January 25, 1926, Woolaroc Archive.

165 Grif Graham to Frank Phillips, letter, February 8, 1926, Woolaroc Archive.

166 Grif Graham to Frank Phillips, letter, February 15, 1926, Woolaroc Archive.

167 *Ibid.*

168 Grif Graham to Frank Phillips, letter, March 6, 1926, Woolaroc Archive.

169 Grif Graham to Frank Phillips, telegram, May 11, 1926, Woolaroc Archive.

170 Grif Graham to Frank Phillips, telegram, February 4, 1927, Woolaroc Archive.

171 "City in Need of Wildcat Fighter," *Tulsa Daily World,* February 22, 1928.

172 "Capture Two Wildcats On Frank Phillips Ranch," *Bartlesville Daily Enterprise* (Bartlesville, Oklahoma), February 21, 1928, Woolaroc Archive.

173 Frank Phillips to E. W. Evans, letter, June 6, 1930, Woolaroc Archive.

174 W. E. Evans to Frank Phillips, letter, October 16, 1930, Woolaroc Archive.

175 A. E. Gray to Frank Phillips, letter, January 3, 1934, Woolaroc Archive.

176 D. C. Zühlke to Frank Phillips, letter, June 22, 1937, Woolaroc Archive.

177 Frank Phillips to W. J. Compton, letter, September 9, 1921, Woolaroc Archive.

178 W. J. Compton to Frank Phillips, letter, Novemebr 12, 1930, Woolaroc Archive.

179 Frank Phillips to John Seward, letter, January 14, 1942, Woolaroc Archive.

180 Frank Phillips Appointment Calendar, 1934.

181 M. S. Kerr to C. B. Tibbett, letter, May 11,1934, Woolaroc Archive.

182 C. B. Tibbitt to Frank Phillips, letters, May 4 and May 17, 1934, Woolaroc Archive.

183 Marjorie Karch to Fern Butler, letter, May 18, 1934, Woolaroc Archive.

184 Henry Well and Dave Ware to Frank Phillips, letter 17 June 1938 (Woolaroc Archive). Spelling and punctuation are exactly transcribed from the original.

185 Frank Phillips to Dave Ware, letter, July 7, 1938, Woolaroc Archive.

186 Don C. Zühlke to Frank Phillips, letter, July 7, 1938, Woolaroc Archive.

187 Don Zühlke to Frank Phillips, letter, July 21, 1938, Woolaroc Archive.

188 Grif Graham to Frank Phillips, letter, undated, Woolaroc Archive. In a letter of November 9, 1938, Frank Phillips mentions this undated letter was received on the same day as a letter dated July 15, 1938.

189 Maxwell M. Mahaney to Frank Phillips, letter, January 13, 1939, Woolaroc Archive.

190 I. S. Horne to Frank Phillips, letter, February 2, 1926, Woolaroc Archive.

191 *Ibid.*

192 I. S. Horne to Frank Phillips, letter, March 24, 1926, Woolaroc Archive.

193 I. S. Horne to Frank Phillips, letter, April 12, 1926, Woolaroc Archive.

194 Horne file, 1926, Woolaroc Archive.

195 Grif Graham to Frank Phillips, letter, October 21, 1926, Woolaroc Archive.

196 Marjorie Loos to I. S. Horne, letter, October 18, 1926, Woolaroc Archive.

197 Grif Graham to I. S. Horne, telegram, October 21, 1926, Woolaroc Archive.

198 Frank Phillips to Horne's Zoological Arena, letter, November 13, 1926, Woolaroc Archive.

199 Frank Phillips to E. M. Livasy, letter, November 29, 1926, Woolaroc Archive.

200 I. S. Horne to Frank Phillips, letter, December 19, 1926, Woolaroc Archive.

201 "Mr. Rogers Has Discovered What Ruined 48 of Our Cities," *New York Times* (New York, New York), September 28, 1928.

202 Frank Phillips to I. S. Horne, letter June 27, 1926, Woolaroc Archive.

203 Frank Phillips to I. S. Horne, letter, April 21, 1926, Woolaroc Archive.

204 E. W. Lenders to Frank Phillips, letter, May 5, 1926, Woolaroc Archive.

205 Horne file, 1926.

206 "Uses Riches to Preserve the Spirit of the West." *Kansas City Star,* November 21, 1926.

207 Horne files, 1926 and 1927.

208 Grif Graham to Frank Phillips, letter, February 6, 1926, Woolaroc Archive.

209 Frank Phillips to I. S. Horne, telegram, August 5, 1926, Woolaroc Archive.

210 Frank Phillips to I. S. Horne, letter, June 16, 1927, Woolaroc Archive.

211 Frank Phillips to I. S. Horne, letter, July 14, 1927, Woolaroc Archive.

212 C. C. Nickel to Frank Phillips, letter, July 29, 1928, Woolaroc Archive.

213 Frank Phillips to John T. Benson, letter, April 3, 1928, Woolaroc Archive.

214 "Statement covering items 9, 14 and 15 on W. G. Moyle Memorandum;" Kaibab National Forest file, Woolaroc Archive.

215 I. S. Horne to Frank Phillips, letter, September 7, 1928, Woolaroc Archive.

216 John T. Benson to Frank Phillips, letter, July 6, 1927, Woolaroc Archive. This is John Ringling of the Ringling Brothers Circus, a friend of the Miller Brothers.

217 Frank Phillips Appointment Calendar, 1927.

218 Carl Hagenbeck to Frank Phillips, letter, July 28, 1927, Woolaroc Archive.

219 Frank Phillips to John T. Benson, letter, October 8, 1927, Woolaroc Archive.

220 Frank Phillips Appointment Calendar, 1928.

221 Frank Phillips to Heinrich Hagenbeck, letter, August 18, 1928, Woolaroc Archive.

222 John T. Benson to Frank Phillips, letter, April 22, 1929, Woolaroc Archive.

223 Frank Phillips to I. S. Horne, letter, November 4, 1929, Woolaroc Archive.

224 Frank Phillips to I. S. Horne, letter, February 7, 1931, Woolaroc Archive.

225 I. S. Horne to Frank Phillips, letter, April 28, 1931, Woolaroc Archive.

226 I. S. Horne to Frank Phillips, letter, September 3, 1931, Woolaroc Archive.

227 John N. Seward, "Winter Feeding," attachment to a letter John N. Seward to Frank Phillips, December 14, 1940, Woolaroc Archive.

228 Grif Graham to Frank Phillips, letter, January 9, 1926, Woolaroc Archive.

229 Grif Graham to Frank Phillips, letter, December 16, 1925, Woolaroc Archive.

230 Frank Phillips to Grif Graham, letter, January 11, 1926, Woolaroc Archive.

231 Grif Graham file, Woolaroc Archive.

232 Grif Graham to Frank Phillips, letter, March 8, 1926, Woolaroc Archive.

233 John A. Bell to Frank Phillips, letter, November 27, 1926, Woolaroc Archive.

234 Toalson Farm was east of town on Toalson Road, now Adams Boulevard, in the area which is now the Woodland Park development.

235 Frank Phillips to John Bell, letter, May 2, 1929, Woolaroc Archive.

236 Frank Phillips to John Lagle, letter, November 2, 1925; Don Zühlke to Frank Phillips, letter, November 21, 1938, Woolaroc Archive.

237 Frank Phillips to Fred Phillips, letter, August 14, 1946, Woolaroc Archive.

238 Charles Schwab to Frank Phillips, letter, November 12, 1928, Woolaroc Archive.

239 E. W. Evans to Frank Phillips, letter, October 16, 1930, Woolaroc Archive.

240 E. W. Evans to Frank Phillips, letter, November 26, 1930, Woolaroc Archive.

241 Record of Intradermal Tuberculin Test, Oklahoma State Board of Agriculture, October 17, 1930, Woolaroc Archive.

242 E. W. Evans to Frank Phillips, letter, October 23, 1930, Woolaroc Archive.

243 Frank Phillips to E. W. Evans, letter, October 27, 1930, Woolaroc Archive.

244 Dr. J. E. Ewers to Dr. L. J. Allen, letter, November 23, 1930; Dr. C. C. Nickel to Frank Phillips, letter, December 5, 1930; E. W. Evans to Frank Philips, letter, November 21, 1930, Woolaroc Archive.

245 Frank Phillips to E. W. Evans, letter, November 29, 1930, Woolaroc Archive.

246 Ewers to Allen and Nickel to Phillips, letters.

247 Frank Phillips to E. W. Evans, letter, January 7, 1931, Woolaroc Archive.

248 "Hog Analysis—FP Ranch 3-15-32," Woolaroc Archive.

249 "Move to Preserve Texas Longhorns," *New York Times,* May 16, 1928.

250 Frank Phillips to J. M. Davis, letter, August 20, 1928, Woolaroc Archive.

251 Frank Phillips to Amon Carter, letter, December 23, 1929, Woolaroc Archive.

252 George L. Miller to Caesar Kleberg, letter, February 13, 1928; Caesar Kleberg to Frank Phillips, letter, March 24, 1928 Woolaroc Archive.

253 Robert Kleberg to Frank Phillips, letter, April 4, 1928, Woolaroc Archive.

254 Sherm Ewing, *The Ranch: A Modern History of the North American Cattle Industry,* (Missoula: Mountain Free Press, 1995), p. 178.

255 "American Brahman Breeders Association History & Background,"http://www.brahman.org/history.html. 1998.

256 C. E. Byrne to Frank Phillips, letter, April 22, 1929, Woolaroc Archive.

257 Frank Phillips to A. P. Borden, letter, April 6, 1929; A. P. Borden to Frank Phillips, letter, April 11, 1929, Woolaroc Archive.

258 James W. Sartwelle to W. E. West, letter, June 28, 1929, Woolaroc Archive.

259 James W. Sartwelle to Frank Phillips, letter, March 23, 1931, Woolaroc Archive.

260 James W. Sartwelle, American Brahman Breeders Association, to Frank

Phillips, letter, March 23, 1931; E. W. Evans to Frank Phillips, letter, November 21, 1930 Woolaroc Archive.

261 John T. Benson to Frank Phillip, letter, December 3, 1931, Woolaroc Archive.

262 Ranch Report October, 1933, Woolaroc Archive. This report is unsigned and some of the names have been blacked out.

263 Frank Phillips to W. I. Compton, letter, February 24, 1932, Woolaroc Archive.

264 Frank Phillips to E. W. Evans, letter, October 27, 1930, Woolaroc Archive.

265 Frank Phillips to Mrs. Wesley Fisher, letter, July 15, 1936, Woolaroc Archive.

266 E. W. Evans to Frank Phillips, letter, February 2, 1931, Woolaroc Archive.

267 Frank Phillips to W. I. Compton, letter, February 24, 1932, Woolaroc Archive.

268 Frank Phillips to Don Zühlke, letter, March 25, 1938; "Crystal Springs Farmyear 1941," September 17, 1941, Woolaroc Archive.

269 Don Zühlke to Frank Phillips, letter, January 23, 1936, Woolaroc Archive.

270 Frank Phillips to Hiram D. Scott, letter, September 28, 1936, Woolaroc Archive.

271 Frank Phillips to John D. Mayo, letter, November 5, 1937, Woolaroc Archive.

272 Frank Phillips to Don Zühlke, letter, March 25, 1938; Don Zühlke to Frank Phillips, letter, March 29, 1938, Woolaroc Archive.

273 Fern Butler to Marjorie Loos, letter, June 16, 1926 Woolaroc Archive. This must have been a response to the first air mail letter, for Fern wrote a note at the bottom, saying it appeared worth while.

274 *Phillips: The First 66 Years,* pp. 29-52.

275 Calendar, 1927; There are many accounts of the Dole Contest, *Oil Man,* pp. 236-242, has a dramatic recounting of the events of the race.

276 Calendar, 1927.

277 "Woolaroc Airplane Will Be Displayed At Phillips Ranch." *The Morning Examiner.* December 16, 1928.

278 Endacott, "Woolaroc's Early Years." p. 7.

279 Frank Phillips Appointment Calendar, 1929.

280 "Phillips Will Preserve Woolaroc," *Tulsa World,* July 18, 1929.

281 "Goebel, Woolaroc In Air For Last Time," *Tulsa World,* August 13, 1929.

282 Hugh Amick. "Meet the Master of Woolaroc Lodge: He Thinks of Posterity While Enriching the Passing Hour." *U. S. Air Services,* (August 1929).

283 *Ibid.*

284 Woolaroc Bulletin (Summer, 1987), special edition.

285 Frank Phillips to A. R. Reeves, letter, October 27, 1925, Woolaroc Archive.

286 *Tulsa Daily World,* May 16, 1926.

287 "A Remarkable Preserve in Oklahoma," *Outdoor Oklahoma* (May 1927).

288 Richard W. Hill to Frank Phillips, letter, April 9, 1929, Woolaroc Archive.

289 "Phillips Folks on an Outing Today," *Bartlesville Enterprise,* July 24, 1926; "Phillips Employees To Picnic At Ranch," *Bartlesville Morning Examiner,* July 23, 1926.

290 "Wild West Show Staged on Frank Phillips Ranch," *The Morning Examiner,* September 3, 1926.

291 Calendar, 1926.

292 John G. Phillips remarked in his 1932 travel diary that people in La Paz, Bolivia really drank tea at tea parties, not like New York. From this it might be inferred they had afternoon cocktails at Mildred's tea party. John G. Phillips diary, March 29, 1932.

293 Bartlesville Enterprise, November 27, 1926.

294 Calendar, 1926; "Phillips Ranch Guests," Bartlesville Enterprise, December 13, 1926.

295 Frank Phillips to Roy Hoffman, telegram, December 22, 1927, Woolaroc Archive.

296 Frank Phillips to Amon Carter, letter, December 29, 1927. The guest list included General and Mrs. Hoffman, Mr. And Mrs. Walter Harrison, Judge and Mrs. Charles Mason, Judge and Mrs. Frank Burford, and Mr. And Mrs. Fred Capshew from Oklahoma City, and local guests L. E., Clyde Alexander, John Kane, Bill Davis, Burdette Blue, Vernon Foster, Fred Dunn, and their wives

297 Frank Phillips to Hired Hand, telegram, December 31, 1927; Frank Phillips to Amon Carter, letter, January 7, 1928, Woolaroc Archive.

298 Gid Graham to Frank Phillips, letter, January 5, 1927; Frank Phillips to Gid Graham, letter, January 20, 1927, Woolaroc Archive.

299 "Frank Phillips Is Host To Waltonites," *Bartlesville Morning Examiner,* May 6, 1927.

300 "Miss Mabel Boes Pupils Picnicking," Bartlesville Enterprise, May 18, 1927; "Entertains At Woolaroc,"

Bartlesville Morning Examiner, May 18, 1927.

301 "Rail Magnates Pleased With Bartlesville," *Bartlesville Enterprise,* January 20, 1928.

302 "Schwab Entertained At Woolaroc Lodge," *Bartlesville Morning Examiner,* October 20, 1928.

303 Menu, March 12, 1930, Woolaroc Archive.

304 Menu, October 3, 1930, Woolaroc Archive.

305 "Two Boyhood Friends Guests of Frank Phillips Here Today," *Bartlesville Enterprise,* January 28, 1933.

306 "Host To Early Day Cowboys," *Bartlesville Enterprise,* June 3, 1927.

307 "Cow Thieves, Outlaws Mix," *Bartlesville Morning Examiner,* October 25, 1929.

308 Wallis, *Oil Man,* pp. 79-82.

309 Text copy of display case information on Henry Wells, Woolaroc Archive.

310 "Frank Phillips Adopted By the Osage Indians. First White Man To Be So Honored," *The Phillips Gas Tank,* September-October 1930, 7.

311 Wallis, *Oil Man,* p. 269.

312 Frank Phillips Appointment Calendar, 1931; "Entertaining at F. P. Ranch," 1926-34 Woolaroc Archive.

313 Frank Phillips to Richard Conner, letter, November 17, 1933, Woolaroc Archive.

314 Wallis, *Oil Man,* p. 357. Phillips: The First 66 Years, p. 73.

315 K. S. "Boots" Adams (1899-1975). Adams began working for Phillips Petroleum Company in 1920 as a shipping clerk. Adams said that this episode with Chief Bacon Rind was the first time he ever met Frank Phillips. He came to the favorable attention of Mr. Phillips by coming up with a plan to save money on insurance premiums. By the early 1930s he was rising rapidly in the company. In 1938 Frank recommended that Adams succeed him as company president. After Frank's death, Adams went on to become chairman of the board, retiring in 1965.

316 *Ibid.,* 272.

317 Frank Phillips to Fred Lookout, letter, September 30, 1930, Woolaroc Archive.

318 Frank Phillips to Gen. R. L. Bullard, letter, October 25, 1930, Woolaroc Archive.

319 "Osages Confer Tribal Rights Upon Phillips," *The Morning Examiner,* March 29, 1931.

320 Chief Bacon Rind to Frank Phillips, letter, March 31, 1931, Woolaroc Archive.

321 Fred Lookout, Julia Lookout to Frank Phillips, letter, March 30, 1931, Woolaroc Archive.

322 Walter M. Harrison to Frank Phillips, letter, December 31, 1926, Woolaroc Archive.

323 E.P. Earle to Frank Phillips, letter, February 14, 1927, Woolaroc Archive.

324 "G.O.P. Group Meet David W. Mulvane," *Bartlesville Enterprise,* January 8, 1928.

325 Frederick H. Harbison to Frank Phillips, letter, July 3, 1943, Woolaroc Archive.

326 "Oklahoma and Kansas Governors And Wives To Be Guests Of Honor," *Bartlesville Enterprise,* October 1, 1935; "Daily Broadcasts Planned For Show,"*Bartlesville Morning Examiner,* October 2, 1935; "Sardinian Donkeys To Be Exhibited At Show," *Bartlesville Morning Examiner,* October 2, 1935.

327 "President's Son Was Visitor Here Today," *Bartlesville Enterprise,* December 3, 1935.

328 Elliott Roosevelt to Frank Phillips, telegram, December 3, 1935, Woolaroc Archive.

329 Iva Chandler Jones to Frank Phillips, letter, June 29, 1936, Woolaroc Archive.

330 E. W. Marland to Frank Phillips, letter, July 21, 1938, Woolaroc Archive.

331 Merrill C. Meigs to Frank Phillips, letter, September 30, 1938, Woolaroc Archive.

332 Bob Lynn to Frank Phillips, letter, September 27, 1938, Woolaroc Archive.

333 Ken Miller to Frank Phillips, letter, October 4, 1938, Woolaroc Archive.

334 R. C. Jopling to Frank Phillips, letter, December 16, 1938, Woolaroc Archive.

335 Olin D. Johnston to Frank Phillips, letter, October 12, 1938, Woolaroc Archive.

336 W. C. Smoot to Frank Phillips, letter, July 10, 1939; Marge L. Karch to Frank Phillips, letter, July 8, 1939, Woolaroc Archive.

337 Lucille Zühlke to Forrest E. Clements, letter, July 10, 1939, Woolaroc Archive.

338 Bryce L. Twitty to Coke Stephenson, letter, October 20, 1941, Woolaroc Archive.

339 Calendar, 1927.

340 Calendar, 1926.

341 Calendar, July 17, 1927.

342 Calendar 1927.

343 T. A. Latta, "On Life's Highway," *Tulsa World*, January 8, 1928.

344 *Ibid.*

345 Frank Phillips to Tom Latta, letter, January 11, 1928, Woolaroc Archive.

346 Frank Phillips to Mrs. Peggy Gaddis, letter, December 29, 1927, Woolaroc Archive.

347 "Buffalo Milk Sends Scribe Into Ecstasy," *Tulsa World*, n.d.; J. C. Nichols to Frank Phillips, letter, October 5, 1940, Woolaroc Archive.

348 Clyde Nichols, Jr. to Frank Phillips, letter, January 5, 1936, Woolaroc Archive.

349 Frank Phillips to J. C. Nichols, Jr., letter, January 13, 1936, Woolaroc Archive.

350 Frank Phillips to Mrs. Frank M. Breene, letter, June 28, 1926, Woolaroc Archive.

351 Marguerite Riley to Frank Phillips, letter, about April 1929, Woolaroc Archive.

352 Ruth and Little Annie Rooney to Frank Phillips, letter, n.d., Woolaroc Archive.

353 Ruth Alexander, Ph.D. to Frank Phillips, letter, April 12, 1941, Woolaroc Archive. Node Phillips was L.E. Phillips' wife.

354 Wallis, *Oil Man*, p. 276.

355 M. L. Karch to Frank Phillips, letter, February 29, 1939; C. I. Pontius to Frank Phillips, letter, February 27, 1939, Woolaroc Archive.

356 A. M. Hughes to M. L. Karch, letter, October 27, 1939, Woolaroc Archive.

357 Edward L. Queen, Stephen R. Prothero, and Gardiner H. Shattuck, *The Encyclopedia of American Religious History* (New York: Facts On File, 1996), p. 394. She suffered a nervous breakdown in 1930, and she died of an accidental barbiturate overdose in 1944.

358 Secretary to Edith Williams, letter, June 21, 1934, Woolaroc Archive.

359 Frank Phillips to M. H. Aylesworth, letter, October 20, 1938, Woolaroc Archive.

360 "History of St. John Catholic Church," computer database read in telephone conversation with church office July 26, 1999; Archive Office, Tulsa Diocese, telephone conversation with archivist, Mary Jones July 29 and August 2, 1999. Fr. John Van den Hende, born October 9, 1873 Renaix, Belgium, died July 25, 1951. He was the first resident priest at St. John Catholic Church in Bartlesville 1906 to 1925. He built the Rectory in 1907, the church in 1910, and started St. John's Catholic School in 1912. In 1925 he was assigned to Concho Indian School at El Reno, Oklahoma.

361 Calendar, 1929

362 Jane Phillips Diary, 1935.

363 *Ibid.*

364 Francis C. Kelley to W. C. Smoot, letter, December 10, 1938, Woolaroc Archive.

365 F. J. Spellman to Frank Phillips, letter, June 1, 1940; F. J. Spellman to Frank Phillips, letter, June 27, 1940, Woolaroc Archive.

366 July 29, 1999 telephone conversation with Diocesan librarian in Tulsa.

367 "Famous Circus Man Visits Here," *Bartlesville Enterprise*, February 20, 1928.

368 "French Envoy To Visit Phillips Home," Tulsa Tribune (Tulsa, Oklahoma), July 4, 1928; "French Visitor Guest At Woolaroc," *Bartlesville Examiner*, July 4, 1928.

369 Russell S. Rhodes to Frank Phillips, letter, March 3, 1945, Woolaroc Archive.

370 Halifax to Frank Phillips, letter, May 14, 1945, Woolaroc Archive.

371 1930 files, no date or source, Woolaroc Archive.

372 E. W. Evans to Roy E. Lewis, letter, October 18, 1930, Woolaroc Archive.

373 1930 files, no date, handwritten on John G. Phillips stationary, Woolaroc Archive.

374 Frank Phillips, letter, October 26, 1936. Sent to J. M. Davis; R. B. White, President Western Union; E. P. Earle; E. E. Loomis; A. S. Woods ,Markle Foundation; J. L. Johnston, The Lambert Co; H. M. Addinsell, First Boston; Gould Dietz; Amon Carter; R. L. Cochran, Gov. Nebraska; Clyde Tingley, Gov. New Mexico; J. Taylor; Wm. T. Kemper, Woolaroc Archive.

375 E. P. Earle to Frank Phillips, letter, October 28, 1936, Woolaroc Archive.

376 Gould to Frank Phillips, letter, October 28, 1936, Woolaroc Archive.

377 E. E. Loomis to Frank Phillips, letter, October 29, 1936, Woolaroc Archive.

378 J. M. Davis to Frank Phillips, letter, October 29, 1936, Woolaroc Archive.

379 H. L. Jones to Frank Phillips, letter, July 18, 1938, Woolaroc Archive.

380 Frank Phillips to W. B. Lerch, letter, July 20, 1926, Woolaroc Archive.

381 W. B. Lerch to Frank Phillips, report, September 3, 1926, Woolaroc Archive.

382 Frank Phillips to E. E. Dale, letter, February 14, 1928, Woolaroc Archive.

383 Edwin L. O'Neil to T. A. Latta, let-

ter, January 9, 1928, Woolaroc Archive.

384 Frank Phillips to Edwin L. O'Neil, letter, January 13, 1928, Woolaroc Archive.

385 "Cow Thieves, Outlaws Mix," *Bartlesville Examiner,* October 25, 1928.

386 Amon Carter to Frank Phillips, letter, August 13, 1929, Woolaroc Archive.

387 Frank Phillips, gift enclosure, December 30, 1929, to Waite and Genevieve Phillips; Mr. and Mrs. Johnson D. Hill; Mr. and Mrs. Fred Phillips; Mr. and Mrs. H. N. Greis; Mr. and Mrs. Hal C. Moore; Henry McGraw; Mr. and Mrs. W. G. Skelly; Mrs. Fannie McGraw; Mr. and Mrs. John D. Mayo; Mr. and Mrs. Frank L. Moore; Mr. and Mrs. M. M. Doan; Mr. and Mrs. R. Otis McClintock; Mr. and Mrs, F. L. Dunn; Mr. and Mrs. Charles B. Peters; Mr. and Mrs. R. C. Sharp; Mr. and Mrs. George S. Bole; Mrs. Frank M. Breen, Woolaroc Archive.

388 Karch to S. F. Butler, memorandum enclosure, February 14, 1935 "Liquor Supplies Used in Bartlesville January 1, 1926 to November 7, 1934," Woolaroc Archive.

389 Jane Phillips Diary, 1935 in possession of Robert Phillips, copy at Woolaroc.

390 Grif Graham to Frank Phillips, letter, July 28, 1927, Woolaroc Archive.

391 Frank Phillips to Grif Graham, letter, August 26, 1927, Woolaroc Archive.

392 "These People Worked in the Era 1935-1937," information from Joe Billiam Woolaroc Archive.

393 Grif Graham to Frank Phillips, letter, April 1, 1937, Woolaroc Archive.

394 "More Woolaroc Visiting Days As Visitors Increase," *Tulsa Tribune,* October 18, 1939.

395 "Charles 'Pop' Shirley dies; services Monday," *Examiner Enterprise,* February 23, 1979.

396 RFH to R. D. Best, letter, June 20, 1929, Woolaroc Archive.

397 Frank Phillips to Richard A. Addison, letter, December 15, 1927, Woolaroc Archive.

398 Gertrude Smith to Frank Phillips, letter, May 29, 1929, referring an application from Waite's office. Frank was still looking. Marjorie Loos to W. F. Barton, letter, July 27, 1929, West was manager by this date Woolaroc Archive.

399 W. E. West, "following is a list of F. P. Ranch organization." n.d. from among 1930 papers Woolaroc Archive.

400 E. W. Evans to Frank Phillips, letter, March 14, 1930, Woolaroc Archive.

401 E. W. Evans to Frank Phillips, letter, April 25, 1930, Woolaroc Archive.

402 E. W. Evans to Frank Phillips, letter, September 2, 1930, Woolaroc Archive.

403 Frank Phillips to W. E. West, letter, December 29, 1930, Woolaroc Archive.

404 Frank Phillips to W. E. West, letter, January 13, 1931, Woolaroc Archive.

405 E. W. Evans to Frank Phillips, letter, February 2, 1931, Woolaroc Archive.

406 W.E. West, "Following is a list of the F. P. Ranch organization," Woolaroc Archive.

407 E. W. Evans to Frank Phillips, letter, June 6, 1930, Woolaroc Archive.

408 Interview with niece Bernadine Knotts, Bartlesville, Oklahoma, June 10, 1999.

409 Frank Phillips to W. I. Beavers, letter, April 1, 1932, Woolaroc Archive.

410 Unsigned ranch report, October 1933, Woolaroc Archive.

411 A. H. Riney to Frank Phillips, letter, November 20, 1933, Woolaroc Archive.

412 "Statement Covering Items 9, 14 and 15 on W. G. Moyle Memorandum."

413 Marjorie Loos Karch to Fern Butler, letter, March 15, 1934, Woolaroc Archive.

414 M. S. Kerr to Mrs. Karch, letter, March 4, 1935, Woolaroc Archive.

415 Arthur S. Phillips to Frank Phillips, letter, March 24, 1935, Woolaroc Archive.

416 Frank Phillips to Arthur S. Phillips, letter, March 26, 1935, Woolaroc Archive.

417 Gordon Matzene to Frank Phillips, letter, April 24, 1940, Woolaroc Archive.

418 Don Zühlke to Frank Phillips, letters August 11, 1936, and June 22, 1937, Woolaroc Archive.

419 M. L. Karch to Frank Phillips, letter, February 12, 1932, Woolaroc Archive.

420 I. S. Horne to Frank Phillips, letter, May 1, 1930, Woolaroc Archive.

421 Marjorie L. Karch to S. F. Butler, letter enclosure "Statement of Ranch Deductions—Year 1930 to Date (November 1st)," December 9, 1930, Woolaroc Archive.

422 J. R. Baradel to Frank Phillips, letter, September 16, 1933, Woolaroc Archive.

423 F. W. Alexander to Frank Phillips, telegram, July 18, 1933, Woolaroc Archive.

424 Hy Byrd to W. C. Smoot, letter, September 14, 1939, Woolaroc Archive.

425 R. M. Summers, K.S. Adams, T. V. Stevens to Frank Phillips, letter, May 25, 1933, Woolaroc Archives.

426 S. F. Butler to Frank Phillips, memorandum, September 14, 1934, Woolaroc Archive.

427 Walter A. Cooper to P. W. Fitzkee, letter, September 11, 1934, Woolaroc Archives.

428 Frank Phillips to Phillips Petroleum Company, invoice, November 28, 1934, Woolaroc Archive.

429 T. A. Latta.

430 "Petrified Wood," unsigned, undated essay; T. C. Sherwood to Frank Phillips, letter October 27, 1926, Woolaroc Archive. Evidently the fossil in question was a section of, not an entire, trunk of Calamites, preserved as a silica replacement and not a mold of the plant. There is no indication of exactly how large the fossil may have been. It is no longer at Woolaroc and no one knows what became of it.

431 Frank Phillips to T. C. Sherwood, letter, November 5, 1926, Woolaroc Archive.

432 Grif Graham to Frank Phillips, letter, May 7, 1926, Woolaroc Archive.

433 Frank Phillips to Albert Friedrich, letter, March 31, 1926, Woolaroc Archive.

434 Bert Gaddis to Frank Phillips, letter, December 23, 1925; Grif Graham to Frank Phillips, letter, February 15, 1926, Woolaroc Archive.

435 Grif Graham to Frank Phillips, letter, March 8, 1926, Woolaroc Archive.

436 Frank Phillips to Louis Weber, letter, September 8, 1926, Woolaroc Archive.

437 E. W. Lenders to Frank Phillips, letter, April 15, 1926, Woolaroc Archive.

438 *Gilcrease Journal* (Spring 1993), p.37.

439 Frank Phillips to E. W. Lenders, letter, July 31, 1926, Woolaroc Archive.

440 Frank Phillips to E. W. Lenders, letter, April 7, 1927, Woolaroc Archive.

441 Frank Phillips to E. W. Lenders, letter, April 23, 1927, Woolaroc Archive.

442 Robert Lindneux to Frank Phillips, letter, December 7, 1927, Woolaroc Archive.

443 Fern Butler to Marjorie Loos, letter, February 19, 1930, Woolaroc Archive.

444 Henry Balink to Frank Phillips, letter, March 9, 1925, Woolaroc Archive.

445 According to *Mantle Fieldings Dictionary,* Stanley Arthurs was a Delaware artist, listed as a mural painter, he was a student of Howard Pyle.

446 Frank Phillips to A. Felix du Pont, letter, May 20, 1926, Woolaroc Archive.

447 Frank Phillips to A. N. Ruble, letter, May 20, 1926, Woolaroc Archive.

448 Frank Phillips to Dr. Richard L. Sutton, letter, June 14, 1926, Woolaroc Archive.

449 Frank Phillips to Mr. and Mrs. J. S. Leach, letter, September 4, 1926, Woolaroc Archive.

450 H. V. Foster to Frank Phillips, letter, September 10, 1926; Frank Phillips to Henry Vernon Foster, letter, September 20, 1926, Woolaroc Archive.

451 Frank Phillips to John Irwin, letter, November 3, 1926, Woolaroc Archive.

452 R. A. Broomfield to Frank Phillips, letter, November 29, 1926,Woolaroc Archive.

453 Grif Graham to Frank Phillips, letter, January 25, 1926, Woolaroc Archive.

454 C. Jonas to Frank Phillips, letter, April 20, 1934, Woolaroc Archive.

455 E. W. Lenders to Frank Phillips, letter, April 15, 1926, Woolaroc Archive.

456 Frank Phillips to A. P. Hill, letter, July 30, 1928, Woolaroc Archive.

457 Marjorie Loos to A. P. Hill, letter, June 18, 1929; A. P. Hill to Marjorie Loos, letter, June 20, 1929, Woolaroc Archive.

458 Woolaroc Memorandum, February 11, 1927, Woolaroc Archive.

459 Frank Phillips to Gen. Roy Hoffman, letter, February 11, 1927, Woolaroc Archive.

460 Roy Hoffman to Frank Phillips, letter, February 13, 1927, Woolaroc Archive. The common name is Marco Polo's sheep.

461 Theodore Roosevelt to Roy Hoffman, letter, February 17, 1927, Woolaroc Archive.

462 Roy Hoffman to Frank Phillips, letter, May 3, 1927, Woolaroc Archive.

463 Frank Phillips to L. D. Bertillion, letter, August 20, 1928, Woolaroc Archive.

464 Frank Phillips to Heinrich Hagenbeck, letter, February 28, 1929, Woolaroc Archive.

465 Frank Phillips to Heinrich Hagenbeck, letter, March 12, 1929, Woolaroc Archive.

466 Inventory, April 15, 1929; Memorandum, M. G. Terry, April , 1929, Woolaroc Archive.

467 Marjorie Loos to Geo. B. Spencer, letter, October 4, 1929, Woolaroc Archive.

468 C. F. Meyer to Frank Phillips, letter, July 7, 1931, Woolaroc Archive.

469 Nanette Morrison, "Examiner Reporter Presents Woolaroc," *Bartlesville Morning Examiner, May* 20, 1934.

470 L. D. Bertillion to Frank Phillips, letter, December 16, 1926, Woolaroc Museum.

471 Frank Phillips to Mrs. L. D. Bertillion, letter, May 30, 1945, Woolaroc Archive.

472 John I. White to Director Woolaroc Museum, letter and enclosure, June 6, 1976. "Enclosed is a short item on Texan, L. D. Bertillion, that is being considered for use in a forthcoming book," Woolaroc Archive.

473 L. S. Zühlke to Frank Phillips, letter, May 2, 1939, Woolaroc Archive.

474 Frank Phillips to Amon Carter, letter, May 9, 1939, Woolaroc Archive.

475 J. M. Davis to Frank Phillips, letter, September 7, 1927, Woolaroc Archive.

476 J. M. Davis to Frank Phillips, letter, September 24, 1927, Woolaroc Archive.

477 Frank Phillips to J. M. Davis, letter, October 4, 1927, Woolaroc Archive.

478 J. M. Davis to Frank Phillips, letter, October 8, 1927, Woolaroc Archive.

479 Frank Phillips to J. M. Davis, letter , October 10, 1927, Woolaroc Archive.

480 *U. S. Air Services.*

481 Frank Phillips to Paul J. McIntyre, letter, November 10, 1926, Woolaroc Archive.

482 Smug Byler to Frank Phillips, letter, May 4, 1928, Woolaroc Archive.

483 Smug Byler to Frank Phillips, letter, May 24, 1928, Woolaroc Archive.

484 Smug Byler to Frank Phillips, letter, June 18, 1928, Woolaroc Archive.

485 John G. Phillips diary; Roy Chapman Andrews to Frank Phillips, letter, March 11, 1932, Woolaroc Archive.

486 C. O. Dobbins to Frank Phillips, letter, August, 1936, Woolaroc Archive.

487 Phillip R. Phillips to Frank Phillips, letter, June 8, 1939, Woolaroc Archive.

488 W. E. Carlin to George H. Hunter, letter, June 21, 1939, Woolaroc Archive.

489 Frank Phillips to Mrs. H. V. Foster, letter, October 25, 1940, Woolaroc Archive.

490 Frank Phillips to Marie Foster, letter, December 12, 1940, Woolaroc Archive.

491 Warren E. Nyer to Woolaroc Museum, letter, May 5, 1953, Woolaroc Archive.

492 Nanette Morrison, "Examiner Reporter Presents Woolaroc," *Bartlesville Morning Examiner,* May 20, 1934.

493 "Articles Presented To Mr. Frank Phillips For Woolaroc Lodge," undated memorandum, probably from 1927, Woolaroc Archive.

494 Rev. O. M. Millsap to Frank Phillips, letter, January 5, 1928, Woolaroc Archive

495 Calendar, 1928.

496 "Phillips Adds Historic Stage To Collection," *Bartlesville Morning Examiner,* July 15, 1928.

497 Nanette Morrison, "Examiner Reporter Presents," *Bartlesville Morning Examiner,* May 20, 1934.

498 Bert G. Phillips to Frank Phillips, letter, June 25, 1939, Woolaroc Archive.

499 Ralph C. Martinez to Frank Phillips, letter, June 19, 1939, Woolaroc Archive.

500 V. M. Locke to P. J. Hurley, letter, April 27, 1931, Woolaroc Archive.

501 Frank Phillips to P. J. Hurley, letter, January 10, 1931, Woolaroc Archive.

502 Grif to M. L. Karch, letter, January 3, 1939, Woolaroc Archive.

503 M. L. McClure to Frank Phillips, letter, February 23, 1928, Woolaroc Archive.

504 A. W. Paine to Frank Phillips, letter, May 7, 1927, Woolaroc Archive.

505 Frank Phillips to George B. Keeler, letter, June 5, 1927, Woolaroc Archive.

506 P. J. Hurley to Frank Phillips, letter, February 5, 1927, Woolaroc Archive.

507 Frank Phillips to Grant Foreman, letter, February 8, 1927, Woolaroc Archive.

508 Grant Foreman to Frank Phillips, letter, July 28, 1927, Woolaroc Archive.

509 Grant Foreman to Frank Phillips, letter and enclosure, October 18, 1927, Woolaroc Archive.

510 Frank Phillips to Grant Foreman, letter, December 14, 1927, Woolaroc Archive.

511 Grant Foreman to Frank Phillips, letter, May 18, 1938, Woolaroc Archive.

512 Frank Phillips to Grant Foreman, letter, May 20, 1938, Woolaroc Archive.

513 W. B. Bissell to Frank Phillips, letter, November 8, 1927, Woolaroc Archive.

514 Calendar, 1928.

515 Frank Phillips to E. E. Dale, letter, February 14, 1929, Woolaroc Archive.

516 Betty Kirk to Frank Phillips, letter, July 17, 1929, Woolaroc Archive.

517 Frank Phillips to Ellsworth Collings, letter, October 21, 1937, Woolaroc Archive.

518 William Finders Petrie was the famous archaeologist who discovered Tutankhamen's tomb in Egypt.

519 Wallis, *Oil Man,* p. 407.

520 J. W. Hale to Frank Phillips, letter, December 10, 1935, Woolaroc Archive.

521 Barbara Page, "Artifacts Reveal 12th Century Culture," *The Gilcrease Magazine of American History and Art* (July, 1981).

522 Frank Phillips Appointment Calendar, 1936.

523 Harry Lysee to Frank Phillips, letter, July 15, 1936, Woolaroc Archive.

524 John C. Pfalzgraf to Frank Phillips, letter and inventory, September 14, 1936, Woolaroc Archive.

525 Jack Reid to Frank Phillips, letter, August 7, 1936, Woolaroc Archive.

526 Frank Phillips to Jack Reid, letter, August 10, 1936, Woolaroc Archive.

527 Jack Reid to Frank Phillips, letter, September 5, 1936, Woolaroc Archive.

528 Lucille Zühlke to Forrest E. Clements, letter, September 16, 1936, Woolaroc Archive.

529 Lucille Zühlke to Forrest Clements, letter, October 27, 1936, Woolaroc Archive.

530 Forrest Clements to Lucille Zühlke, letter, January 12, 1938, Woolaroc Archive.

531 Lucille Zühlke to Forrest Clements, letter, October 12, 1938, Woolaroc Archive.

532 Forrest Clements to Lucille Zühlke, letter, November 4, 1938, Woolaroc Archive.

533 Forrest Clements to Frank Phillips, letter, December 11, 1938, Woolaroc Archive.

534 Sarah White to Mrs. Don Zühlke, letter, February 8, 1939, Woolaroc Archive.

535 Forrest E. Clements to Frank Phillips, letter and enclosure, "Account of Expenditures from the Frank Phillips Foundation Inc.," November 29, 1939, Woolaroc Archive.

536 Sarah White to Lucille Zühlke, letter, February 27, 1940, Woolaroc Archive.

537 Sarah White to Frank Phillips, letter, April 18, 1941, Woolaroc Archive.

538 Sarah White to Frank Phillips, letter, April 28, 1941, Woolaroc Archive.

539 Sarah Clements to Frank Phillips, letter, September 16, 1941, Woolaroc Archive.

540 Sarah Clements to Frank Phillips, letter, January 2, 1942, Woolaroc Archive.

541 Lucille Zühlke to Sarah White, letter, April 6, 1940, Woolaroc Archive.

542 Sarah White to Frank Phillips, letter, October 24, 1940, Woolaroc Archive. R. Gordon Matzene (1880-1950) was born in London, and educated in Denmark and Italy. As a young man he was an overseer on a Thomas Lipton tea plantation in Ceylon. He was in China during the Boxer Rebellion where he began a large collection of oriental and South Seas art. He was a photographer, with studios in New York, Chicago, and Los Angeles. He photographed many early stars of the stage and screen, also several members of European royalty, and every living maharajah in India. After becoming close friends with Mr. and Mrs. Charles Calkins in Ponca City, he moved there in 1927. He gave a large oriental art collection to the University of Oklahoma, and made other generous gifts in Ponca City.

543 Forrest E. Celments to Frank Phillips, letter, July 22, 1940, Woolaroc Archive.

544 Frank Phillips to Sarah White, letter, November 9, 1940, Woolaroc Archive.

545 Sarah White to Frank Phillips, letter, December 18, 1940, Woolaroc Archive.

546 Frank Phillips to Sarah White, letter, December 27, 1940, Woolaroc Archive.

547 Forrest Clements to Frank Phillips, letter, January 23, 1941, Woolaroc Archive.

548 *Ibid.*

549 Sarah White to Frank Phillips, letter, April 28, 1941, Woolaroc Archive.

550 Frank Phillips Appointment Calendar, 1942.

551 Sarah White to Frank Phillips, letter, June 22, 1941, Woolaroc Archive.

552 John P. Harrington to Forrest Clements, letter, April 29, 1940, Woolaroc Archive.

553 Marjorie Karch to Sam Tilden, letter, August 5, 1940, Woolaroc Archive.

554 Sarah Clements to Frank Phillips, letter, April 7, 1942, Woolaroc Archive.

555 John G. Phillips, travel diary, 1932.

556 John Phillips to Frank Phillips, letter, December 25, 1932, Woolaroc Archive.

557 John G. Phillips to Frank Phillips, letter, December 25, 1933, Woolaroc Archive.

558 "Articles Purchased From Rudolph Rhein, Tulsa, Feb. 6, 1937," Woolaroc Archive.

559 "South American Collection," P.3, 5. Woolaroc Archive.

560 *Ibid.*

561 Ellsworth Collings to Frank Phillips, letter, July 27, 1945, Woolaroc Archive.

562 L. M. Tidd to Frank Phillips, letter, December 23, 1927, Woolaroc Archive.

563 "List of Blades Collection J. A. Richards," January 1, 1930, Woolaroc Archive.

564 Marjorie L. Karch to A. V. Muzzy, letter, March 14, 1931, Woolaroc Archive.

565 L. E. Phillips to Frank Phillips, letter, June 15, 1938, Woolaroc Archive.

566 Frank Phillips to Phil Phillips, letter, November 12, 1940, Woolaroc Archive.

567 E. W. Lenders to Frank Phillips, letter and handwritten instrument by Emil W. Lenders, September 30, 1930, Woolaroc Archive.

568 E. W. Lenders to Frank Phillips, letter, November 6, 1930, Woolaroc Archive.

569 Frank Phillips to Carrico V. Lenders, letter, May 22, 1934, Woolaroc Archive.

570 Marjorie Karch to Frank Phillips, undated internal memorandum, probably June 25, 1935, Woolaroc Archive.

571 *Gilcrease,* (Spring, 1993), p. 38.

572 Frank Phillips to R. S. Kerr and S. H. Lynn, letter, June 17, 1937, Woolaroc Archive.

573 Jos. S. Kidder to Pat Patterson, letter, May 19, 1959, Woolaroc Archive.

574 C. M. Shachet, "He Lives As A Cowboy To Paint The Wild West," *The Kansas City Star Magazine* (Kansas City, Missouri), June 13, 1926.

575 Gordon Hines to Frank Phillips, letter, April 3, 1933, Woolaroc Archive.

576 Woolaroc Catalog No. McL149.

577 C. E. Hochstetler to Frank Phillips, letter, June 28, 1935, Woolaroc Archive.

578 Woolaroc Catalog No. McL153.

579 Woolaroc Catalog No.151, 1935.

580 Ellsworth Collings Collection file, Woolaroc Archive.

581 Frank Phillips to Zack T. Miller, letter, February 7, 1938, Woolaroc Archive.

582 T. S. Terry to Frank Phillips, letter, February 9, 1938, Woolaroc Archive.

583 George F. Jordan to Frank Phillips, letter, March 1, 1938, Woolaroc Archive.

584 Frank Phillips to Zack Miller, letter, October 31, 1940, Woolaroc Archive.

585 Frank Phillips to Mabel Mix, letter, March 16, 1942, Woolaroc Archive.

586 Pat Patterson to Eldon K. Everett, letter, March 25, 1960, Woolaroc Archive.

587 Woolaroc Catalog, No. McL 155.

588 "The following lists given to Pat Patterson February 21, 1942, to be returned in due course to Bartlesville files," Woolaroc Archive.

589 Woolaroc Catalog No. 7

590 Margaret Elliott to Sarah White, letter, December 1, 1940, Woolaroc Archive.

591"Suggestions for lighting in museum," memorandum Margaret Elliott to Frank Phillips, undated Woolaroc Archive.

592 J. Steinfeld to Frank Phillips, letter, September 21, 1927, Woolaroc Archive.

593 Joesph Thoburn, "Shameless Acts of Vandalism Damage Valuable Works of Art in Oklahoma," undated newspaper article, probably from 1936; Mary Bridgewater, "John Noble's Western Painting Home Again," *Tulsa World*, May 22, 1936.

594 John Shelby Metcalf to Frank Phillips, letter, April 5, 1937, Woolaroc Archive.

595 Paul Gardner to J. C. Nichols, letter, April 26, 1937, Woolaroc Archive.

596 Frank Phillips to James J. Kelleher, letter, December 11, 1939, Woolaroc Archive.

597 Frank Phillips to J. C. Nichols, letter, April 19, 1937, Woolaroc Archive.

598 Fern Butler to Frank Phillips, letter, March 17, 1928, Woolaroc Archive.

599 S. F. Butler to Frank Phillips, letter, December 7, 1936, Woolaroc Archive.

600 Marjorie Karch to Fern Butler, letter, September 19, 1938, Woolaroc Archive.

601 Marjorie Karch to Cornelius J. Sullivan, letter, December 28, 1936, Woolaroc Archive.

602 Z. T. Miller to Frank Phillips, letter, September 12, 1929, Woolaroc Archive.

603 Calendar, January 29, 1937.

604 Frank Phillips Appointment Calendar, March 29, 1941.

605 Gordon Matzene to Frank Phillips, letter, March 20, 1941, Woolaroc Archive.

606 Gordon Matzene to Frank Phillips, letter, May 12, 1941, Woolaroc Archive.

607 *Ibid.*

608 Calendars 1936, 1937.

609 Adah S. Sanders to Frank Phillips, letter, December 27, 1936, Woolaroc Archive.

610 Frank Phillips to Willard E. Johnson, letter, October 9, 1939, Woolaroc Archive.

611 Paul J. Baumgarten to Frank Phillips, letter, November 6, 1940, Woolaroc Archive.

612 Erwin S. Barrie to Phillip R. Phillips, letter, October 22, 1949, Woolaroc Archive.

613 Mary Sullivan to Frank Phillips, letter, December 18, 1936, Woolaroc Archive.

614 Frank Phillips to Mrs. Will Rogers, letter, February 4, 1937, Woolaroc Archive.

615 Nancy Russell to Frank Phillips, letter, February 15, 1937, Woolaroc Archive.

616 Mary Sullivan to Frank Phillips, letter, February 10, 1937, Woolaroc Archive.

617 Frank Phillips to S. F. Butler, letter, March 2, 1939, Woolaroc Archive.

618 Conversation with John Hughes, October 15, 1999. *Oil Man* has a good description of the case, p.377-379.

619 Frank Phillips Appointment Calendar, 1938.

620 Medical report Dr. Joseph Lintz, March 30, 1938, Woolaroc Archive.

621 Medical report Lindsay S. Milne, M.D., April 27, 1938.

622 Dr. Arthur W. Proetz to Dr. Lawrence Post, letter, September 20, 1938, Woolaroc Archive.

623 Thomas H. Johnson, M.D. to Frank Phillips, letter, August 2, 1938, Woolaroc Archive.

624 Frank Phillips to Willard E. Johnson, letter, October 9, 1939, Woolaroc Archive.

625 "Paintings at Frank Philips Ranch," January 18, 1988, Woolaroc Archive.

626 Marjorie Karch to Fern Butler, letter, January 29, 1939, Woolaroc Archive.

627 Marjorie Karch to Fern Butler, letter, January 20, 1939, Woolaroc Archive.

628 Fern Butler to Marjorie Karch, letter, March 1 and March 3, 1939, Woolaroc Archive.

629 R. Gordon Matzene to Frank Phillips, letter, January 13, 1939, Woolaroc Archive.

630 Marjorie Karch to C. F. Calkins, letter, June 16, 1939, Woolaroc Archive.

631 Gordon Matzene to Frank Phillips, letter, April 18, 1939, Woolaroc Archive.

632 Frank Phillips to Gordon Matzene, letter, May 10, 1939, Woolaroc Archive.

633 Gordon Matzene to Frank Phillips, letter, January 22, 1940, Woolaroc Archive.

634 Gordon Matzene to Mrs. Clubb, letter, October 4, 1939, Woolaroc Archive.

635 L. A. Clubb to Mr. Matzene, letter, October 4, 1939, Woolaroc Archive.

636 Gordon Matzene to Frank Phillips, letter, December 9, 1939, Woolaroc Archive.

637 *Ibid.*

638 Frank Phillips to Gordon Matzene, letter, December 11, 1939, Woolaroc Archive.

639 Frank Phillips to Gordon Matzene, letter, January 18, 1940, Woolaroc Archive.

640 Gordon Matzene to Frank Phillips, letter, June 24, 1940, Woolaroc Archive.

641 Frank Phillips to Gordon Matzene, letter, June 27, 1940, Woolaroc Archive.

642 *Ibid.*

643 Gordon Matzene to Frank Phillips, letter, July 1, 1940, Woolaroc Archive.

644 Frank Phillips to Gordon Matzene, letter, July 5, 1940, Woolaroc Archive.

645 Gordon Matzene to Frank Phillips, letter, April 25, 1940; Craig Sheppard to Mr. Matzene, letter, Tuesday, Woolaroc Archive.

646 Frank Philips to Gordon Matzene, letter, June 3, 1940, Woolaroc Archive.

647 Gordon Matzene to Frank Phillips, undated letter, Woolaroc Archive.

648 Gordon Matzene to Professor O. B. Jacobson, undated letter, Woolaroc Archive.

649 O. B. Jacobson to Gordon Matzene, letter, October 29, 1941, Woolaroc Archive.

650 Unsigned to Sarah, letter, November 1, 1941, Woolaroc Archive. Only Frank's secretary, Marjorie Karch, would have had access to these quotations.

651 Gordon Matzene to Frank Phillips, letter, July 8, 1940, Woolaroc Archive.

652 Gordon Matzene to Frank Phillips, letter, July 9, 1940, Woolaroc Archive. This is where the Frederick Jackson Turner historiography of the West is first articulated. Turner proposed that the West was settled by an advancing frontier in stages, first of trappers, then cowboys, then farmers.

653 Frank Phillips to Gordon Matzene, letter, July 16, 1940, Woolaroc Archive.

654 Frank Phillips to Dorothy Wentz, letter, August 23, 1927; Frank Phillips to Frank B. Burford, letter, July 2, 1928, Woolaroc Archive.

655 Gordon Matzene to Frank Phillips, letter, October 28, 1940 Woolaroc Archive.

656 Gordon Matzene to Frank Phillips. Letter, November 14, 1940.

657 Odd Halseth to Frank Phillips, letter, May 15, 1940, Woolaroc Archive.

658 J. H. Sharp to Clay Smith, letter, February 16, 1940, Woolaroc Archive.

659 Gordon Matzene to Frank Phillips, letter, October 4, 1940, Woolaroc Archive.

660 Gordon Matzene to Frank Phillips, letter, October 28, 1940, Woolaroc Archive.

661 Gordon Matzene to Frank Phillips, letter, July 9, 1940, Woolaroc Archive.

662 Frank Phillips to Gordon Matzene, letter, June 27, 1940, Woolaroc Archive.

663 Gordon Matzene to Frank Phillips, letter, January 9, 1941, Woolaroc Archive.

664 Gordon Matzene to Margaret Elliott, letter, November 18, 1940, Woolaroc Archive.

665 Frank Phillips to Gordon Matzene, letter, September 2, 1941, Woolaroc Archive.

666 Frank Phillips to Gordon Matzene, letter, February 21, 1942, Woolaroc Archive.

667 Gordon Matzene to Frank Phillips, letter, undated, Woolaroc Archive. This letter was probably written in November 1940 because it discusses the mural.

668 Frank Phillips to W. C. Thompson, letter, January 22, 1941, Woolaroc Archive.

669 E. W. Marland to Frank Phillips, letter, March 11, 1940, Woolaroc Archive.

670 Gordon Matzene to Nan Sheets, letter, April 18, 1940, Woolaroc Archive.

671 Gordon Matzene to Frank Phillips, letter, July 7, 1940, Woolaroc Archive.

672 Gordon Matzene to Frank Phillips, letters, July 19, 1940, and August 6, 1940, Woolaroc Archive.

673 Powder River Jack to Frank Phillips, letter, July 15, 1938, Woolaroc Archive.

674 Powder River Jack Lee to Frank Phillips, letter, February 16, 1936, Woolaroc Archive.

675 Frank Phillips to Powder River Jack Lee, letter, March 7, 1936, Woolaroc Archive.

676 G. T. Nelson to Frank Phillips, letter, December 23, 1939, Woolaroc Archive.

677 Frank Phillips to Harry Carr, letter, January 31, 1940, Woolaroc Archive.

678 Frank Phillips to Betty Rogers, letter, January 31, 1940, Woolaroc Archive.

679 Harry Carr to Frank Phillips, letter, February 5, 1940, Woolaroc Archive.

680 Frank Phillips to Harry Carr, letter, February 6, 1940, Woolaroc Archive.

681 Frank Phillips to K. S. Adams, letter, March 13, 1940, Woolaroc Archive.

682 *Ibid.*

683 Jim to KSA, memorandum, March 16, 1940, Woolaroc Archive.

684 Unsigned memorandum, March 20, 1940, Woolaroc Archive.

685 Frank Phillips to Nancy Russell, letter, February 21, 1940, Woolaroc Archive.

686 Frank Phillips to Nancy Russell, letter, March 2, 1940, Woolaroc Archive.

687 Gordon to Frank Phillips, telegram, March 10, 1940, Woolaroc Archive.

688 Frank Phillips to Betty Rogers, letter, March 12, 1940, Woolaroc Archive.

689 Frank Phillips to Lucille Zühlke, letter, March 12, 1940, Woolaroc Archive.

690 Gordon Matzene to Frank Phillips, letter, March 19, 1940, Woolaroc Archive.

691 Gordon Matzene to Frank Phillips, letter, March 19, 1940, Woolaroc Archive.

692 Bob Stivers to Dave, letter, May 13, 1940, Woolaroc Archive.

693 Bob Stivers to D. C. Hemsell, letter, October 25, 1940, Woolaroc Archive.

694 John W. Donner to D. C. Hemsell, letter, May 17, 1941, Woolaroc Archive.

695 John W. Donner to David C. Hemsell, letter, May 15, 1942, Woolaroc Archive.

696 Marjorie Karch to Fern Butler, letter September 19, 1938, Woolaroc Archive.

697 W. R. Leigh to Frank Phillips, letter, February 13, 1943, Woolaroc Archive.

698 Thomas Gilcrease to Frank Phillips, letter, January 26, 1944, Woolaroc Archive.

699 Ernie Pyle, "Ernie Finds One Millionaire Who Really Enjoys Money," *Washington Daily News* (Washington, D. C.), May 2, 1939.

700 *Ibid.*

701 *Ibid.*

702 "318 Families Given Beef Through W.A.," *Bartlesville Morning Examiner,* August 1, 1934.

703 M. L. Karch to M. B. Heine, memorandum, December 17, 1940; M. B. Heine to Dulin Gill, letter, December 23, 1940, Woolaroc Archive.

704 W. C. Smoot to Frank Phillips, memorandum, November 6, 1940, Woolaroc Archive.

705 Frank Phillips to A. N. Ekstrand, letter, July 7, 1938, Woolaroc Archive.

706 H. W. Meyer to Frank Phillips, letter, January 26, 1928, Woolaroc Archive.

707 E. V. Hoopingarner to Frank Phillips, letter, April 23, 1940, Woolaroc Archive.

708 T. P. Scott to Frank Phillips, letter, May 20, 1936, Woolaroc Archive.

709 Erwin Levold. levolde@rockvax.rockefeller.edu, "Markle," private e-mail message to Gale Kane, March 25, 1999. Dr. Levold is the archivist for the Markle

Foundation. He kindly looked up the dates of Frank Phillips' service, though there is no longer any record of the specific contributions Frank may have made to the Board. John Markle died in 1933. "It wasn't until 1935/1936 that a concrete plan of action was decided upon, but from 1936-1945 the foundation primarily supported medical research (627 grants for 336 projects)."

710 Hy Byrd to Frank Phillips, letter, August 20, 1938, Woolaroc Archive.

711 Hy Byrd to Frank Phillips, and Walter A. Cooper to Frank Phillips, letters, October 13, 1937, Woolaroc Archive.

712 S. Morgan Friedman. "Inflation Calculator." http://www.westegg.com/inflation/. September 19, 1999. Frank's $2300 worth of small bequests translates into $25,548 in 1998 dollars.

713 "Foundation Contributions Approved by Mr. Phillips...11-1-37" Woolaroc Archive.

714 W. C. Smoot to Frank Phillips, letter, March 8, 1938; Hy Byrd to W. C. Smoot, letter, March 21, 1938, Woolaroc Archive.

715 Frank Phillips to Hy Byrd, telegram, April 4, 1938, Woolaroc Archive.

716 S.F. Butler to W. C. Smoot, letter, January 24, 1938, Woolaroc Archive.

717 W. B. Bizzell to Frank Phillips, letter, April 24, 1938, Woolaroc Archive.

718 W. C. Smoot to Rev. C. L. Schultz, letter, March 20, 1939, Woolaroc Archive.

719 "Uncle Frank," *Christian Science Monitor* (Boston, Massachusetts), November 17, 1938.

720 "Oil Man May Pay Off City Church Debts," *The Daily Oklahoman* (Oklahoma City, Oklahoma), December 8, 1938.

721 Friedman. "Inflation Calculator." $100,000 in 1938 dollars translates to $1,110,789 in 1998 dollars.

722 W. C. Smoot to Frank Phillips, two letters, July 7, 1938, Woolaroc Archive; "Scout Leaders Begin Laying Plans For Beneficial Uses Of Frank Phillips' Big Gift," *Bartlesville Morning Examiner,* July 9, 1938.

723 Frank Phillips to Miss Mary Kimbrough, letter, July 13, 1938, Woolaroc Archive.

724 "Phillips Church Debt Plan Hailed by Pastor," *Oklahoma News* (Oklahoma City, Oklahoma), December 8, 1938.

725 Frank Phillips to W. C. Smoot, letter, December 16, 1938, Woolaric Archive.

726 "Phillips Petroleum Head Rents Ranch to Company," *New York Times,* January 13, 1939.

727 Margot Tremann to Frank Phillips, letter, June 12, 1938, Woolaroc Archive.

728 Lizzie Crane to Frank Phillips, undated letter from 1940, Woolaroc Archive.

729 Rhea Folger to W. C. Smoot, letter, November 15, 1939, Woolaroc Archive.

730 Friedman, "Inflation Calculator." $50.000 in 1939 dollars becomes 566,151 in 1998 dollars.

731 F. O. Nordstrom to J. E. Bacon, letter, August 1, 1939, Woolaroc Archive.

732 Friedman, "Inflation Calculator." $66,000 in 1940 dollars becomes $757,930 in 1998 dollars.

733 Bishop to Frank Phillips, letter, March 16, 1939, Woolaroc Archive.

734 Friedman, "Inflation Calculator." $5,000 in 1942 becomes $54,143 in 1998 dollars.

735 W. C. Smoot to R. A. Gerkin, letter, March 30, 1942, Woolaroc Archive.

736 Francis C. Kelley to Frank Phillips, letter, July 9, 1938, Woolaroc Archive.

737 *Ibid.*

738 Francis C. Kelley to W. C. Smoot, letter, November 2, 1938, Woolaroc Archive.

739 Francis C. Kelley to W. C. Smoot, letter, December 10, 1938, Woolaroc Archive.

740 W. K. Warren to Frank Phillips, letter, October 13, 1941, Woolaroc Archive.

741 Sister Mary Annunciation to Frank Phillips, letter, January 30, 1942, Woolaroc Archive.

742 Frank Phillips to Robert S. Kerr, letter, October 27, 1943, Woolaroc Archive.

743 J. Howard Williams, "The Rising Tide," The Baptist Messenger, December 9, 1943. Friedman, "Inflation Calculator." $100,000 in 1943 dollars translates to $978,199 in 1998 dollars.

744 W. G. Angel to C. H. Wright, letter, March 12, 1948, Woolaroc Archive.

745 Lee Slater, "Woolaroc Director Slaps Modern Art," *Tulsa Daily World,* January 21, 1968. See also *Oil Man.*

746 Pat Patterson to Frank Phillips, letter, February 1, 1942, Woolaroc Archive.

747 Sarah Clements to Frank Phillips, letter, February 12, 1942; Gordon Matzene to Frank Phillips, letter, June 9, 1942, Woolaroc Archive.

748 Pat Patterson to Frank Phillips, letter, October 4, 1942, Woolaroc Museum.

749 Pat Patterson to Frank Phillips, memorandum, September 11, 1945, Woolaroc Archive.

750 Wallis, *Oil Man,* p. 455.

INDEX

GENTS